# GUITAR
## FAMILY TREES

# GUITAR
## FAMILY TREES
### THE HISTORY OF THE WORLD'S MOST ICONIC GUITARS

TERRY BURROWS

Foreword by
ZAKK WYLDE

NEW BURLINGTON

A Quintessence Book

This edition published in 2017 by

New Burlington Books
The Old Brewery, 6 Blundell Street,
London, N7 9BH

All rights reserved. No part of this publication
may be reproduced, stored in a retrieval system or
transmitted in any form or by any means, electronic,
mechanical, photocopying, recording or otherwise,
without the permission of the copyright holder.

ISBN: 978-0-85762-179-5
QSS.GCOL2

Reprinted in 2018

This book was designed and produced by
Quintessence Editions Ltd.
The Old Brewery, 6 Blundell Street,
London, N7 9BH
Copyright © 2011 Quintessence Editions Ltd.

**Editors:** Philip Contos, Simon Hartley,
Frank Ritter
**Designer:** Alison Hau

**Editorial Director:** Ruth Patrick
**Publisher:** Philip Cooper

Colour reproduction by KHL Chromagraphics, Singapore
Printed in China by Toppan Leefung Printing Ltd.

# CONTENTS

# FOREWORD BY ZAKK WYLDE

Guitars — what more can I say? THEY RULE!!! From the first time I picked up an acoustic guitar n could play "Smoke on the Water" n "Iron Man" on the Low E String, and then plugging in an electric guitar into a distortion pedal, that otherworldly magic that is music has made me a disciple ever since. We, as guitarist's have made the guitar our musical weapon of choice, n there r many to choose from — just as anybody who picks up a guitar is unique, so is every guitar. You've got your Les Paul Custom guys, your Les Paul Standard guys, Strat guys, Tele guys, Flying V, Explorer, Moderne n whatever other crazy shaped guitar you could think of inbetween. Thats the beauty n just one of things that makes the guitar so awesome. Whereas I love the thick, meaty, warm, raw tone of my Les Paul Customs, I also love the amazing liquidy single coiled tones of the legendary Robin Trower's army of Strats.

Thats why as FAR AS RECOMENDING
WHAT TYPE OF GUITAR to BUY, Its
ALL UP TO the INDIVIDUAL. I WOULD
RECOMEND HAVING SOMEBODY with
Knowledge OF GUITAR OR A GUITARIST
to hELP YOU FIND A GOOD PLAYING
INSTRUMENT to MAKE LEARNING EASIER.

OBVIOUSLY Look TO SOME OF YOUR
FAVORITE PLAYERS OR TRY EVERYTHING
TIL YOU FIND WHAT YOU LOVE. LIKE I
SAID, JUST AS BO DIDLEY'S "BOX
GUITAR" IS UNIQUE TO HIM, A "LES
PAUL STANDARD" IS TO JIMMY PAGE.

WITH SO MANY GADGETS N PEDALS
N AMAZING AMPS FOR EVERY STYLE
OF ELECTRIC GUITAR, TO NYLON
STRING N STEEL STRING ACOUSTICS,
THE MUSICAL SOUNDSCAPE IS
AN ENDLESS ROAD — ONE LAST
RECOMENDATION, BECOME A DISCIPLE
OF ThE RELIGION KNOWN AS GUITAR AND
YOU WILL TRULY
BE BLESSED

SDMF
TBLO
B&S

# INTRODUCTION

For more than half a century, popular culture has enjoyed an intense and unprecedented love affair with the guitar, in both its acoustic and electric forms. Although the guitar is an instrument with roots dating back several thousand years to pre-Babylonian times, it was not until the late nineteenth century that it was first treated as a serious musical entity worthy of a place on the concert platform. Indeed, such has been its popularity in every imaginable musical sphere from then onward that few would disagree that the guitar stands as *the* instrument of the twentieth century.

The reasons for this explosion in popularity are varied and sometimes quite curious. For Andrés Segovia, the most important classical guitarist of the twentieth century, the instrument was the perfect vehicle for his own masterful musical expression. "The guitar is a small orchestra," enthused Segovia. "It is polyphonic. Every string is a different color, a different voice."

In the period between the two world wars, Segovia took the instrument to hitherto unknown heights of virtuosity and premiered works by some of the greatest composers of his era. In the hands of Segovia and others that followed in his wake, including many of the later masters of the electric guitar in the fields of jazz, rock, and metal, the instrument was heard to be capable of hugely sophisticated musical statements. Yet at the time of Segovia's rise, the guitar simultaneously emerged as a popular domestic folk instrument. Commonly used by black American blues musicians, the guitar began to reach wider audiences during the 1930s with the emergence of Hollywood "singing cowboys" such as Roy Rogers and, in particular, Gene Autry. It was in this role that the essential appeal of the guitar lay; a handful of easy-to-learn, open-string chords could provide a simple musical accompaniment for any kind of song. Perhaps it is this duality as both sophisticated solo instrument and simple means of accompaniment that makes the guitar such a unique musical force.

Equally, the guitar can be a very simple instrument. Keith Richards of the Rolling Stones once memorably remarked that "Guitar is easy, all it takes is five strings, three notes, two fingers, and one arsehole." (By "five strings," Richards refers to a further personalized simplification—the removal of the bottom E string.) On the guitar, absolutely anybody can begin to achieve "instant" results after a few days of dedicated practice.

Of course, the electrification of the guitar is the single most significant aspect of the instrument's varied history. It was at first merely a practical solution to the problem of competing with louder acoustic instruments, but from the late 1950s the electric guitar was to have a galvanizing effect on musical culture. Indeed, a great deal of the popular music that emerged subsequently simply could not have existed without electric guitars, loud amplification, and electronic effects, such as distortion. Prolific guitarist and composer Frank Zappa acknowledged the nature of its attraction to musicians: "The guitar can be the single most blasphemous device on the face of the earth. That's why I like it. . . . The disgusting stink of a too-loud electric guitar: now that's my idea of a good time."

Such was the shift in musical sensibilities in the 1950s and '60s that the electric guitar began to find itself positioned as a symbol of intergenerational divide and rebellious intent, the scourge of every middle-class parent, who suddenly felt locked out of a newly emerging cultural climate. To quote from "Welcome To The Machine" by Pink Floyd's Roger Waters, "You bought a guitar to punish your ma, you didn't like school, and you know you're nobody's fool."

Of course, the electric guitar is now regarded as a mainstream instrument. Indeed, by the late 1990s, the U.K. had elected its own Stratocaster-wielding prime minister—as a long-haired Oxford undergraduate in the early 1970s, Tony Blair had fronted Ugly Rumours, a rock band in the style of the Rolling Stones. The guitar's reputation as a tool of revolution was perhaps permanently quashed.

Nevertheless, the instrument has proven itself to be surprisingly versatile, and successive generations of musicians continue to come up with intriguing new ways to use (and abuse) the guitar. This alone seems certain to ensure its status as the world's most popular musical instrument well into the twenty-first century.

Inside this book are profiles of more than 200 guitars. These combine to provide an overall picture of the way the instrument has developed, and how individual models relate to one another. Instruments are presented alphabetically by manufacturer or luthier, and, within that, by type, chronology, or specific model. Each instrument is dated according to when it first appeared on the market, with the main image illustrating an example from as close to that date as possible. One-off guitars—typically those with no specific model identity built by pre-twentieth-century luthiers—are dated simply as the year in which the guitar shown was built. Each guitar profile features a technical specification panel with data relevant to the time the instrument was launched. Most featured guitars are accompanied by a photograph of a celebrity player using the instrument and details of an album on which the guitar can be heard.

An unusual feature of this book is the inclusion of fourteen family trees. Each one attempts to show in a linear fashion the ways in which guitars of a specific manufacturer have evolved over time. These are by no means exhaustive in content—that would require a book devoted exclusively to large family trees.

Of course, the actual content of this book is all about personal preference. Connoisseurs of the instrument would probably agree on perhaps fifty key instruments, which here leaves about 150 models up for debate. My list of the rest draws perhaps on some of my left-field tastes. I hope you find the choices interesting. Some of you may scratch your heads at the unusual or obscure retro Italian and Japanese models from the 1960s, or perhaps the so-ugly-they're-beautiful 1970s British Shergolds. I'm happy also to confess a special fondness for the maverick luthiers, such as Jim Burns (Burns), Semie Moseley (Mosrite), and Ralph Jones (Micro-Frets); original thinkers like Emmett Chapman, Allan Gittler, and Ulrich Teuffel; and many of the modern day boutique brands that continue to refine classic American electric guitar design. Feel free to vent indignation at my whimsical inclusions or willful exclusions—I know I certainly would!

# ACOUSTIC BLACK WIDOW 1972

producing high-end solid-state systems for guitar and bass.

In 1972, Acoustic made its only foray into guitar production with the Black Widow. This instrument has a somewhat convoluted history beginning the previous decade when early Rickenbacker pioneer Paul Barth began producing this long-scale design under the Bartell name. In 1972 he agreed to produce a revamped version of the Black Widow for Acoustic, but quickly found his facilities were unable to build the numbers required. A manufacturing deal was struck with Matsumoto Moko in Japan, who would produce most of the thousand or so Black Widows in existence—1975 saw production switch back briefly to the U.S., where Mosrite's Semie Moseley claims responsibility for the last 200 units before Acoustic decided, once more, to concentrate on amplification.

The end of the 1960s saw a shift in guitar technology, as valve amplification became increasingly usurped by cheaper, more reliable solid-state circuitry. Acoustic Control Corporation specialized in

▲
**Jimi Hendrix plays one of Paul Barth's pre-Acoustic Black Widows. Although he used the guitar in the studio we have no idea on which tracks it may be heard. Other noted players of the guitar included Frank Zappa and Jeff Baxter of the Doobie Brothers/Steely Dan.**

▼
**Jazz fusion star Larry Coryell was endorsing the Black Widow around the time of the 1973 debut of his new group, The Eleventh House.**

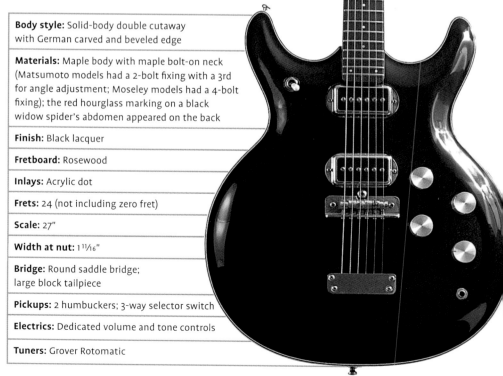

**Body style:** Solid-body double cutaway with German carved and beveled edge

**Materials:** Maple body with maple bolt-on neck (Matsumoto models had a 2-bolt fixing with a 3rd for angle adjustment; Moseley models had a 4-bolt fixing); the red hourglass marking on a black widow spider's abdomen appeared on the back

**Finish:** Black lacquer

**Fretboard:** Rosewood

**Inlays:** Acrylic dot

**Frets:** 24 (not including zero fret)

**Scale:** 27"

**Width at nut:** 1 $^{11}/_{16}$"

**Bridge:** Round saddle bridge; large block tailpiece

**Pickups:** 2 humbuckers; 3-way selector switch

**Electrics:** Dedicated volume and tone controls

**Tuners:** Grover Rotomatic

# AIRLINE RES-O-GLAS 1964

W ith man's conquest of space no longer seemingly a sci-fi fantasy, America in the early 1960s became obsessive about the future. The electric guitar was still a relatively recent innovation, and there were designers intent on taking the guitar into the twenty-first century. Looking like something straight out of *The Jetsons*, the 1964 Airline Res-O-Glas is a case in point.

Airline began making instruments in 1958; by the early 1960s the brand was applied to guitars produced in the U.S. by Valco. This model, once generally known as the "J. B. Hutto," (after the bluesman), is now uniquely associated with Jack White of The White Stripes.

Interestingly, the Airline marks one of the earliest uses of composite materials in guitar manufacture. The body is made from "Res-O-Glas," a type of glass fiber chosen less for any particular acoustic properties than to create an instrument that would last longer than conventional wood. The body comprised two molded, chambered halves. The seam was then hidden with a strip of white vinyl binding around the edge.

▲
The White Stripes emerged in 1997 with an unusual stripped-back sound of just drums, electric guitar, and vocals.

▼
Jack White's Airline can be heard on all of The White Stripes' albums. Recorded on an eight-track in Jack White's living room, De Stijl (2000) is particularly recommended.

| | |
|---|---|
| Body style: | Double cutaway chambered semi-hollow body |
| Materials: | Res-O-Glas glass fiber; bolt on maple neck |
| Finish: | Unpainted Res-O-Glas |
| Fretboard: | Rosewood |
| Inlays: | Block |
| Frets: | 20 (not including zero fret) |
| Scale: | 25 ½" |
| Width at nut: | 1 ¹¹⁄₁₆" |
| Bridge: | Tune-o-matic style |
| Pickups: | 2 single-coil pickups; 3-way selector switch |
| Electrics: | Dedicated volume and tone controls for each pickup; master volume |

# ALEMBIC 001 "JACK CASADY" 1972

Alembic Inc. was founded in 1969 by former Ampex electronics expert Ron Wickersham, initially working with high-profile West Coast bands, such as the Grateful Dead and Jefferson Airplane, consulting on methods of improving both concert sound systems and their live recordings. Among Alembic's early experiments was the development of a low-impedance pickup, its signal boosted by an "active" onboard preamplifier. This enabled a wider audio bandwidth than was possible with the high-impedance pickups normally used in electric guitars and basses. These systems—the most advanced of their kind—were successfully installed on instruments owned by the Grateful Dead.

Alembic's first foray into guitar building came in 1972 with an active bass built for Jack Casady of Jefferson Airplane. The bass was made from unusual woods, such as zebrawood and purpleheart. The instrument's most unusual feature was its pair of movable pickups that could slide along two brass tubes fitted to the body.

The pointed protrusion—on what would become the Series 1 body shape—was supposedly there to encourage players to use a guitar stand.

▲
Jack Casady seen in 1973 playing his unique Alembic bass with Hot Tuna—an offshoot band of Jefferson Airplane, formed by Jack Casady with Airplane guitarist Jorma Kaukonen.

▼
Casady's Alembic 001 bass features on Hot Tuna's fourth album, *The Phosphorescent Rat* (1974).

| | |
|---|---|
| **Body style:** | Double cutaway solid body |
| **Materials:** | Hand-carved zebrawood body; maple and purpleheart laminated straight-through neck |
| **Finish:** | Natural |
| **Fretboard:** | Ebony |
| **Inlays:** | "Tree of life" design in abalone and silver wire |
| **Frets:** | 24 |
| **Scale:** | 32" |
| **Width at nut:** | 1 ¾" |
| **Bridge:** | Adjustable |
| **Pickups:** | 2 active, hand-made moveable pickups on brass tracks |
| **Electrics:** | Dedicated volume and tone controls for each pickup; tone circuitry |

# ALEMBIC TENOR 1973

Although Alembic made a number of six-string guitars, it was for the bass instruments that its reputation began to emerge. One of Alembic's early converts was jazz fusion star Stanley Clarke, then a part of the crossover band Return To Forever, with Chick Corea and Al Di Meola. Clarke redefined the role of the electric bass and in doing so became the first celebrity bass guitarist.

Clarke's Gibsonesque Alembic has a short scale (30¾") and is also restrung as a so-called "tenor bass," where each string is a perfect fourth higher than standard tuning. Thus, Clarke's bass is tuned A-D-G-C, which enhances upper register and was integral to his melodic playing style during this period. (He also sometimes used "piccolo" tuning—each string one octave higher than standard.)

Stanley Clarke and Mark King, singer and bassist of Level 42, are the only players to have been honored with Alembic signature models.

Following the attention earned by the Casady bass, Alembic decided to go into the manufacturing business. By 1974 the workshop was producing in the region of a hundred guitars and basses a year, all made to the highest specification at prices only the most successful musicians could afford.

▲
**Stanley Clarke has used Alembic bass guitars exclusively since 1973.**

▼
**The title track of Stanley Clarke's *School Days* (1976) is a genre classic. Clarke himself suggests: "Anyone who seriously wants to learn to play the bass has to buy that record and learn to play that song."**

| | |
|---|---|
| **Body style:** | Double cutaway solid body |
| **Materials:** | Mahogany body with maple inlays; maple and walnut laminated "pinstripe" straight-through neck (assorted top laminates later available) |
| **Finish:** | Natural; high gloss polyester finish on body with satin neck |
| **Fretboard:** | Rosewood (later ebony) |
| **Inlays:** | Abalone |
| **Frets:** | 24 |
| **Scale:** | 30¾" |
| **Width at nut:** | 1½" (or 1¾") |
| **Bridge:** | Adjustable, independent tailpiece |
| **Pickups:** | 2 pickups; 3-way selector switch |
| **Electrics:** | Dedicated volume and tone controls for each pickup; tone switching |

# AMPEG ASB-1 "DEVIL BASS" 1966

The Ampeg name is, above all, associated with the history and development of bass amplification. The story began in the 1940s when bass player Everett Hull designed a microphone pickup to be fitted on the end of an upright bass. He dubbed it the Amplified Peg—"Ampeg" for short. In 1949 the Ampeg Bassamp Company was founded, and over the next three decades it would be responsible for many innovations in the field: the Portaflex bass combo in 1960; the Reverberocket—the first guitar amplifier to incorporate a spring reverb; and, in 1969, the development of Super Valve Technology used to create a 300-watt amplifier—then the most powerful musical instrument amplifier yet built.

During the 1960s, Ampeg also began to dabble in the instrument market, with a range of guitars and basses. A business sideline, most of these models were built in small quantities for Ampeg and, although they were not hugely popular, were always quite distinctive—both visually and in their features.

Initially, Ampeg produced electric upright basses. When the company's first bass guitars appeared in 1966, this heritage was honored in the scrolled headstock design and rear-pointing tuners. Less than a thousand of the first so-called "scroll" basses were produced, either as fretted (AEB-1) or fretless (AUB-1) instruments.

Produced briefly from the end of 1966, the ASB-1 (and fretless AUSB-1) were inspired by the stylings of the earlier Danelectro Longhorn. With its red and black sunburst finish and sharp horns, the ASB-1 quickly acquired the tag "Devil Bass."

Unpopular even among Ampeg employees, no more than an estimated one hundred were built, a quarter of which were fretless. Unsurprisingly, they are now highly collectible.

▼
**The first of Ampeg's scroll basses, the AEB-1/AUB-1 were almost identical in hardware features to the Devil Bass.**

| | |
|---|---|
| **Body style:** | Double cutaway solid frame |
| **Materials:** | Maple with birch plywood body (solid maple on later models) with bolt-on maple neck; glued plastic scrolls on headstock |
| **Finish:** | Red and black sunburst |
| **Fretboard:** | Rosewood or ebony |
| **Inlays:** | Acrylic dot |
| **Frets:** | 20 (not including zero fret) |
| **Scale:** | 35" |
| **Width at nut:** | 1¾" |
| **Bridge:** | Adjustable with end-stop tailpiece |
| **Pickups:** | Described in Ampeg literature as the mystery pickup—2 large magentic coils cast in a large epoxy block, mounted beneath the bridge under a thin steel diaphragm plate |
| **Electrics:** | Master volume and tone control |

# AMPEG DAN ARMSTRONG 1969

Ampeg had grown out of the world of jazz. Even if their scroll basses were visual curiosities, they had been aimed less at young rock musicians than jazz players switching from upright bass. In 1968 Ampeg, knowing that their market was limited, engaged well-respected guitar and amplifier technician Dan Armstrong to look at modernization.

Armstrong would enjoy a long and varied career, but the innovation for which he is best remembered is the see-through guitar made from Plexiglass, an extremely strong, clear plastic. Available both as guitar and bass, the instruments had enormous on-stage visual appeal—it was as if it were carved from glass—but that was not the only reason for Armstrong's choice. The density of the material gave the instruments greater levels of sustain. They were also electronically innovative in that they were designed for use with an assortment of slot-in "quick-change" pickups: six for the guitar; two for the bass.

Seen on stage with the Rolling Stones, the Plexiglass models became very desirable, but production was ended suddenly in 1971 following an insurmountable contractual row between Ampeg and Armstrong.

▲
**Bill Wyman of the Rolling Stones played an Ampeg Dan Armstrong bass during the early 1970s. Fellow Stone Keith Richards would regularly use the six-string counterpart.**

▼
**The Ampeg Dan Armstrong bass can be heard on the Rolling Stones' 1970 live album *Get Yer Ya-Ya's Out*.**

| | |
|---|---|
| **Body style:** | Twin cutaway solid body |
| **Materials:** | Plexiglass body with bolt-on maple neck |
| **Finish:** | Clear |
| **Fingerboard:** | Rosewood |
| **Inlays:** | Acrylic dot |
| **Frets:** | 24 |
| **Scale:** | 30" |
| **Width at nut:** | 1 ⅝" |
| **Bridge:** | Rosewood with compensated brass saddles |
| **Pickups:** | Interchangeable "slot-in" pickups: stacked coil bright bass and deep bass |
| **Electrics:** | Master volume and tone control; tone switch |

# ANTORIA LG-30 1957

"basic," and popular simply because there was nothing else available.

But when rock 'n' roll hit the shores of Great Britain in the late 1950s there was scant choice for fledgling electric guitarists. An import embargo made U.S. models all but impossible to find—and even then retailed at prices affordable only to the wealthy.

Spotting a market gap, a small U.K. company named J.T. Coppock based in Leeds began importing cheap guitars from Japan. The first models were stock Guyatones rebadged with the Antoria brand, most notably the single-pickup LG-30 and twin-pickup LG-50. These were not carefully crafted instruments: a high action made them demanding to play and the sound they produced was limited. But what makes these such significant instruments is that, for many novice guitarists of the late 1950s, they were the only practical of way of joining an emerging musical revolution.

The history of the electric guitar is logically told as an unfolding timeline of benchmark developments, most of which took place in America throughout the 1950s. There is rarely room for the inclusion of a brand that produced instruments that were

▲
Hank Marvin of The Shadows performed on an Antoria LG-50 before his famous purchase of Britain's first Fender Stratocaster in 1959.

▼
Hank Marvin used his Antoria LG-50 on some tracks on Cliff Richard's 1959 debut album. At this time The Shadows were still known as The Drifters.

| | |
|---|---|
| **Body style:** | Single cutaway solid body |
| **Materials:** | Laminated body with maple top; bolt-on maple neck |
| **Finish:** | Grey cellulose, blonde maplewood |
| **Fretboard:** | Rosewood |
| **Inlays:** | Block |
| **Frets:** | 20 |
| **Scale:** | 25 ½" |
| **Width at nut:** | 1 ⅝" |
| **Bridge:** | Fixed |
| **Pickups:** | 1 single-coil (LG-30) pickup or 2 single-coil (LG-50) pickups; 3-way pickup selector on LG-50s |
| **Machine heads:** | Open |
| **Electrics:** | Master volume and tone control |

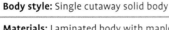

# ARIA DIAMOND ADSG-12T 1967

いい楽器を求めるコツはマークをマークすること

荒井貿易株式会社

their woods split and their glues became unstuck. In 1964, Arai moved production to Matsumoku, which solved these issues by using stronger glues and woods that had been dried for at least two years.

The first Arai/Matsumoku electric guitars appeared in 1966, branded either Arai, Aria, Diamond, or Arita. These models—like the Diamond ADSG electric twelve-string (*see right*)—represent some of the best Japanese guitar manufacture of the period, in particular the three-piece maple necks, which matched anything produced by the major U.S. factories.

In 1975, Arai adopted the Aria Pro II brand which, along with Yamaha and Ibanez, formed the vanguard of Japan's challenge to the established market leaders in America. Many of the company's innovative new designs were the work of Nobuaki Hayashi—widely known under the pseudonym "H. Noble."

Aria was founded in 1956 by Shiro Arai. Initially operating as an importer and retailer of classical guitars, in 1960 Arai contracted Guyatone to manufacture guitars for export to the U.S. However, these early Arai models did not adjust well to the dryer American climate;

▲
A 1968 Japanese magazine advertisement for a Telecaster-style Diamond, which also illustrates the slim three-ply maple neck. Throughout the 1970s Aria produced high-quality imitations of classic Fender and Gibson guitars, as well as its own original designs.

| | |
|---|---|
| **Body style:** | Cresting wave solid body |
| **Materials:** | Laminate body with bolt-on 3-ply maple neck |
| **Finish:** | Sunburst |
| **Fretboard:** | Rosewood |
| **Inlays:** | Left-justified acrylic dot |
| **Frets:** | 21 |
| **Scale:** | 24 ¾" |
| **Width at nut:** | 1 ⅝" |
| **Bridge:** | Integral bridge and tailpiece with vibrato mechanism |
| **Pickups:** | 2 single-coil pickups; 3-way pickup selector switch |
| **Electrics:** | Master volume and tone control |

# ARIAS 1870

<V>icente Arias was born in Alcazar de San Juan, Ciudad Real, in 1833. He trained as a cabinet maker and began to build guitars in around 1860. He remained in his home town for most of his life, only moving his workshop to Madrid in 1900. Little more is known about his life and yet, despite having built relatively few guitars—only twenty-four are currently known—he and Manuel Ramirez are considered the only nineteenth-century luthiers capable of producing instruments to rival those of Torres.

Arias instruments are characterized by their lightness and personality. They were decorated around the rose with such intricate detail that every model was visually unique.

During the course of his career, Arias received prestigious prizes at exhibitions in Barcelona, Madrid, Brussels, and Buenos Aires. Indeed, such was the esteem in which he was held that Francisco Tárrega—the greatest virtuoso of his time—commissioned him to make a small guitar that he could carry under his cape to use to strengthen his fingers out of sight while traveling.

Arias continued making guitars up until his death in 1914.

▲
Francisco Tárrega (1852–1909), guitarist and composer of the Romantic era, commissioned a small travel guitar from Vicente Arias.

▼
Belgian guitarist Raphaëlla Smits uses an 1899 eight-string Arias on this 1999 album of pieces by composer Antonio Jiménez Manjón.

| | |
|---|---|
| **Body style:** | Small-body classical |
| **Materials:** | Brazilian rosewood back and sides; German spruce top |
| **Finish:** | French polish, shellac |
| **Fretboard:** | Ebony |
| **Inlays:** | None, but the rosette around the sound hole is unique, as on all Arias guitars |
| **Frets:** | 19 (partial 19th fret) |
| **Scale:** | 25 17/36" |
| **Bridge:** | Ebony with bone saddle |
| **Tuners:** | Originally violin-style tuning pegs, here replaced by more reliable brass tuners |
| **Bracing:** | Torres-style fan bracing |

# ASHBORN 1850

James Ashborn could lay claim to having been the first guitar maker to apply the principles of mass production to the guitar.

Born in England in 1816, Ashborn is thought to have been trained either as a clock maker or machinist. In his early twenties he emigrated to the United States, basing himself in Torrington, Connecticut. Torrington was a rural wagon-building town surrounded by mills, with a plentiful supply of wood and a suitably skilled workforce.

The workshop Ashborn devised was highly innovative in applying a division of labor. Workers were employed according to their skills, and given specific suitable tasks. Thus, one man would machine tuners; another would fret the fingerboards; another would French-polish the finished guitar.

Ashborn was also willing to take advantage of the sophisticated new machinery being used by wagon builders—band saws, table saws, and routers, powered by the flow of water in the Naugatuck River.

With these radical new methods Ashborn quickly established himself as America's most prolific maker of guitars and banjos, his tiny workforce sometimes creating more than a hundred instruments a month. The majority of these guitars are labeled "William Hall and Son"—the New York company that distributed his instruments to retailers.

Ashborn's guitars were themselves unusual in design, combining the small-bodied English parlor tradition of Louis Panormo with the kind of interior fan-bracing found in Spanish classical instruments. And although his manufacturing process may have been highly mechanized for its time, he produced high-quality instruments, with sophisticated design features that also required significant amounts of highly skilled handwork.

▼

James Ashborn designed and manufactured banjos as well as guitars. Those he built during the 1850s are highly esteemed by present-day banjo players.

| | |
|---|---|
| **Body style:** | Hollow body with Panormo-style parlor peanut shape |
| **Materials:** | Rosewood-veneered maple on back and sides; spruce front; chestnut or butternut glued neck with Indian rosewood veneer and a butt joint at the 12th fret |
| **Finish:** | Shellac French-polished |
| **Fretboard:** | Rosewood |
| **Inlays:** | None |
| **Frets:** | 19 |
| **Scale:** | 24 ⁵⁄₈" |
| **Width at nut:** | 1 ²⁹⁄₃₂" |
| **Bridge:** | Rosewood with saddles |
| **Tuners:** | Brass |

# ASHBORY 1986

When Leo Fender introduced his Precision bass guitar in 1951 he had little idea of the impact this new instrument would have on the role of the bass player: by the end of the decade, the acoustic upright bass was all but dead in popular music. There have since been attempts to integrate aspects of the upright sound with a standard bass guitar, such as removing the frets. Arguably, however, none have come closer to capturing the tone of an acoustic bass than the Ashbory.

Developed in 1985 by Alun Ashworth-Jones and Nigel Thornbory, the Ashbory is to a considerable degree capable of reproducing the deep, resonant tone of a plucked double bass. Unfortunately the design has one severe downside: with a scale length of 18 inches—almost half the size of a standard bass guitar—it is decidedly difficult to master accurately, even with the fret positions marked on the

fingerboard. Nonetheless, despite its toylike appearance, the Ashbory is a remarkable instrument.

To create its unique tone, the bass is fitted with silicone rubber strings that are stretched across an acoustic piezo-transducer pickup fitted into the non-adjustable bridge. Initial tuning can be problematic: when a new set of strings is fitted, the bottom E and A both require time to "bed in" before tuning may be considered stable.

The Ashbory is most effectively played with the fingers rather than a pick, and because of the natural grip of the rubber, dusting the strings with chalk or talcum powder is necessary to enable nimble movement.

The Ashbory bass was produced by Guild Guitars from 1986–88, using a one-piece poplar body and neck. Production then ceased until 1999 when it was re-introduced by Fender under the DeArmond brand, this time using cheaper agathis wood.

▼
**The Ashbory bass, compared in size to a standard bass guitar.**

| | |
|---|---|
| **Body style:** | Solid body "stick" |
| **Materials:** | 1-piece instrument carved from agathis (originally poplar) |
| **Finish:** | Black, frost red, and moon blue; nitrocellulose coating |
| **Fretboard:** | Plastic |
| **Inlays:** | Dot |
| **Frets:** | None (markers from 1 to 24) |
| **Scale:** | 18" |
| **Width at nut:** | 1 ¹¹⁄₁₆" |
| **Bridge:** | Ashworth transducer bridge |
| **Pickups:** | Ashworth piezo with active circuitry |
| **Machine heads:** | Open |
| **Electrics:** | Single volume control; active bass and active treble controls |

# Bartolini 20-4V 1962

Italy's guitar-building heritage had traditionally been concentrated in the country's industrial north. The end of the 1950s, however, saw an explosion of activity around Castelfidardo on the eastern coast— the manufacturing base for the world's finest accordions.

The aftermath of Italy's wartime defeat had already laid low a once-thriving region. Matters deteriorated with the advent of rock 'n' roll, as the popularity of the accordion began to decline. Alvaro Bartolini, like other accordion makers in Castelfidardo, responded by introducing guitars.

As with most electric models launched in Italy from the early 1960s, a glance at the sparkling body and pearloid fingerboard of the Bartolini 20-4V tells us that expertise acquired from decades of accordion production was not discarded overnight. Indeed, Italian electric guitars, many of which found their way to different export markets under a wide variety of brand names, had a lot in common with one another. Similarities were not only cosmetic: compare the unusual arrangement of four pickups and the impressive line of rocker switches and rotary dials on the 20-4V with the Crucianelli Elite or the better known Eko models—all of which were built in the Castelfidardo region at that time. Also notable is the ornately decorated scratchplate, which, in common with all Bartolinis, follows the shape of the body over much of its surface.

Italian electric guitars of the 1960s once had little more than kitsch interest for collectors, but with the market for even modest vintage American models now fully exploited, instruments like the Bartolini—which might easily have been picked up in junk shops during the 1980s—have seen an appreciation in value. It's not difficult to see why: they are fun, stylish, full of retro charm, and an original in mint condition can look quite spectacular.

▼
A rare Bartolini bass. Standard guitar tuners were used; bass tuners were not then available in Italy.

| | |
|---|---|
| **Body style:** | Double cutaway solid body |
| **Materials:** | Basswood body with set maple neck |
| **Finish:** | Celluloid sparkle finish in assorted colors |
| **Fretboard:** | Pearloid |
| **Inlays:** | Painted dot |
| **Frets:** | 21 |
| **Scale:** | 25½" |
| **Width at nut:** | 1¹¹⁄₁₆" |
| **Bridge:** | Nonadjustable bridge with vibrato on independent tailpiece |
| **Pickups:** | 4 single-coil pickups with combination rocker switches |
| **Electrics:** | Master volume and tone vertical rotary dials |

# B.C. RICH WARLOCK 1981

Three years later, "B.C. Rich" produced its first batch of electric instruments—ten electric guitars and ten basses inspired respectively by Gibson's Les Paul and EB-3 models. In 1972, Rico produced the Seagull, its visually distinctive body shape indicating the company's direction.

The first B.C. Rich guitar to achieve widespread recognition was the Mockingbird (ranked the "coolest guitar of all time" by *Guitar World* magazine in 2010). This was swiftly followed by the Eagle and Bich models.

The Warlock emerged in 1981, and is considered to be the final entry in B.C. Rich's "classic five shapes." Its unique claw-like appearance was adopted widely within the booming metal culture of the period.

During the 1980s there was a significant vogue for unorthodox guitar shapes: many of the best of these can be traced back to B.C. Rich originals.

For a name so indelibly linked with the metal scene, the B.C. Rich marque emerged from an unlikely source. In 1966 an accomplished acoustic guitarist named Bernardo Chavez Rico began building flamenco guitars at his workshop in Los Angeles, California.

▲
**Kerry King was one of the founding members of Slayer. He has used B.C. Rich guitars since the band formed in the early 1980s.**

▼
**Released in 1985, *Hell Awaits* is Slayer's second album. It established the band as one of thrash metal's "big four"—along with Metallica, Anthrax, and Megadeth.**

| | |
|---|---|
| **Body style:** | Double cutaway solid body |
| **Materials:** | Agathis wood body with a maple bolt-on neck |
| **Finish:** | Painted onyx |
| **Fretboard:** | Rosewood |
| **Frets:** | 24 |
| **Inlays:** | Pearloid dots |
| **Scale:** | 24 ½" |
| **Width at nut:** | 1 ⅝" |
| **Bridge:** | B.C. Rich Quad |
| **Pickups:** | 2 B.C. Rich BDSM ("Broad Dynamic Sonically Matched") humbuckers; 3-way selector switch |
| **Electrics:** | Master volume and control |
| **Tuners:** | B.C. Rich die cast |

# B.C. Rich Bich 1978

When the original B.C. Rich Bich guitar emerged in 1978, the curious body shape—with its "rear cutaway"—was never going to be popular outside of the hard rock fraternity, which embraced its gothic horror visuals. B.C. Rich would continue to play along with this image, in the future even offering coffin-shaped flight cases.

The rear cutaway was not merely aesthetic, however, but served a specific purpose. The Bich was a ten-string guitar—the tuners for the standard six strings were fitted to the headstock in the usual fashion; the four additional tuners were fitted behind the bridge.

Instruments with ten strings *have* existed in the past, but they have usually featured five "courses" of strings tuned in unison or octaves, like most of the post-Renaissance acoustic guitars, or have ten independent strings—such as the Chapman Stick. The Bich 10 is played as a standard guitar but has the top four strings doubled up—the two at the bass end are single strings. Stock tuning pairs the top two strings in unison and the middle two strings tuned an octave apart. This creates a very full sound when chords are played with distortion, with the single bottom strings providing a clear tone.

**Dave Mustaine was an early member of Metallica, during which time he played a B.C. Rich Bich. He later found success in his own thrash metal band, Megadeth.**

**Mustaine can be heard on Megadeth's 1985 debut album *Killing Is My Business . . . And Business Is Good.***

| | |
|---|---|
| **Body style:** | Double cutaway solid body |
| **Materials:** | Maple straight-through neck with basswood fins attached to each side |
| **Finish:** | Painted onyx |
| **Fretboard:** | Ebony |
| **Frets:** | 24 |
| **Inlays:** | Diamond blocks |
| **Scale:** | 24 ⅝" |
| **Width at nut:** | 1 ⅝" |
| **Bridge:** | B.C. Rich Quad |
| **Pickups:** | 2 Rockfield Mafia humbuckers; 3-way selector switch |
| **Electrics:** | Dedicated volume controls for each pickup; master tone control |
| **Tuners:** | 10 B.C. Rich die cast—6 mounted on headstock; 4 on the lower bout behind the bridge |

# BIGSBY MERLE TRAVIS 1947

the vibrato on his Gibson L-10 he asked Bigsby to look into the problem. Rather than repairing what he saw as a poor design, Bigsby came up with a mechanism of his own—the now famous, and still widely used, Bigsby vibrato system.

A year later, over lunch, Travis showed Bigsby a sketch of an idea he'd had for a new guitar and asked if he thought he could build such an instrument. Bigsby's apocryphal response—"I can make anything!"—has now passed into guitar folklore.

The resulting instrument can reasonably lay claim to be the first *true* solid-body electric guitar. Les Paul's Log experiment may have been built several years earlier, but Bigsby's instrument was purpose-built.

Travis was also friends with a certain Leo Fender. It seems highly likely that the Bigsby Merle Travis played a part in influencing the early Fender production-line instruments.

**P**aul Bigsby was a skilled engineer at the Crocker Motorcycle Company in Los Angeles. It was here that in 1945 he first met and befriended the celebrated country picker and motorbike enthusiast Merle Travis. When Travis experienced tuning problems with

▲
**One of the most important guitar players of the 1940s, Merle Travis introduced "Travis Picking," a technique featuring alternating bass notes picked with the thumb.**

▼

*Guitar Rags And A Too Fast Past* (1994) is a five-CD collection of Merle Travis' early work, some of which features the Bigsby Travis guitar.

| | |
|---|---|
| **Body style:** | Single cutaway solid body (with hollowed wings) |
| **Materials:** | Maple body with straight-through neck; maple wings |
| **Finish:** | Natural |
| **Fretboard:** | Rosewood |
| **Frets:** | 19 (frets 16–19 are partial and do not span the entire width of the fingerboard) |
| **Inlays:** | Playing-card symbols |
| **Scale:** | 22 ½" |
| **Bridge:** | Adjustable |
| **Tailpiece:** | Trapeze |
| **Pickups:** | 1 single-coil pickup |
| **Electrics:** | Single volume control; 2 tone controls; filter switching |

# BIGSBY GRADY MARTIN 1952

Although he produced a solid-body electric guitar a full three years before Leo Fender, Paul Bigsby did not pursue production-line ambitions. His Merle Travis guitar quickly attracted commissions from other top players, such as Billy Byrd, Butterball Paige, and Grady Martin. Bigsby, who had set up a small workshop next to his home in Downey, California, was unable to keep up with demand and waiting lists grew to beyond two years. As he kept no formal records of his work, it is unknown how many instruments Bigsby ultimately produced.

When his health failed in the 1960s, Bigsby sold his business to former Gibson president Ted McCarty, who focused his attention on the Bigsby vibrato systems. Still in production today, Bigsby vibratos are now manufactured by Gretsch.

The doubleneck instrument shown here was built for Nashville session player Grady Martin in 1952. The guitar is augmented by a mandolin neck that extends from the upper treble bout.

▲
**Grady Martin was a member of the elite "Nashville A-Team," a group of top session musicians who backed country's biggest stars during the 1950s and 1960s.**

▼
**Although not one of the Johnny Burnette Trio, Martin, with fellow A-Teamer Bob Moore, provided backing for Burnette's early rockabilly hits.**

| | |
|---|---|
| **Body style:** | Single cutaway solid body |
| **Materials:** | Maple body with straight-through maple guitar and mandolin necks |
| **Finish:** | Natural |
| **Fretboard:** | Rosewood |
| **Frets:** | 20 on each neck |
| **Inlays:** | Dots, blocks, and diamonds |
| **Bridge:** | Adjustable |
| **Tailpiece:** | Trapeze with Bigsby vibrato mechanism |
| **Pickups:** | 3 single-coil pickups on guitar, 1 single-coil pickup on mandolin; 3-way selector switch |
| **Electrics:** | Single volume control; 2 tone controls; function switch |

# BOHMANN HARP GUITAR 1910

strings varies, but twelve, enabling all the notes of the octave to be played, is most common.

The first harp guitars appeared in Europe at the end of the eighteenth century. Quite rare, they have been used by such classical masters as Mauro Giuliani, Ferdinando Carulli, and Julian Bream.

Joseph Bohmann was born in Bohemia in 1848, emigrating to the United States thirty years later. As the self-styled "World's Greatest Instrument Maker," Bohmann won eight international competitions between 1888 and 1904.

A curious hybrid, the harp guitar is a conventional six-string guitar with a second neck supporting a series of "unstopped" strings—the pitch of these cannot be altered by fretting; instead they are tuned and either plucked or allowed to vibrate "in sympathy" with the guitar strings. The number of extra

**Chicago guitar virtuoso Signor Emilio Calamara poses with a Bohmann harp guitar from 1895.**

▼
**The guitar hybrid can be heard on *Harp Guitars Under The Stars* (2010), an album of duets by Muriel Anderson and John Doan. Modern-day instruments are used on this recording.**

| | |
|---|---|
| **Body style:** | Harp guitar |
| **Materials:** | Brazilian rosewood back and sides, spruce top; laminated maple necks |
| **Finish:** | Natural |
| **Fretboard:** | Rosewood |
| **Inlays:** | Concentric circle in mother-of-pearl with diamond block on 5th fret |
| **Frets:** | 20 (including partials) |
| **Scale:** | 25" |
| **Bridge:** | Rosewood |
| **Harp:** | 12 strings; 4 internal "sympathy" strings made from copper, brass, steel, and German silver, tuned via wing-nuts on the body |

# BRIAN MAY RED SPECIAL 1963

rian May was never the most conventional of rock stars. An academic child, it was not until May was researching his PhD in astrophysics that he decided to become a professional guitarist. His chosen instrument was also unorthodox: not one of the popular American classics,

but a guitar he had designed as a sixteen-year-old and built with his father, Harold—an aviation engineer.

They began to work on the guitar in August 1963, most of the wood coming from a reclaimed eighteenth-century oak mantel. The body construction was chambered and covered with two mahogany sheets to give the appearance of a solid body. The unusual coloring was achieved using many layers of Rustin's plastic coating.

The Red Special features a set of three Burns Tri-Sonic pickups. Customized by May with a reverse wind/polarity, the coils were set with Araldite epoxy to reduce microphonics.

May has used his home-built guitar throughout his career, and had a number of replicas built. In 1983 he allowed the Guild Guitar Company to issue a production version, and in 2001 a highly regarded Korean-built Burns copy emerged. The Red Special is now made by Brian May Guitars.

▲
**Brian May plays his Red Special in concert with Queen in 1980.**

▼
The unique tones of the Red Special are heard on Queen's album *A Night At The Opera* (1975), most notably May's definitive rock guitar solo on "Bohemian Rhapsody."

| | |
|---|---|
| **Body style:** | Double cutaway, chambered solid body |
| **Materials:** | Oak and blockboard body covered front and back with mahogany sheet; straight-through oak neck |
| **Finish:** | Natural red-brown color resulting from application of Rustin's plastic varnish |
| **Fretboard:** | Painted oak |
| **Inlays:** | Hand-carved from mother-of-pearl buttons |
| **Frets:** | 24 (not including zero fret) |
| **Scale:** | 24" |
| **Width at nut:** | 1 17/20" |
| **Bridge:** | Adjustable; tremolo mechanism built from old motorcycle parts |
| **Pickups:** | 3 single-coil customized Burns Tri-Sonics; on/off switch for each pickup |
| **Electrics:** | Master volume and tone control; phase switch for each pickup |

# BURNS : THE STORY

J im Burns, a legendary figure who was never far from the epicenter of the U.K.'s electric guitar industry from the late 1950s through to the 1980s, is probably the only Briton whose contribution to guitar design and production deserves the sobriquet of "Britain's Leo Fender."

Born in 1925 in County Durham, England, James Ormston Burns had taught himself to build his first electric guitar while serving in the Royal Air Force, and in 1952 sold his first instruments. In 1958, Burns' first line of guitars was launched using the Supersound brand, the company itself being a general manufacturer/retailer of musical instruments, audio, and movie equipment. The first Supersound guitar was the Telecaster-inspired Ike Isaacs Short Scale, endorsed by Britain's top jazz player of the day. It is thought to have been Britain's first ever mass-produced electric guitar. ①

A year later, the ambitious Burns teamed up with Henry Weill to manufacture guitars under the Burns-Weill banner. Under this designation they produced two new models—the Fenton and the Super Streamline, one of the most visually bizarre early electric guitars, and known widely as "the Martian Cricket Bat." ② The partnership soon foundered, and in 1960 Burns went solo, founding Ormston Burns London Ltd.

The timing of the "Burns London" guitars was critical to the brand's success over the next five years. It coincided with the Beat Boom, a period that saw an explosion in demand for electric guitars. At the same time, a period of high trade tariffs on U.S. goods meant that the Fenders, Gibsons, and Gretschs used by the big American stars were unavailable. Thus, Burns set about producing what he termed "mass-produced one-offs"— instruments that were produced in large quantities but that had the personal quirks of an individually made instrument. Nowhere is this truer than the with early Burns models like the Sonic or Vibra Artist, ③ where the neck proportions might vary greatly according to who was doing the work. This uniqueness was enhanced on more expensive, heavily handcrafted models, such as the Bison. ④

First built in 1962, the Bison was the first high-end luxury Burns instrument. From its striking black finish, gold hardware, unique double cutaway horns, four Ultra-Sonic pickups, and versatile Split-Sound circuitry, it was an electric guitar the like of which had never before

A 1958 advert in the *Melody Maker* for the Supersound Ike Isaacs guitar in 1958.

The Burns-Weill Super Streamline bass—widely known as the "Martian Cricket Bat."

The Vibra Artist— top of the range in the first Burns catalog.

**1925**
James Ormston Burns born in County Durham, England

**1958**
Burns designs the first British electric guitar for Supersound

**1959**
Burns founds the short-lived Burns-Weill with Henry Weill

**1960**
Jim Burns launches his own Burns London brand of guitars

**1962**
The Burns Black Bison is the first British luxury electric guitar

**1964**
Burns produces the Marvin model for Hank Marvin of The Shadows

**1965**
Burns bought by U.S. Baldwin Piano & Organ Company

been built outside of the U.S. Only fifty of the original Bisons were built before the specification was simplified. And this was a good example of the extremes of Jim Burns' personality. Burns was a classic "ideas man" who worked during the night and slept during the day. He was evidently not at all technically minded, and often drew designs on the back of a cigarette packet, but managed to draw together a skilled team capable of fleshing out his ideas. Unfortunately, his ability and desire to innovate always outstripped his business acumen.

The brand's success peaked in 1964 when Jim Burns was able to convince Britain's most popular guitar instrumental band, The Shadows, to endorse his guitars. The band's guitarists, Hank Marvin and Bruce Welch, reported that they were having difficulties keeping their Fender Stratocasters in tune and collaborated with Burns on the development of a replacement. What emerged was the finest guitar the company ever produced—the Burns Marvin.  As the Shadows toured and performed on TV with their new Burns guitars (including the Shadows bass), the brand's profile on the British music scene rocketed.

Once again, however, the truth was that, despite being a great innovator, Jim Burns was a poor businessman. Although he was the highest-profile British guitar maker during a time of unprecedented demand for electric guitars, by 1965 Burns was so heavily in debt that the company had to be sold. Under the new owner, the Cincinatti-based Baldwin Piano & Organ Company, the Burns brand dwindled and within two years had been laid to rest.

Burns himself was rarely idle, however. Contractually unable to use his own name, he formed Ormston Steel Guitars in 1966; in 1970 he was part of the Hayman operation; from 1974 to 1977 he ran Burns UK; and from 1979 to 1983 he ran Jim Burns Actualisers Ltd, continuing to produce characterful guitars such as the Scorpion and the Steer.

In 1992, Barry Gibson resuscitated the Burns brand, hiring Jim Burns as a consultant until his death in 1998. Leaning very heavily on classic designs from the first half of the 1960s, the company has since successfully achieved what its originator never could: building guitars to a high standard *and* staying in business.

The Burns Bison was arguably Europe's first luxury production-line electric guitar.

The Burns Marvin—the most collectible of all Burns guitars.

The Shadows (here with Cliff Richard, right) and other 1960s groups gave valuable publicity to Burns guitars.

**1967** Baldwin ends production of Burns guitars

**1970** Jim Burns works on the short-lived, London-based Hayman brand

**1974** Jim Burns founds Burns UK, and enjoys cult success with the Flyte guitar—modeled on the Concorde supersonic aircraft

**1979** Produces guitars under the Jim Burns Actualisers Ltd brand

**1992** Employed as a consultant by Burns London Ltd which successfully builds replicas of instruments designed between 1960 and 1965

**1998** Jim Burns dies

# BURNS : THE FAMILY TREE (1958-PRESENT)

Jim Burns has been described as "Britain's own Leo Fender." While his impact on the world of music has been considerably more modest, he remains the single most important British luthier. An innovator he may have been, but his business skills were not of the same order. During his lifetime he founded or collaborated in a number of well-known brands, which produced fine instruments but invariably ended in commercial failure. This family tree covers Supersound, Burns-Weill, Ormston Burns, Baldwin, Hayman, Burns UK, and Jim Burns Actualisers.

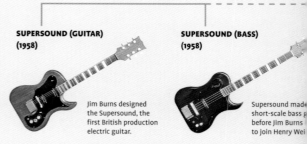

**SUPERSOUND (GUITAR) (1958)**

Jim Burns designed the Supersound, the first British production electric guitar.

**SUPERSOUND (BASS) (1958)**

Supersound made short-scale bass g before Jim Burns to join Henry Wei

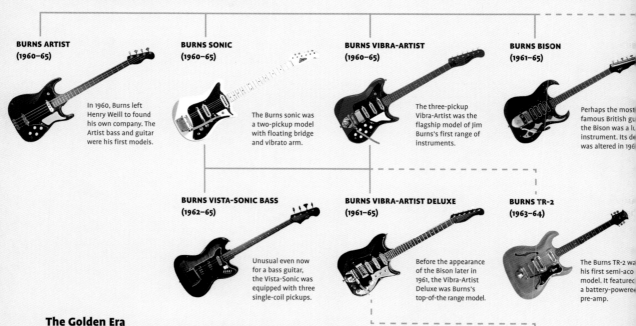

**BURNS ARTIST (1960–65)**

In 1960, Burns left Henry Weill to found his own company. The Artist bass and guitar were his first models.

**BURNS SONIC (1960–65)**

The Burns sonic was a two-pickup model with floating bridge and vibrato arm.

**BURNS VIBRA-ARTIST (1960–65)**

The three-pickup Vibra-Artist was the flagship model of Jim Burns's first range of instruments.

**BURNS BISON (1961–65)**

Perhaps the most famous British gu the Bison was a lu instrument. Its de was altered in 196

**BURNS VISTA-SONIC BASS (1962–65)**

Unusual even now for a bass guitar, the Vista-Sonic was equipped with three single-coil pickups.

**BURNS VIBRA-ARTIST DELUXE (1961–65)**

Before the appearance of the Bison later in 1961, the Vibra-Artist Deluxe was Burns's top-of-the range model.

**BURNS TR-2 (1963–64)**

The Burns TR-2 wa his first semi-aco model. It feature a battery-powere pre-amp.

## The Golden Era

Of the many guitar companies that Jim Burns operated it is Ormston Burns London Ltd, which ran between 1960 and 1965, that is best remembered. Two guitars in particular stand out from this period, the black Bison—which first appeared in 1961 with four pickups—and the Marvin, Burns' own take on the Fender Stratocaster. In 1992 a new business emerged, with Jim Burns contributing as a consultant until his death in 1998; Burns London has continued to produce highly regarded reissues of his 1960s classics.

**BURNS VIBRA-SLIM (1964–65)**

A semi-acoustic w briefly added to t Burns "Vibra" ran shortly before the Baldwin buy-out.

## The Baldwin Years

In 1965 Jim Burns accepted an offer of $380,000 from the Baldwin Piano and Organ Company of Cincinnati, Ohio. Existing models were assigned numbers (the Bison became the 511, the Marvin became the 524) and the Baldwin name was often crudely attached. This period saw a decline in quality of Burns-made instruments.

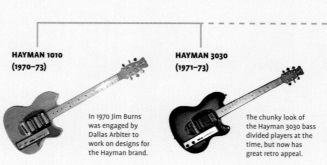

**HAYMAN 1010 (1970–73)**

In 1970 Jim Burns was engaged by Dallas Arbiter to work on designs for the Hayman brand.

**HAYMAN 3030 (1971–73)**

The chunky look of the Hayman 3030 bass divided players at the time, but now has great retro appeal.

**SHERGOLD MODULATOR (1976–82)**

Shergold had prov the woodwork fo Hayman guitars. Burns's influence the design is clea

**BURNS-WEILL FENTON
(1959–60)**

The Burns-Weill Fenton guitar (and also bass) were modeled on Japanese Guyatone models.

**BURNS-WEILL
SUPER STREAMLINE (GUITAR)
(1959–60)**

With its unorthodox body shape, the Burns-Weill Super Streamline was known as the "Martian Cricket Bat."

**BURNS-WEILL
SUPER STREAMLINE (BASS)
(1960)**

Burns-Weill also made the the Super Streamline, available as a twin-pickup bass guitar.

**BURNS JAZZ SPLIT SOUND
(1962–65)**

Split Sound pickups combined the treble strings/bridge pickup with the bass strings/neck pickup.

**BURNS DOUBLE SIX
(1964–65)**

The Double Six was Burns's first electric twelve-string guitar.

**BURNS MARVIN
(1964–65)**

Created for Hank Marvin and Bruce Welch of The Shadows, the Marvin is a highly collectible guitar.

**BURNS SHADOWS BASS
(1964–65)**

A bass counterpart, also with a scrolled headstock, was made for The Shadows' bass player, John Rostill.

**AMPEG WILD DOG EG1
1963–64)**

In 1963, Burns signed an export deal with Ampeg. The Wild Dog EG1 was a stock Jazz Split Sound.

**BALDWIN 712R/T
(1967–70)**

Although Jim Burns played no part in the Baldwin era, new models were added in the Burns style.

## Burns Tri-Sonic Pickups

The Tri-sonic, found on most early 1960s Burns guitars, is the company's best-known pickup design. Unlike most pickups, the Tri-sonic's coil is not held in a rigid shape, but squashed into an oval and fitted around three ceramic magnets. The "random" direction in which the coils point produces a richer harmonic content than conventional winding, but the looseness of the coil makes the Tri-sonic microphonic, causing unwanted feedback. This would be eliminated by "potting" the unit to prevent movement.

**URNS VIRGINIAN
1965)**

The most popular of the semi-acoustics, the Virginian was produced throughout the Baldwin era.

**BURNS UK FLYTE
(1974–77)**

Jim Burns reappeared in 1974 as Burns UK with a guitar based on the Concorde supersonic jet.

**BURNS UK MIRAGE
(1976–77)**

Burns UK produced the unusual Mirage in 1976. Like the Flyte, it featured Burns's own Mach One pickups.

**BURNS UK LJ24
(1977)**

Featuring Mach Two pickups, the visually more conventional LJ24 was unable to save Burns UK in 1977.

**M BURNS SCORPION
1979–83)**

The Scorpion was the first "Jim Burns" guitar. Its unique rear "pincer" horns recalled the Bison of 1961.

**JIM BURNS STEER
(1979–83)**

The Jim Burns Steer was a twin-pickup semi-acoustic, available with or without a cutaway.

**JIM BURNS MAGPIE
(1980–83)**

Featuring a Fender-influenced body, the Magpie appeared in two versions.

**JIM BURNS BANDIT
(1983)**

The Bandit was the last original Jim Burns design to be produced.

# BURNS VIBRA ARTIST 1960

In 1959 the Burns-Weill company produced two guitars, each with a matching bass—the Guyatone-inspired Fenton and the bizarre Super Streamline, known widely as the "Martian Cricket Bat." But the first attempt by a British company to produce a range of "serious" electric guitars would be ill-fated. The difficult working relationship between Jim Burns and Henry Weill quickly deteriorated, and the partners went their separate ways. The following year Weill started up the Fenton-Weill brand, and Burns launched his own line. Beginning with a range of three models, Burns introduced the Sonic, the twin-pickup Artist, and the top-of-the-range Vibra Artist.

In an era when American guitars were not widely available to British musicians, Burns set out on a mission to produce instruments that were at least superior to the cheap Japanese models being imported at the time.

The Vibra Artist featured a simple but original body shape, its twin cutaway with oddly asymmetric horns giving access to the upper notes of a full two-octave fingerboard—indeed, among the many future innovations Jim Burns might claim is the creation of the first production twenty-four-fret fingerboard on an electric guitar.

Early Burns guitars such as the Vibra Artist were somewhat anachronistic, with frequent whimsical characteristics in design and construction. Burns often used reconstituted countertops rescued from pub renovations in his bodies, so the woods used were not necessarily even the same.

The Vibra Artist was an excellent instrument, its three Tri-Sonic pickups and electrics giving plenty of scope for creating very specific tones. But retailing for U.S.$220 (£78), it was a serious investment when compared to the ubiquitous Guyatone GL-50 which was available for U.S.$80 (£29).

▼
Jim Burns—the "British Leo Fender"— was a great innovator but a poor businessman. Yet in spite of many setbacks he always seemed to return with something new.

| | |
|---|---|
| **Body style:** | Solid body double cutaway |
| **Materials:** | Mahogany body; set maple neck (early Burns guitars are notorious for variations in woods used, sometimes using whatever happened to be available) |
| **Finish:** | Assorted—most commonly red |
| **Fretboard:** | Rosewood |
| **Inlays:** | Dot |
| **Frets:** | 24 (not including zero fret) |
| **Scale:** | 24 ¾" |
| **Width at nut:** | 1 ¹¹⁄₁₆" |
| **Bridge:** | Adjustable with chrome cover; vibrato mechanism on tailpiece |
| **Pickups:** | 3 single-coil Tri-Sonic pickups; multiple switching |
| **Electrics:** | Dedicated volume and tone controls for each pickup |

# Burns Bison 1961

▲
**Henry Dartnall of English trio Young Knives plays a reissue Burns Bison.**

▼
**Young Knives' 2006 album *Voices Of Animals And Men* was the band's first album to reach the U.K. Top 30.**

the Bison would surely be immediately recognizable in silhouette. Also notable was the narrow six-in-line headstock with its underside bat wing shape.

The original Bison, issued in 1961, was striking in its black finish and gold hardware, with four Ultra-Sonic pickups developed with the Goldring company (better known for hi-fi cartridges), so-called "Boomerang" vibrato arm, and the extremely versatile Split-Sound circuitry. Finally, concealed in the neck heel was a "gear box" truss rod system.

No British guitar with such features had been built before. And this was reflected in a retail price of £157. (At a time when the average weekly wage in Britain was under £10 a week, the Bison would have been equivalent to around £2,700 [over $4,000] at today's prices.) Impractical to manufacture, just fifty examples of the original Bison were made before a successful simplified redesign was launched.

The Burns Bison was arguably the first truly great electric guitar produced outside of the United States. Visually it has a number of interesting features. The double cutaway horns from which the guitar takes its name are certainly more pronounced than on any other guitar—

| | |
|---|---|
| **Body style:** | Double cutaway solid body with asymmetric curved horns |
| **Materials:** | Sycamore body (other hardwoods used on later versions) with set maple neck (bolt-on after 1961) |
| **Finish:** | Black (other colors available on later models) |
| **Fretboard:** | Ebony |
| **Inlays:** | Dot |
| **Frets:** | 22 (not including zero fret) |
| **Scale:** | 24 ¾" |
| **Width at nut:** | 1 ⅝" |
| **Bridge:** | Adjustable bridge with Boomerang vibrato (Rez-O-Tube vibrato after 1963) |
| **Pickups:** | 4 Ultra-Sonic single-coil pickups (3 Rez-O-Matiks on models after 1963); rotary combination selector switches |
| **Electrics:** | Master volume; Split-Sound circuitry |

# BURNS MARVIN 1964

A typical Shadows instrumental was free of flash or bluster, consisting of a simple guitar melody played cleanly with a touch of echo and some gentle working of the vibrato arm. It was a unique sound that made The Shadows the biggest band in the pre-Beatles era. Marvin's significance, though, is as *the* musician who inspired a generation of teenagers to take up the instrument.

In 1963 the band's two guitarists, Marvin and Bruce Welch, approached Jim Burns to produce a new guitar that wouldn't easily go out of tune, as their Fenders had done. The instrument that emerged was the Burns Marvin, a three-pickup model with an unusual scrolled headstock. It also incorporated the Rez-o-Tube vibrato, enabling Hank to twang away *and* stay in tune.

Only around three hundred original Marvins were made, and these are the most collectible of all Burns guitars. A limited edition 40th Anniversary model was issued in 2004.

Hank Marvin found fame when his band, The Drifters, began backing a young singer named Cliff Richard in 1958. Discovering that an American group of the same name existed, they became The Shadows, and soon began an impressive string of hits of their own.

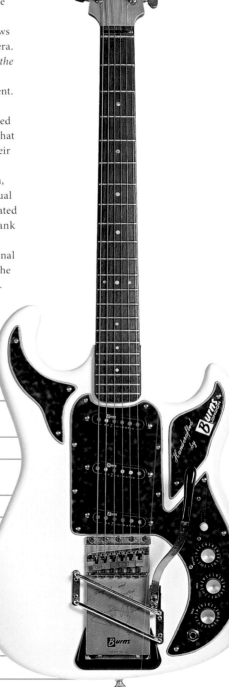

▲
**The Shadows are England's most successful instrumental band, having notched up an incredible thirty-five hit singles—and a further thirty-four backing Cliff Richard.**

▼
**Recorded in 1965, *The Sound Of The Shadows* features Hank Marvin and the band playing their new Burns instruments.**

| | |
|---|---|
| **Body style:** | Double cutaway solid body |
| **Materials:** | Honduras mahogany body (alder on reissues) with Canadian rock maple bolt-on neck |
| **Finish:** | White and red |
| **Fretboard:** | Indian rosewood (also maple on reissue models) |
| **Inlays:** | Dot |
| **Frets:** | 21 (not including zero fret) |
| **Scale:** | 25 ½" |
| **Width at nut:** | 1 ⅝" |
| **Bridge:** | Adjustable with Rez-O-Tube vibrato system |
| **Pickups:** | 3 single-coil Rez-O-Matik pickups; 5-way selector switch; additional push/pull pickup selector from the tone controls |
| **Electrics:** | Master volume and 2 tone controls |

# BURNS UK FLYTE 1975

arrangement was ended following a company reorganization.

Burns next emerged in 1974 with the Burns UK brand. Moving his manufacturing base from London to his native Newcastle-upon-Tyne in the northeast of England, Burns achieved a degree of success with one of his most unusual guitars. Originally to be named after the Concorde supersonic jet, it appeared in 1974 as the Flyte. The guitar featured two Burns Mach One Humbuster pickups and was capable of variety of tones, although the body shape made access to the top frets extremely difficult.

The Flyte was briefly popular toward the end of the Glam Rock era in the 1970s and was sported in television concerts by such likely names as Slade and Marc Bolan's T. Rex.

Burns UK folded in 1977, but the Flyte was relaunched by Burns London in 2003, the fret access issue addressed by the appearance of a cutaway.

Under Baldwin ownership, the original Burns line came to an end in 1970. And although legally prevented from using his name, Jim Burns himself carried on regardless. In the 1970s he was engaged by Dallas-Arbiter to design guitars under the Hayman brand; this

▲
A 1975 Burns UK Ltd. catalog highlights the new Flyte guitar, designed to "facilitate ease of playing with maximum comfort."

▼
The Space Age looks of the Flyte appealed to Marc Bolan of T. Rex. He played one in the video of "London Boys," a track of *Futuristic Dragon* (1976).

| | |
|---|---|
| **Body style:** | Delta shape |
| **Materials:** | Body created from selected hardwoods; bolt-on Canadian rock maple neck |
| **Finish:** | White or silver; bass also in natural |
| **Fretboard:** | Ebony finish |
| **Inlays:** | Acrylic dot |
| **Frets:** | 22 (not including zero fret) |
| **Scale:** | 24 ¾" |
| **Width at nut:** | 1 ⅝" |
| **Bridge:** | Dynamic Tension bridge; individually adjustable saddle; overall height adjustment |
| **Pickups:** | Burns Mach One Humbuster pickups with Alcomax 4-bar magnets; 3-way selector switch |
| **Electrics:** | Master volume and tone controls |

# BUSCARINO VIRTUOSO 1994

**B**ased in Franklin, North Carolina, John Buscarino works alone, hand-building exquisite guitars for some of the finest (not to mention wealthiest) jazz and rock musicians.

Buscarino learned his art as apprentice to two very different luthiers: classical guitar builder Augustine LoPrinzi and famed archtop builder Robert Benedetto. His instruments are built using traditional techniques that he has refined over the past forty years.

Buscarino's instruments are prized not just for their sound and playability but for their aesthetic beauty, and have already found their way into major collections. Indeed, in 1996, Buscarino was one of twenty-two leading luthiers commissioned by guitar collector extraordinaire, the late Scott Chinery, to produce a blue guitar. The resulting exhibition took place at the Smithsonian in Washington, D.C.

Buscarino makes classical and solid-body guitars, but it is for his archtop models that he is best known. At the top of the range is the Virtuoso, with its burl wood headstock, ebony tailpiece, and powerful floating humbuckers, designed by Kent Armstrong to eliminate unwanted feedback.

Jazz guitarist and composer Bob Shimizu favors the Buscarino Virtuoso for recording work.

▼

George Benson's Buscarino can be heard on the 2006 album *Givin' It Up*, recorded with Al Jarreau and stars from the jazz fusion world, such as Herbie Hancock, Stanley Clarke, and Marcus Miller.

| | |
|---|---|
| **Body style:** | Hollow-body archtop with single Venetian cutaway |
| **Materials:** | Back and sides: choice of seasoned, figured flame maple or aged European cello woods; top: seasoned Sitka spruce or aged European cello wood; 3-piece flame maple neck |
| **Finish:** | Natural, honey blonde, vintage natural, blush, sunburst, or custom color |
| **Fretboard:** | Ebony |
| **Inlays:** | Abalone "tree of life" on neck |
| **Frets:** | 22 |
| **Scale:** | 25" |
| **Bridge:** | Adjustable |
| **Pickups:** | Buscarino floating humbucker (or built-in humbucker) |
| **Electrics:** | Master volume and tone controls (on or hidden beneath pickguard) |

# CAMPBELL AMERICAN TRANSITONE 2006

employees learned their skills at the Guild factory in nearby Rhode Island, discarded when Guild was bought out.

Concentrating on a small range of designs, the most popular model produced by Campbell American is the Transitone, an instrument that, interestingly, owes little visually to the American classics on which most custom guitars are based—indeed it brings to mind some of the more outré designs that appeared in Europe and Japan from the 1960s.

As a custom-built guitar, the Transitone is typically available in a far wider range of options than the "name" brands could ever hope to offer. The pickup choices, for example, include Seymour Duncan Jazz or JBs, Dimarzio Bluesbucker, Lollar, or TV Jones selections. So although it's difficult to define any Transitone "sound," the appeal is having a finely crafted instrument that can be tailored to the requirements of the player.

Founded in Blackstone Valley, New England, in 2002, Campbell American is one of the leaders of a growing number of U.S. "boutique" guitar makers. The company's mission statement is to "build guitars here in America using old New England craftsmanship." Indeed, a number of

▲
British guitarist Bill Nelson came to prominence in the band Be-Bop Deluxe. He has his own signature Campbell American Transitone—the Nelsonic.

▼
The Nelsonic Transitone can be heard on many of Bill Nelson's recent albums, among them 2009's *Here Comes Mr. Mercury*.

| | |
|---|---|
| **Body style:** | Single cutaway solid body |
| **Materials:** | American linden (ash, maple, mahogany, or sapele may also be specified) |
| **Finish:** | Wide assortment of natural and color finishes; nitro-cellulose lacquer finishes |
| **Fretboard:** | Maple, rosewood, or ebony |
| **Inlays:** | Acrylic dot |
| **Frets:** | 22 |
| **Scale:** | 25 ½" |
| **Bridge:** | Adjustable Gotoh (optional Gotoh or Bigsby vibrato) |
| **Pickups:** | 2 or 3 single-coil pickups or humbuckers (Seymour Duncan Jazz or JBs, Dimarzio Bluesbucker, Lollar, TV Jones); 3-way selector switch |
| **Electrics:** | Master volume control and tone |

# CARVIN H2 "HOLDSWORTH" 1996

Founded in 1948 as Kiesel Electronics, producing pickups and accessories, Carvin began to produce guitars, basses, and amplifiers in 1954. Unusual in the world of musical instrument sales, almost all of Carvin's products are sold via mail order from the company's headquarters in San Diego, California. The appeal of the Carvin name is that these guitars represent exceptionally good value: since they are built to order they are effectively custom instruments, but with no distributors or retailers cutting into their profits they can be sold at surprisingly competitive prices. And endorsements from such names as Frank Zappa and Steve Vai suggest that these are serious instruments.

Best-known for playing the groundbreaking Synthaxe (*see page 235*), British-born fusion guitarist Allan Holdsworth first came into contact with Carvin when he moved to California in the 1980s. The most unusual aspect of his two signature models—the single-pickup H1 and the twin-pickup H2—was its semi-hollow body construction, which featured two "i-beam" braces into which the neck was set. The top of the body was glued into place without coming into contact with the two beams.

▲
A stalwart of Britain's jazz-rock scene, Allan Holdsworth found a wider audience when he was championed by Eddie Van Halen in the 1980s. He is widely admired for the speed and complexity of his single-note playing.

▼
Holdsworth plays both electric guitar and Synthaxe on 2000's *The Sixteen Men Of Tain.*

**Body style:** Semi-hollow single cutaway

**Materials:** Alder body with set alder neck; optional maple tops

**Finish:** Customer-specifiable colors with options of quilted or flamed maple tops

**Fretboard:** Ebony

**Frets:** 24 (jumbo frets)

**Scale:** 25 ½"

**Width at nut:** 1 ⅝"

**Bridge:** Vibrato

**Pickups:** H22 humbuckers with 3-way selector switch; optional coil-splitting switches

**Electrics:** Master volume and tone control

**Tuners:** Sperzel locking tuners

# CASIO MG-500/510 1987

Founded in Tokyo, Japan, in 1946, Casio is now one of the world's major manufacturers of domestic electronics. Casio's fortunes were based almost entirely around having developed the world's first all-electric compact calculator in 1957. During the 1970s, Casio produced such era-defining products as the Mini calculator, which sold over 10 million units worldwide, and the Casiotron combined watch/calculator/calendar.

In 1980, Casio joined the musical instrument market with the Casiotone compact synthesizer. Little more than an adult toy, it nonetheless generated an unlikely worldwide hit single, "Da Da Da" by German group Trio.

Casio's first attempts at producing a MIDI guitar controller came in 1987, in the MG-500/510 models. The MG-510 (*left*) had a conventional Stratocaster-shaped body, the MG-500 (*right*) more futuristic lines, in keeping with the period aesthetic. Essentially the same instrument, both were also kitted with hexaphonic pickups alongside the bridge, enabling the movements of each string to be converted to MIDI data. This could then be passed down a cable and used to trigger sounds on an external MIDI unit, such as a synthesizer, sampler, or drum machine.

▲
Casio used Erasure's Vince Clarke, one of the best-known electronic musicians of the 1980s, to advertise the new "MG" MIDI guitars.

▼
Despite the differing body shapes, the MG-500 and 510 were essentially the same instrument.

| | |
|---|---|
| **Body style:** | Solid body with single cutaway (MG-500); or double cutaway (MG-510) |
| **Materials:** | Basswood body with bolt-on maple neck |
| **Finish:** | White, red, or black |
| **Fretboard:** | Rosewood |
| **Frets:** | 22 |
| **Scale:** | 25 ½" |
| **Width at nut:** | 1 ¾" |
| **Bridge:** | Adjustable with separate Vibrato |
| **Pickups:** | 3 EMG pickups—2 single-coil (neck and center), one humbucker (bridge); hexaphonic MIDI converter pickup; 5-way selector switch |
| **Electrics:** | Master volume and tone control; multifunction MIDI control panel |
| **Tuners:** | Gotoh |

# CASIO DG-20 1987

synthesizer with the keyboard replaced by a guitar neck. Plucking the string sent MIDI pitch and gate signals to the onboard synth—the sound you heard was dependent on the preset sound you selected. The DG-20 was also kitted out with an internal amplifier and speaker, making it a self-contained instrument.

There are few good reasons why the DG-20 was not treated overly seriously. Casio's market reputation was established at the lower end, specializing in cheap instruments for beginners, so expectations of the DG-20 were low. Furthermore, as an instrument it was unpleasant for an experienced guitarist to play, with no bending notes or vibrato possible. Finally, the in-built voices, with accompanying drum machine, were rather tacky.

Where the DG-20 did score, however was that it enabled guitarists to input MIDI data into sequencers without having to acquire basic keyboard skills.

**M**any guitarists who lived through the 1980s would doubtless baulk at the idea of even calling the Casio DG-20 a guitar. To begin with, this curious box with its six nylon B-strings had no acoustic sound of its own. It was, in effect, a standard budget Casio

▲
"I think I need a 1983 Casio DG-20 electric guitar ... set to electric mandolin ... some drums ... yeah!" New Zealand's Flight Of The Conchords namecheck a legend but erroneously—the date should be 1987.

▼
McKenzie's "Digital Guitar" features in the song "Boom" on The Conchords' eponymous first album (2008).

| | |
|---|---|
| **Body style:** | Single cutaway plastic body |
| **Materials:** | Molded plastic |
| **Finish:** | Gray/silver |
| **Fretboard:** | Plastic, with plastic molded frets |
| **Frets:** | 21 |
| **Bridge:** | All in one non-adjustable |
| **Electrics (Front):** | Power switch; main volume control; drum machine volume control; start/stop key; synchro/fill key; mute key; 4 miniature drum pads (snare; hi tom; lo tom; cymbal) |
| **Electrics (Side):** | Tone selectors (assorted acoustic guitars; assorted electric guitars; harp; glockenspiel; funky clavinet; organ; mandolin; trumpet; flute; clarinet); drum machine presets (rock; pop; reggae; country; enka; swing; blues; bossa nova; waltz; tango); drum machine tempo buttons |
| **Connections:** | MIDI output; footswitch; headphones; line out |

# CHAPMAN STICK 1974

At first glance, the Chapman Stick appears to be little more than a long, wide guitar neck. But although the Stick resembles a guitar, the playing technique is very different. The Stick is a "tapping" instrument: sounds are produced by pressing the strings against the frets rather than by plucking them. The original Stick (as shown) featured ten strings: the right hand taps the upper five strings while the left hand taps the lower five. In this way the adept player can double up combinations of bass parts, chords, and lead lines, making it more comparable to a keyboard instrument than a guitar.

The Stick was conceived in the late 1960s by American jazz guitarist Emmett Chapman who had developed his own double-handed tapping style on a long-scale guitar but now sought an instrument on which the technique could be developed. Launched in 1974, the early models were made from solid ironwood with a split pickup that enabled the bass and treble strings to be channeled to different amplifiers.

Mainly thanks to the Stick's inventor and his persistent efforts to further develop his niche instrument, the Stick is now well established with thousands of ardent players across the globe.

▲
One of the elite of session bass, Tony Levin has worked with such diverse artists as Peter Gabriel, King Crimson, John Lennon, Buddy Rich, and Alice Cooper.

▼
Tony Levin's Chapman Stick can be heard fulfilling bass duties on King Crimson's 1981 album *Discipline*.

**Body style:** Elongated fretted fingerboard

**Materials:** Ironwood (later models have been built from ebony, padauk, Indian rosewood, tarara, maple, wenge, mahogany, and bamboo, injection-molded polycarbonate resin, and graphite epoxy)

**Finish:** Natural (colors available on later models)

**Inlays:** Mother-of-pearl

**Frets:** 25 (not including zero fret)

**Scale:** 36"

**Width at nut:** 3 ¼" (3 ¾" for 12-string version)

**Bridge:** Individual adjustable screw saddles; combined bridge and tailpiece on modern Sticks

**Pickups:** Passive 2-channel split pickup (EMG active pickups available on newer models)

**Electrics:** Master volume and tone control

# CHARVEL MODEL 4 1986

Fender Stratocasters. At the end of 1978 Charvel sold his share of the business to one of his employees, Grover Jackson, under whose management the brand would evolve from customization to guitar production.

Early Charvel users included Eddie Van Halen, Bon Jovi's Richie Sambora, Warren DeMartini of Ratt, and Twisted Sister's Eddie Ojeda.

During the 1980s, having worked with guitarist Randy Rhoads, Jackson set up a sister brand that took his own name. Charvel guitars gradually shifted production to Japan and became widely known for their souped-up, high-performance, Strat-inspired instruments with the characteristic pointy headstocks.

Featuring all of the standard superstrat accoutrements, such as fast fingerboard, powered pre-amp, and locking tremolo system, the Charvel Model 4 is viewed by some as one of the finest imported guitars made.

The Charvel brand is part of the "superstrat" story that is integral to the history of the 1980s rock guitar.

Founded in 1974 by Wayne Charvel in Azusa, California, Charvel Repairs specialized in hardware upgrades to existing production guitars—often

▲
Throughout the 1980s, Eddie Ojeda of Twisted Sister used a custom Charvel, its pink and black bullseye pattern recognizable from the band's videos. The guitar above is a later replica built by Wayne Charvel.

▼
Revisit the world of 1980s glam metal with *Big Hits And Nasty Cuts: The Best Of Twisted Sister* (1992).

| | |
|---|---|
| **Body style:** | Solid body with double cutaway |
| **Materials:** | American basswood body; maple neck |
| **Finish:** | Black, cobalt blue, red, pearl white, black cherry |
| **Fretboard:** | Rosewood (maple on Model 4M) |
| **Inlays:** | Mother-of-pearl dot (black dot on Model 4M; shark's tooth on later models) |
| **Frets:** | 22 |
| **Scale:** | 25 ½" |
| **Width at nut:** | 1 ¹¹⁄₁₆" |
| **Bridge:** | First models featured Kahler locking tremolo; later models had Jackson Floyd Rose-style system |
| **Pickups:** | 2 Jackson J200 pickups and 1 J50BC pickup (later models had Jackson EMGs) |
| **Electrics:** | Volume and tone control; Jackson pre-amp with mid-range boost (powered by 9-volt battery); 3 mini-toggles (2-way) |

# CHARVEL SURFCASTER 1992

In spite of many celebrity users, the Charvel/Jackson business was struggling financially by the late 1980s. As Jackson himself admitted: "I didn't understand money. I was just thinking about the product . . . If I could do something better I'd throw every nickel at it." So Jackson surrendered sole ownership in favor of investment from the Texas-based International Music Corporation. However, cost-cutting measures were quickly applied, and in 1989, when IMC decided on large-scale job cuts, Jackson sold his remaining shares and walked away from the business.

The musical tide was also turning against Charvel/Jackson as 1980s rock gave way to '90s grunge, and suddenly the guitars fell from fashion.

This period saw the birth of the most curious guitar ever to bear the Charvel name. The Surfcaster appeared to be a modern high-performance composite of 1950s retro American guitar design. It featured a body that combined a Fender Jaguar outline with Rickenbacker stylings and a pair of newly designed Danelectro-style pickups. Now something of a cult item, production was ended when the Jackson/Charvel name was bought by the Fender Corporation in 2002.

▲
Bilinda Butcher, one of the guitarists with My Bloody Valentine, used a Charvel Surfcaster when the band reunited for a series of live events in 2007. The Surfcaster is fast developing into a cult instrument.

▼
The Surfcaster playing of New York metal band Prong's Tommy Victor can be heard on *Cleansing* (1994).

| | |
|---|---|
| **Body style:** | Double cutaway, offset waist hollow body with Rickenbacker-style slash sound hole |
| **Materials:** | Mahogany or basswood with bolt-on maple neck |
| **Finish:** | Seafoam green, sunburst, orange |
| **Fretboard:** | Rosewood, ebony, or maple |
| **Inlays:** | Shark's tooth |
| **Frets:** | 24 (including partial frets) |
| **Scale:** | 25 ½" |
| **Width at nut:** | 1 ⅝" |
| **Bridge:** | Jackson JT-490 tremolo or C stop tail |
| **Pickups:** | 2 lipstick single-coil pickups (on later versions 1 lipstick and 1 humbucker); 3-way pickup switch |
| **Electrics:** | Master volume and tone controls |

# COLLINGS CJSB "LYLE LOVETT" 1999

workshop was little more than a single-car garage, which he used to custom-build one-off models. It wasn't until 1989 that he was able to rent larger premises and hire two assistants. The business then took off quickly, with an order for twenty-four custom Gruhn flat-top acoustic guitars.

The CJ ("Collings Jumbo") range of guitars is, according to Collings himself, based on the Gibson Advanced Jumbo, a flat-top, round-shouldered Dreadnought produced briefly in 1936. In 1999, Collings produced a signature CJ model for country singer Lyle Lovett, a long-term Collings player. The CJ is a loud guitar, but produces a sweet treble tone, making it perfect for chordal accompaniment on stage.

Collings Guitars is now well established as a producer of upmarket classic American designs, its large factory space and staff of over seventy ensuring a high output.

Based in Austin, Texas, Collings Guitars produces acoustic guitars, electric guitars, mandolins, and ukuleles. Most critically lauded, however, are the company's flat-top acoustics.

Established in 1973 by medical school drop-out Bill Collings, the first

▲
Primarily known as a country singer/songwriter, Lyle Lovett makes music that also incorporates folk, swing, blues, jazz, and gospel. He owns a number of Collings guitars.

▼
Released in 1996, Lyle Lovett's *The Road to Ensenada* was awarded a Grammy for Best Country Album.

| | |
|---|---|
| **Body style:** | Round-shouldered Dreadnought style |
| **Materials:** | Rosewood back and sides, spruce top; maple neck (custom options are offered on all models) |
| **Body dimensions:** | Maximum width 16", depth 4 ⅞", length 20 ⅛" |
| **Finish:** | Sunburst |
| **Fretboard:** | Ebony |
| **Inlays:** | Abalone dot |
| **Frets:** | 20 |
| **Scale:** | 25 ½" |
| **Width at nut:** | 1 ¹¹⁄₁₆" |
| **Bridge:** | Ebony |
| **Tuners:** | Waverly |

# CONTRERAS CARLEVARO 1983

One of the most interesting classical guitar makers of the twentieth century, Manuel Contreras was born in Madrid, Spain, in 1928. He first established himself as an expert cabinet maker, and his work came to the attention of master luthier José Ramirez III, who in 1959 invited him to join the noted Ramirez workshop. Three years later, Contreras was able to set up his own Madrid workshop where he quickly forged a reputation as one of Spain's leading luthiers.

Although his first instruments were built according to Spanish guitar traditions, Contreras began to experiment during the 1970s with new approaches to the classical guitar, most successfully with the Double Top model (more accurately described as a "double back" model, as the inner back of the body is lined with the same wood used on the top, improving tone and projection).

In 1983, Contreras constructed an instrument based on the ideas of Uruguayan concert guitarist Abel Carlevaro (1916–2001), who studied under the great master Andrés Segovia. This striking instrument incorporated two very unorthodox elements: no waist on the bass side of the body, and no sound hole. Carlevaro's design was aimed at enhancing clarity and achieving balance between bass and treble.

▲
From 1983 Abel Carlevaro made exclusive use of the guitar Contreras had built for him.

▼
The Contreras Carlevaro can be heard on this 1985 recording in which Carlevaro plays his own compositions.

| | |
|---|---|
| **Body style:** | Single-waisted, hollow-body classical design with no conventional sound hole |
| **Materials:** | Brazilian rosewood back and sides with spruce top |
| **Finish:** | Natural |
| **Fretboard:** | Ebony |
| **Inlays:** | None |
| **Frets:** | 19 (including partial fret) |
| **Scale:** | 25 $\frac{13}{22}$" |
| **Width at nut:** | 2 $\frac{1}{21}$" |
| **Bridge:** | Ebony |
| **Tuners:** | Fustero |

# DANELECTRO : THE STORY

D anelectro is an important name in the history of the electric guitar. Founded in 1947 by Nathan "Nate" Daniel, Danelectro guitars were built using innovative and eye-catching designs, but nonetheless very much with affordability in mind. Rarely treated as serious examples of luthiery by guitar connoisseurs of the time, their retro visual appeal has made them increasingly collectible over the past two decades.

Nathan Daniel was born in New York City in 1912, one year to the day after his parents had arrived in the United States from Lithuania, then ruled by tsarist Russia. A clever child, Daniel developed an interest in radio during his teen years, dropping out of college during the Great Depression to manufacture his own amplifier designs. Founding Daniel Electrical Laboratories in a Lower Manhattan loft, he soon became the exclusive supplier of amplifiers to Epiphone, which it sold with its early electric guitars. His first business was cut short by the U.S. entry into World War II. His electronics expertise prevented him from being drafted and he worked on systems to prevent the engines of military jeeps interfering with battlefield radio messages. After the war he restarted his amplifier business, this time moving out from the city to New Jersey and trading under the name Danelectro (from "Daniel Electrics"). His business break came in the late 1940s when he won contracts to provide cheap amplifiers to two major retail chains. He produced Silvertone models for Sears Roebuck and Airline models for Montgomery Ward.

The first guitars bearing the Danelectro brand appeared in 1954. Unusually for a luthier, Daniel couldn't actually play the guitar or any other instrument himself, nor was he at all interested in popular music, preferring to listen to nineteenth-century composers such as Mendelsohn. Nonetheless, he was able to gauge accurately the requirements of the modern musician. And, above all, he wanted to build guitars that would be affordable to the masses.

The first Danelectro model featured a thin Telecaster-style body cut from poplar and covered in tweed-patterned vinyl. It was the C series  of 1955 that saw the debut of the construction technique for which Danelectro would be remembered. Putting aside all of the standard debates about the merits of assorted tonewoods, Daniel designed a guitar with a body built

**A 1955 Danelectro C series guitar—this model was built for sale by Sears Roebuck and is branded "Silvertone."**

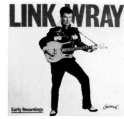

**The cover of the 1956 Danelectro catalog.**

**An album cover showing Link Wray playing a Danelectro Longhorn guitar.**

**1912**
Nathan Daniel born in New York City

**1946**
Daniel founds the Danelectro company, producing amplifiers

**1954**
The first guitar bearing the Danelectro brand is launched

**1955**
Launch of C series, constructed using Masonite

**1956**
The UB-2 is the first ever six-string bass—five years ahead of Fender's

**1958**
Danelectro launches iconic Longhorn and Shorthorn models

**1958**
Daniel moves Danelectro to Neptune, New Jersey

from a pine frame covered top and bottom with a thin piece of Masonite—a material made from heavily compressed woodchips. The body was then covered in vinyl. This technique ensured that guitars could be produced both cheaply and at great speed. That same year, Danelectro launched the U series. Built in the same way, but with bodies painted in an array of unusual colors, these were the first guitars to feature the so-called "lipstick tube" single-coil pickups—the housings of which actually *were* supplied by a cosmetics manufacturer. The U range was expanded with the launch of the UB-2 six-string bass in 1956. ❷ Tuned using a special gauge of strings an octave lower than a regular guitar, the UB-2 predated the more famous, but essentially identical, Fender Bass VI by five years.

The year 1958 saw the launch of the two ranges for which Danelectro is best known, the Longhorn ❸ and Shorthorn models ❹—the former featuring a deep twin cutaway with extraordinary thin elongated horns. Both of these styles were available in guitar and bass form—the Shorthorn was even available as both simultaneously, an early example of a double-neck electric guitar. At the same time, Danelectro continued to produce Silvertone models for Sears Roebuck, including the ingenious 1448 Amp-In-Case model, ❺ regularly seen in recent years on stage with Beck Hansen.

As the 1960s progressed, Daniel continued to innovate, teaming up with New York session guitarist Vinnie Bell to produce the twelve-string Bellzouki as well as the very first electric sitar (under the Coral brand).

In 1966, Daniel sold the Danelectro brand to MCA, but remained involved with the company. The Coral line of guitars was introduced in 1967. Two years later, MCA shut down the factory in Neptune, New Jersey, and Danelectro, in its original form, was no more. During the 1970s, Daniel switched his interests from musical instruments to designing seacraft. He died on Christmas Eve, 1994, at the age of eighty-two.

The Danelectro story picks up again in 1998, when the Evets Corporation, based in San Clemente, California, bought the rights to use the brand name. The new owner produced reasonable-quality Korean-built replicas of original Danelectro and Silvertone models from the 1950s, as well as a bewildering, ever-expanding array of cheap, retro-looking stomp-boxes. ❻

The Danelectro Shorthorn, introduced in 1958.

The Silvertone 1448 Amp-In-Case, designed by Danelectro.

The retro-syled Honeytone battery-powered amp, part of the modern-day Danelectro range.

**1961** Produces the first twelve-string electric guitar—the Bellzouki, designed with guitarist Vinnie Bell

**1966** Daniel sells Danelectro brand name to MCA

**1967** Danelectro makes the first electric sitar, under the Coral brand

**1969** MCA closes down the factory at Neptune, New Jersey

**1994** Nathan Daniel dies—he was 82 years of age

**1998** Evets Corporation of San Clemente, California, relaunches classic Danelectro and Silvertone models

# DANELECTRO : THE FAMILY TREE (1954-1969)

Danelectro instruments were always at the "cheap and cheerful" end of the market. This probably explains why it is only relatively recently that they have begun to interest serious guitar collectors.

From the very beginning, founder Nathan Daniel wanted to make guitars that would reach the widest possible market. Indeed, his earliest commercial successes came from building a range of guitars and amplifiers with the Silvertone brand, exclusively for Sears Roebuck, one of the biggest retail chains in the U.S. Many top players of the 1960s and beyond cut their teeth on Silvertones.

Daniel was also an ingenious yet pragmatic innovator. His desire to produce affordable guitars for the ordinary player led to what is perhaps the Danelectro brand's defining characteristic—the body structure. Whereas other luthiers of the mid-1950s experimented with assorted tonewoods, Daniel designed a simple body built from a pine frame, with vinyl-covered Masonite hardboard on the top and bottom.

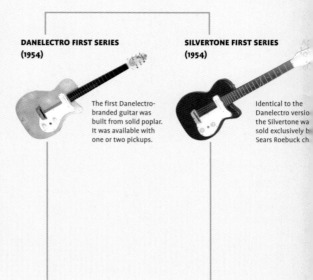

**DANELECTRO FIRST SERIES**
**(1954)**

The first Danelectro-branded guitar was built from solid poplar. It was available with one or two pickups.

**SILVERTONE FIRST SERIES**
**(1954)**

Identical to the Danelectro versio the Silvertone wa sold exclusively b Sears Roebuck ch

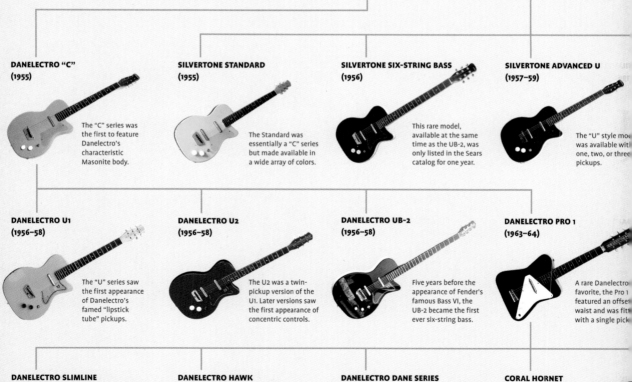

**DANELECTRO "C"**
**(1955)**

The "C" series was the first to feature Danelectro's characteristic Masonite body.

**SILVERTONE STANDARD**
**(1955)**

The Standard was essentially a "C" series but made available in a wide array of colors.

**SILVERTONE SIX-STRING BASS**
**(1956)**

This rare model, available at the same time as the UB-2, was only listed in the Sears catalog for one year.

**SILVERTONE ADVANCED U**
**(1957–59)**

The "U" style mod was available wit one, two, or three pickups.

**DANELECTRO U1**
**(1956–58)**

The "U" series saw the first appearance of Danelectro's famed "lipstick tube" pickups.

**DANELECTRO U2**
**(1956–58)**

The U2 was a twin-pickup version of the U1. Later versions saw the first appearance of concentric controls.

**DANELECTRO UB-2**
**(1956–58)**

Five years before the appearance of Fender's famous Bass VI, the UB-2 became the first ever six-string bass.

**DANELECTRO PRO 1**
**(1963–64)**

A rare Danelectro favorite, the Pro 1 featured an offse waist and was fit with a single pick

**DANELECTRO SLIMLINE**
**(1967–69)**

Semi-solid guitar fitted with two or three pickups. The Slimline's "Durabody" was a new departure.

**DANELECTRO HAWK**
**(1967–69)**

Available as six- and twelve-string guitars, and as a four-string bass, the Hawk series was made from poplar.

**DANELECTRO DANE SERIES**
**(1967–69)**

The Dane appeared in five ranges (denoted "A" to "E"). The one shown here is a Dane E "E2N4" bass.

**CORAL HORNET**
**(1967–69)**

Designed by Vinn Bell, the Hornet s featured instrum named after asso stinging insects.

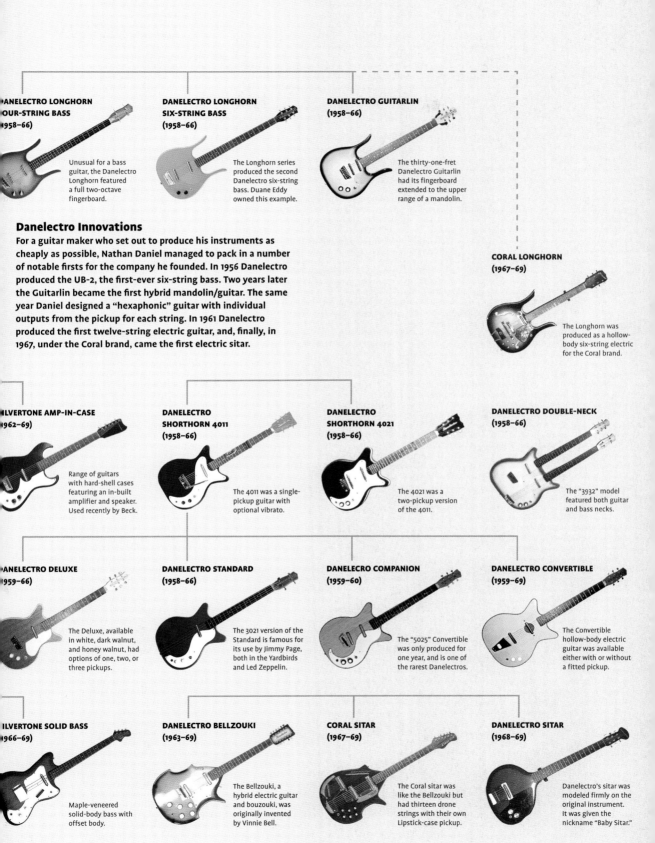

**DANELECTRO LONGHORN FOUR-STRING BASS**
**(1958–66)**

Unusual for a bass guitar, the Danelectro Longhorn featured a full two-octave fingerboard.

**DANELECTRO LONGHORN SIX-STRING BASS**
**(1958–66)**

The Longhorn series produced the second Danelectro six-string bass. Duane Eddy owned this example.

**DANELECTRO GUITARLIN**
**(1958–66)**

The thirty-one-fret Danelectro Guitarlin had its fingerboard extended to the upper range of a mandolin.

## Danelectro Innovations

For a guitar maker who set out to produce his instruments as cheaply as possible, Nathan Daniel managed to pack in a number of notable firsts for the company he founded. In 1956 Danelectro produced the UB-2, the first-ever six-string bass. Two years later the Guitarlin became the first hybrid mandolin/guitar. The same year Daniel designed a "hexaphonic" guitar with individual outputs from the pickup for each string. In 1961 Danelectro produced the first twelve-string electric guitar, and, finally, in 1967, under the Coral brand, came the first electric sitar.

**CORAL LONGHORN**
**(1967–69)**

The Longhorn was produced as a hollow-body six-string electric for the Coral brand.

**SILVERTONE AMP-IN-CASE**
**(1962–69)**

Range of guitars with hard-shell cases featuring an in-built amplifier and speaker. Used recently by Beck.

**DANELECTRO SHORTHORN 4011**
**(1958–66)**

The 4011 was a single-pickup guitar with optional vibrato.

**DANELECTRO SHORTHORN 4021**
**(1958–66)**

The 4021 was a two-pickup version of the 4011.

**DANELECTRO DOUBLE-NECK**
**(1958–66)**

The "3932" model featured both guitar and bass necks.

**DANELECTRO DELUXE**
**(1959–66)**

The Deluxe, available in white, dark walnut, and honey walnut, had options of one, two, or three pickups.

**DANELECTRO STANDARD**
**(1958–66)**

The 3021 version of the Standard is famous for its use by Jimmy Page, both in the Yardbirds and Led Zeppelin.

**DANELECRO COMPANION**
**(1959–60)**

The "5025" Convertible was only produced for one year, and is one of the rarest Danelectros.

**DANELECTRO CONVERTIBLE**
**(1959–69)**

The Convertible hollow-body electric guitar was available either with or without a fitted pickup.

**SILVERTONE SOLID BASS**
**(1966–69)**

Maple-veneered solid-body bass with offset body.

**DANELECTRO BELLZOUKI**
**(1963–69)**

The Bellzouki, a hybrid electric guitar and bouzouki, was originally invented by Vinnie Bell.

**CORAL SITAR**
**(1967–69)**

The Coral sitar was like the Bellzouki but had thirteen drone strings with their own Lipstick-case pickup.

**DANELECTRO SITAR**
**(1968–69)**

Danelectro's sitar was modeled firmly on the original instrument. It was given the nickname "Baby Sitar."

# DANELECTRO U2 1956

The first of Nathan Daniel's guitars to bear the Danelectro brand emerged in 1954—these were tweed-covered instruments made from solid poplar. They had no model designation but are now generally referred to as the "1954." This was followed a year later by the C, with its peanut-shaped body. Both models

were produced until 1956, and the launch of the U series.

The first Danelectros to be produced in any great numbers, the U range comprised the U1, with its single lipstick case pickup and the twin-pickup U2. (A three-pickup U3 was briefly made in 1957.)

The Danelectro U series was the first to utilize the budget construction technique for which the company would become most (in)famous. Instead of a carved solid block of poplar, the body was made using a poplar framework of side, neck, and bridge blocks, covered top and bottom by a ⅜-inch sheet of Masonite—created using wood chips steam-blasted into long fibers and then pressed into boards. This made for an unusually lightweight instrument, but one that many argued lacked the acoustic properties of traditional tonewoods.

Each pickup has a single stacked concentric control, the outer ring for tone and the inner knob for volume.

▲
Danelectro's 1950s advertising makes some bold claims for its instruments: "The best, anywhere. No other electric guitar can touch the Danelectro for consistency of tone." Some collectors agree.

▼
Nels Cline features both Danelectro and Silvertone guitars on his album *Instrumentals* (2002).

| | |
|---|---|
| **Body style:** | Hollow body with single cutaway |
| **Materials:** | Poplar-framed body with Masonite top and bottom, and cream vinyl tape edging; bolt-on maple neck |
| **Finish:** | Black, copper, royal blue, coral red, surf green |
| **Fretboard:** | Rosewood |
| **Inlays:** | Acrylic dot |
| **Frets:** | 21 |
| **Scale:** | 24 ¾" |
| **Width at nut:** | 1 ¹⁷⁄₂₆" |
| **Bridge:** | Standard Danelectro tailpiece with floating rosewood saddle |
| **Pickups:** | 2 lipstick case single-coil pickups (U1 has 1 pickup; U3 has 3 pickups) |
| **Electrics:** | Danelectro concentric pot for each pickup; 3-way tone switch |

# DANELECTRO LONGHORN 1958

▲
**Link Wray plays the Danelectro Longhorn wearing a two-tone jacket; famously, the jacket, guitar, and matching loafers all came from the Sears & Roebuck catalog.**

▼
**After "Rumble" (1958) Wray made a switch unimaginable today— from a Gibson Les Paul to a Danelectro Longhorn. He used the Dano on most of his early recordings.**

S urely one of the most dramatic body shapes of any guitar, the Danelectro Longhorn continues to polarize players: to some it is a late-1950s design classic; to others, one of the ugliest instruments ever made.

Launched in 1958, the Longhorn series was available as a four- or six-string bass, and as the novel "Guitarlin"—a thirty-one-fret instrument with the upper range of a mandolin. Like all "Danos," they were low-cost models, featuring the standard body construction of a poplar frame with Masonite top and bottom and cream vinyl tape around the edges.

A characteristic feature of the Longhorn, and other Danelectros of the period, was the unique shape of the headstock: with its three-a-side array of tuners, it became widely known as the "Coke bottle."

In spite of its low cost, the Longhorn guitar had its professional fans, mostly at the twangy instrumental end of the rock 'n' roll spectrum—the single-coil lipstick case pickups were especially effective for this type of sound.

In 1967, Danelectro produced a hollow-body Longhorn guitar under the Coral brand, but it is the bass, with its distinctive low-end thud, that remains popular as a modern reissue.

**Body style:** Hollow body with double cutaway and heavily extended treble and bass horns

**Materials:** Poplar framed body with Masonite top and bottom; bolt-on maple neck

**Finish:** Bronze sunburst on original instruments; numerous color options on modern reissues

**Fretboard:** Rosewood

**Inlays:** Acrylic dot

**Frets:** 24

**Scale:** 24 ¾"

**Width at nut:** 1 $\frac{17}{26}$"

**Bridge:** Standard Danelectro tailpiece with floating rosewood saddle

**Pickups:** 2 lipstick case single-coil pickups

**Electrics:** Danelectro concentric pot for each pickup (volume in the center; tone on the surround)

# DANELECTRO BELLZOUKI 1963

Vinnie Bell was one of New York's top session guitarists during the late 1950s. He was also something of an inventor, coming up with the concept of a solid-body guitar-and-bouzouki hybrid. The traditional Greek bouzouki has a shorter scale than a standard guitar and features four paired courses of strings. Bell increased the number of strings to six courses, and tuned it as a regular guitar.

Danelectro were interested, and in 1961 the Bellzouki was launched. Initially it took a tear-drop shape and featured two faux tortoise shell pickguards. Later models introduced a notch in the body, making it easier to play sitting down.

As with all Danelectros, while the body appears solid it is in fact a poplar frame covered with Masonite. A maple-capped neck with a rosewood fingerboard was bolted on.

The Bellzouki was not the most radical development in the history of the instrument—it effectively evolved into a twelve-string electric guitar. But Bell would later develop the electric sitar. Issued under the Coral brand, it was famously played by Bell on such classics as "Green Tambourine" (1967) and "Band Of Gold" (1970).

▲
**Count V's guitarist Sean Byrne playing a Bellzouki. The band was immortalized in rock journalist Lester Bangs' essay *Psychotic Reactions And Carburetor Dung.***

▼
**Count V had one major hit single, 1966's "Psychotic Reaction." The Bellzouki can be heard on this "garage" classic.**

| | |
|---|---|
| **Body style:** | Hollow bouzouki body with notched thigh rest |
| **Materials:** | Poplar frame with Masonite cover top and bottom; vinyl strip around edging; bolt-on maple body |
| **Finish:** | Tobacco brown sunburst |
| **Fretboard:** | Rosewood |
| **Inlays:** | Acrylic dot |
| **Frets:** | 21 |
| **Scale:** | 24 1/2" |
| **Width at nut:** | 1 7/8" |
| **Bridge:** | Combined bridge and tailpiece; rosewood saddle |
| **Pickups:** | 1 or 2 Danelectro lipstick case single-coil pickups; 3-way selector switch |
| **Electrics:** | Master volume control; volume and tone controls for each pickup |

# DANELECTRO SHORTHORN 1958

I n 1958 the Les Paul-inspired U series was dropped from the range and replaced with two new designs. The Longhorn and Shorthorn series were both identifiable by the depth of their twin cutaway bodies.

The Shorthorn was available with one, two, or three pickups, and also as a short-scale bass (*right*). Perhaps the most interesting guitar in the range was the model 3923 Shorthorn double-neck guitar, which emerged at around the same time as Gibson's EMS-1235 model. However, unlike Gibson's six-/twelve-string model (which is now seen as standard), Danelectro opted to combine a six-string guitar at the top with a bass guitar at the bottom.

Cosmetic variation aside, the Shorthorns were largely identical to the U series, featuring the same hollow-body construction, lipstick case pickups, and comically crude bridge mechanisms.

These supposed shortcomings did not deter such rock luminaries as Jimmy Page and Eric Clapton, both of whom used their Danelectro Shorthorns at the peaks of their careers: Clapton used his hand-painted psychedelic Shorthorn with Blind Faith; Page used his mainly for playing slide during his Led Zeppelin career.

▲
**JImmy Page used his Shorthorn with Led Zeppelin on live versions of "Kashmir" (1975). The guitar was tuned to DADGAD.**

▼
**Blind Faith, Eric Clapton's ill-fated "supergroup," produced just one album, in 1969, before their dissolution. Clapton used a Danelectro Shorthorn during this period.**

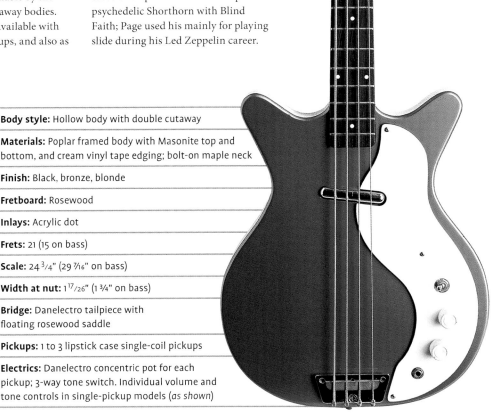

| | |
|---|---|
| **Body style:** | Hollow body with double cutaway |
| **Materials:** | Poplar framed body with Masonite top and bottom, and cream vinyl tape edging; bolt-on maple neck |
| **Finish:** | Black, bronze, blonde |
| **Fretboard:** | Rosewood |
| **Inlays:** | Acrylic dot |
| **Frets:** | 21 (15 on bass) |
| **Scale:** | 24 3/4" (29 7/16" on bass) |
| **Width at nut:** | 1 17/26" (1 3/4" on bass) |
| **Bridge:** | Danelectro tailpiece with floating rosewood saddle |
| **Pickups:** | 1 to 3 lipstick case single-coil pickups |
| **Electrics:** | Danelectro concentric pot for each pickup; 3-way tone switch. Individual volume and tone controls in single-pickup models (*as shown*) |

# D'ANGELICO EXCEL 1936

D'Angelico began learning his trade at the age of nine in the workshop of his uncle, Signor Ciani, known for crafting fine traditional Italian mandolins.

D'Angelico set up his own workshop in 1932 at 40 Kenmare Street, New York City. His guitars were strictly handmade in very limited quantities, production peaking in the late 1930s when he and his tiny workforce were making over thirty instruments a year.

The earliest D'Angelico guitars were modeled on the Gibson L-5 archtop, but he gradually added his Art Deco flourishes, such as the hallmark stairstep pickguard and tailpiece. Even though by the late 1940s D'Angelico's work was admired widely, his guitars were priced much the same as mass-produced Gibsons.

The Excel was popular with jazz musicians, and also found a fan in the great Chet Atkins, who played this model until his Gretsch deal was struck in 1954.

New York master luthier John D'Angelico perfected the archtop acoustic guitar style, casting a shadow over all who followed. In craftsmanship he was rivaled only by his assistant, Jimmy D'Aquisto, who produced his own guitars from 1964. Born in New York City in 1905,

▲
**Oscar Moore (left) played a D'Angelico guitar on his recordings with the influential King Cole Trio. Although Nat King Cole is remembered as one of the top crooners of the 1950s, he had earlier made his mark as a fine jazz pianist.**

▼
**Many of the King Cole Trio's finest recordings from the 1940s are gathered on this compilation.**

| | |
|---|---|
| **Body style:** | Hollow-body archtop with single Venetian cutaway and f-holes |
| **Materials:** | European maple back and sides, solid book-matched, hand-carved spruce top; solid flame maple neck with 3-ply walnut/maple centerstripe |
| **Finish:** | Natural or sunburst, nitrocellulose lacquer |
| **Fretboard:** | Ebony |
| **Inlays:** | Mother-of-pearl blocks |
| **Frets:** | 22 |
| **Scale:** | 25½" |
| **Width at nut:** | 1¹¹⁄₁₆" |
| **Bridge:** | Adjustable ebony bridge; gold-engraved stepped "Art Deco" tailpiece |
| **Pickguard:** | D'Angelico stairstep |
| **Tuners:** | Grover Imperial |

# D'ANGELICO NEW YORKER 1936

In the early days of John D'Angelico's workshop there were only two basic models produced: Style A was the 17-inch budget model; Style B was similar but featured an ornate headstock. These modest guitars were superseded in 1936 by the Excel and New Yorker models.

By the time of his death in 1964, workshop records show that 1,164 D'Angelico guitars had been built. Jimmy D'Aquisto, who completed the ten in progress at that time, bought the workshop from D'Angelico's family and built equally revered archtops.

The New Yorker was first produced in 1936 and became popular with many jazz players. All D'Angelico guitars were custom built, so there is a wide variation in individual specifications.

The mixture of craftsmanship, design, and scarcity has made D'Angelicos highly desirable to modern collectors. Their Art Deco style has even earned them a presence in museum exhibitions. Recreations of D'Angelico's original designs are now produced in New Jersey by D'Angelico Guitars of America.

▲
**Johnny Smith is more likely to be remembered for his Guild and Gibson signature guitars than his music. He was, however, one of the most influential jazz players of the 1950s. He was also a close personal friend of John D'Angelico.**

▼
**Smith's D'Angelico can be seen and heard on the 1960 album *The Sound Of The Johnny Smith Guitar*.**

**Body style:** Hollow-body archtop with single Venetian cutaway and f-holes (non-cutaway models also exist)

**Materials:** European maple back and sides, solid book-matched, hand-carved spruce top; solid flame maple neck with 3-ply walnut/maple centerstripe; 7-ply binding on body and headstock

**Finish:** Sunburst finish, nitrocellulose lacquer

**Fretboard:** Ebony; 3-ply binding

**Inlays:** Mother-of-pearl blocks

**Frets:** 22

**Scale:** 25 ¾"

**Width at nut:** 1 ¹¹⁄₁₆"

**Bridge:** Adjustable ebony bridge with mother-of-pearl inlays; gold-engraved stepped "Art Deco" tailpiece

**Pickguard:** 9-ply leopard tortoise stairstep

**Tuners:** Grover Imperial

# D'AQUISTO 1965

York master luthier John D'Angelico (*see page 54*), producer of high-end archtop guitars. When D'Angelico died in 1964, his assistant bought out the business and moved east from Brooklyn to Long Island, New York.

The first instruments to bear the D'Aquisto name were firmly based on those he had built for his former employer, among them electric archtop jazz guitars.

D'Aquisto's aim was to reinvent the guitar as a modern instrument, and he took a genuinely experimental approach to his work. This was particularly true in the bridge construction, tailpiece (which he made adjustable), and sound hole design, which shifted from the traditional f-shape to an elongated S-shape—and later to even more unorthodox styles.

By the 1980s, James D'Aquisto had established a reputation that made him the most important independent guitar maker of his time.

Vintage guitar guru George Gruhn once described James L. D'Aquisto as "A modern-day Stradivarius . . . a genius at carving archtop guitars."

In 1953, D'Aquisto, then a seventeen-year-old aspiring jazz player, began an apprenticeship with legendary New

▲
**Jim Hall is regarded as one of the most influential post-bop jazz players. He is seen here playing a D'Aquisto electric archtop at a jazz festival in 2001.**

▼
**Hall's D'Aquisto can be heard on this 1999 album of duets with Pat Metheny.**

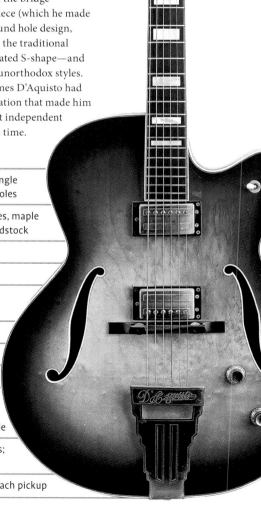

**Body style:** Hollow-body archtop with single Venetian cutaway and S-shaped sound holes

**Materials:** European maple back and sides, maple top; mahogany neck; ebony-covered headstock

**Finish:** Sunburst

**Fretboard:** Créme-bound ebony

**Inlays:** Mother-of-pearl block on fingerboard and headstock

**Frets:** 24 (not including zero fret)

**Scale:** 24 $^{9}/_{10}$"

**Width at nut:** 1 $^{13}/_{16}$"

**Bridge:** 2-piece carved ebony; hinged tailpiece of Macassar ebony with a hinged black-chrome end piece; variations possible

**Pickups:** 2 gold-plated Guild humbuckers; 3-way pickup selector switching

**Electrics:** Volume and tone controls for each pickup

# D'Aquisto Avant Garde 1988

By the time of his unexpected death in April 1995, "Jimmy" D'Aquisto had a ten-year waiting list for new commisions. His instruments may have been startlingly expensive—well beyond the financial reach of all but the wealthiest musicians—but they undoubtedly had a quality to match. Indeed, George Gruhn places them "among an elite group of the finest fretted instruments ever made."

Since each guitar was individually hand crafted (only the tuners and pickups were brought in), D'Aquisto's total manufacturing output over a thirty-year period was actually very low. During the 1970s he was estimated to have built only eight or nine instruments each year, a number that rose to between ten and fifteen during the 1980s. His production was further hampered by taking on occasional repair work for D'Angelico guitars—on which he was obviously the foremost living authority.

D'Aquisto built only custom-order guitars, with specifications tailored to suit the needs of the purchaser. In fact he would refuse any request that he felt lacked merit, but he was always prepared to experiment, as can be seen from his teardrop design with its elongated lower bout ending with sharp point.

Produced from 1988, D'Aquisto's so-called "late period," one of his most unusual designs was the Avant Garde model, striking with its two oval sound holes, raised ebony pickguard, and headstock cut-outs. D'Aquisto evidently built the prototype in 1988 for a wealthy Californian vintage guitar dealer, who contributed construction ideas as well as the model's name. After D'Aquisto's death, prices for his guitars skyrocketed. Eventually the dealer sold his Avant Garde prototype for approaching $150,000—a price that at current market values seems something of a bargain.

▼
**Jimmy D'Aquisto, the modern-day Stradivarius of the guitar. Some experts believe that one of his original instruments is likely to be the first "non-celebrity" guitar to break the million-dollar barrier at auction.**

| | |
|---|---|
| **Body style:** | Jumbo (17" wide) with oval sound holes |
| **Materials:** | Sitka spruce top; laminated flamed maple back and sides; flamed maple binding on body; one-piece maple neck |
| **Finish:** | Natural |
| **Fretboard:** | Ebony |
| **Inlays:** | None |
| **Frets:** | 22 |
| **Scale:** | 25 ½" |
| **Width at nut:** | 1 ⅞" |
| **Bridge:** | Acutone height adjustable |
| **Pickguard:** | Raised; ebony |

# DOBRO MODEL 100 1930

ports or a pair of f-holes in the upper bout. Many players prefer the warmth in tone of a wooden resonator over the slightly harder sound of a metal instrument, but since the majority of slide blues players—who were the earliest group of musicians to take the resonator idea on board—tended to use metal-bodied instruments, for many that represents the "traditional" sound.

During the 1970s, when resonator guitars reached mainstream audiences, Dobro became almost a generic term for a resonator guitar. Subsequently models calling themselves Dobros began to appear from the Far East. When Gibson acquired the rights to the brand name in 1994, the company announced it would strongly defend its right to use the name exclusively.

The only legitimate model to appear on the market recently has been the Phil Leadbetter signature Dobro, a mahogany-bodied instrument based on designs such as this Model 100 from the 1930s.

Although metal-bodied Dobro and National models are arguably the best known resonators, the majority of the guitars produced by Dobro from the late 1920s were standard instruments built from wood, but featuring an internal resonator with a decorative metal covering and either two circular metal

▲
One of the finest modern-day resonator players, Phil Leadbetter was honored with his own signature Dobro.

▼
Leadbetter's Dobro playing on *Slide Effects* (2005) earned him two awards from the International Bluegrass Music Association.

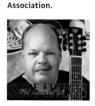

| | |
|---|---|
| **Body style:** | Hollow body, figure-eight, jumbo resonator; 14 ⅛" wide; 3 ⁷⁄₁₆" deep |
| **Materials:** | Matched walnut body with "deluxe" white purfling |
| **Finish:** | Natural |
| **Fretboard:** | Rosewood |
| **Inlays:** | Mother-of-pearl dot |
| **Frets:** | 19 |
| **Scale:** | 25" |
| **Width at nut:** | 1¹¹⁄₁₆" |
| **Bridge:** | Dobro Spider bridge |
| **Resonator:** | Dobro dish shape with fan-design covering and 2 grilled portholes |

# DOBRO MODEL 16 1935

a
*SOUND*
*investment*

Inventor John Dopyera and his brothers had worked at National but left to found Dobro and make single-cone resonators. Dopyera's first problem was a question of patents. National—who had wanted only to produce superior tri-cone resonators— owned the patent for his "biscuit"

design. To get around this, Dopyera developed a new variant, inverting the cone, so that instead of the bridge resting on the cone's apex, it was fitted to a cast aluminum "spider" with eight legs spanning the perimeter of a *downward*-pointing cone.

Following the successful launch of the first Dobros, National also produced a number of single-cone models, using Dopyera's original design, although, in truth, there seems to be little difference in practice between the two systems.

Despite his patent disagreements with National, Dopyera remained a major shareholder in that company, and in 1934, with both companies struggling in the aftermath of the Depression, they were merged into the National-Dobro Corporation.

In 1935, metal-bodied instruments bearing the Dobro brand appeared for the first time, and remained in production until 1941.

▲
A Dobro catalog from 1966. By this time the brand name was being used as a generic term to describe all resonator guitars. Dobros proved popular with the country-rock crossover bands of the the early 1970s, such as the Flying Burrito Brothers. Album credits often listed "dobro" players, even though in most cases the instruments are likely to have been Nationals.

**Body style:** Hollow body, figure-eight, jumbo resonator; 14 ⅛" wide; 3 ⁷⁄₁₆" deep

**Materials:** Brass body with mahogany neck

**Finish:** Ornate engraving around the resonator plate and upper bout

**Fretboard:** Rosewood

**Inlays:** Mother-of-pearl dot

**Frets:** 19

**Scale:** 25"

**Width at nut:** 1 ¹¹⁄₁₆"

**Bridge:** Dobro Spider bridge

**Resonator:** Dobro dish shape with fan-design covering and 2 open portholes

# EGMOND MODEL 3 1965

**n.v. muziekinstrumentenfabriek egmond**
('EGMOND' MUSICAL INSTRUMENTS FACTORY)
**BEST**

E gmond is the best-known guitar brand to emanate from The Netherlands. Egmond fed an explosion in demand from the late 1950s for cheap electric guitars. They were often exported under other brand names, such as Rosetti (best known in the U.K.), Caledonie, Wilson, and Vega. The company began in

1932, when former railwayman Uilke Egmond opened a music shop. Joined by his sons after the end of World War II, together they began building guitars at a workshop in Eindhoven. By the end of the 1950s Egmond was among Europe's largest guitar producers, and in 1961 he moved to a much larger factory in the town of Best.

Many British would-be rockers first learned their licks on an Egmond. George Harrison, Brian May, and Rory Gallagher all cut their teeth on cheap Egmond acoustic guitars; Paul McCartney started off with a Solid 7 electric guitar which he later converted to a bass by using piano wire.

The Egmond Model 3 became available in around 1965, and is clearly modeled on the asymmetric waist of the Fender Jazzmaster. Fender, though, certainly never gave any of their instruments a finish like the unusual sparkly plastic covering on the model shown here.

**The Egmond catalog from 1963 shows the factory at Best.**

**Just fifty of these Egmond double-neck guitar/mandolin models were built.**

| | |
|---|---|
| **Body style:** Solid body, twin cutaway, asymmetric waist | |
| **Materials:** Laminated body; bolt-on maple neck | |
| **Finish:** Plastic covering | |
| **Fretboard:** Rosewood | |
| **Inlays:** Acrylic dot | |
| **Frets:** 20 (not including zero fret) | |
| **Scale:** 25 ½" | |
| **Nut width:** 1 ⅝" | |
| **Bridge:** Adjustable; separate tailpiece with vibrato | |
| **Pickups:** 3 single-coil pickups; "chicken head" selector switch; lead/rhythm switch | |
| **Electrics:** Master volume and tone controls | |

# Eko 700/4V 1961

By the middle of the 1960s almost all of Italy's electric guitars emanated from Castelfidardo, the most significant being Pigini's Eko brand.

The first notable Eko came in 1960. The 400 series Ekomaster was seen in use by some of Italy's early rock 'n' roll performers, such as Adriano Celentano. A year later, it was updated in the form of the 700 series, probably the single most celebrated electric guitar produced in mainland Europe.

With its eye-catching triple cutaway, the 700 was visually unique. Add to that the traditional accordion-maker's "sparkle" (an especially thick plastic coating which Pigini had developed for his guitars), and a four-pickup array with an assortment of tonal switching possibilities, and you have an instrument as easy on the ears and fingers as it is on the eye.

In recent years, early Eko models, especially the 400 and 700 series, have become highly collectible.

Oliviero Pigini, like the other post-war Italian accordion makers of Castelfidardo, near Italy's Adriatic coast, struggled with the advent of rock 'n' roll. Pigini was the first of this group to introduce guitars, taking over his uncle's accordion factory in 1959 and bringing experienced luthiers to the region.

**Adriano Celentano,** seen here playing a four-pickup Eko 400, was Italy's first big rock 'n' roll star.

▼
Celentano's career has encompassed singing, acting, comedy, and directing films. Most of his many greatest hits compilations feature examples of his early work.

| | |
|---|---|
| **Body style:** | Solid body, triple cutaway |
| **Materials:** | Assorted hardwoods were used for the body, including mahogany; set maple neck |
| **Finish:** | Pearl sparkle (sometimes known as "mother-of-toilet seat"); red sparkle; silver sparkle |
| **Fretboard:** | Rosewood |
| **Inlays:** | Plastic "plus" block |
| **Frets:** | 21 |
| **Scale:** | 25" |
| **Width at nut:** | 1 7/10" |
| **Bridge:** | Adjustable Melita-style; separate tailpiece with vibrato |
| **Pickups:** | 4 pickups (grouped in pairs); 6 pickup selector switches on upper bout (M, 1, 4, 1+4, 2+3, 0) |
| **Electrics:** | Master volume and tone controls |

# EPIPHONE : THE STORY

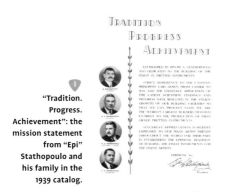

"Tradition. Progress. Achievement": the mission statement from "Epi" Stathopoulo and his family in the 1939 catalog.

The 1936 Epiphone Emperor archtop.

John Lennon playing an Epiphone Casino in 1968.

Nowadays we tend to think of the Epiphone name as a Gibson diffusion line. In fact, Epiphone and Gibson were once equally matched competitors, both producing professional archtop guitars. During the 1930s, the two companies fought a commercial battle every bit as fierce as those later waged between Gibson and Fender.

The roots of the Epiphone Company date back to 1873 and the Ottoman Empire, when Anastasios Stathopoulo began selling ouds—the Arabic equivalent to the European lute. In 1903, Stathopoulo emigrated to Long Island, New York, where he continued to make his original instruments. Following his death in 1915, his son, Epaminondas, took over the workshop and shifted the emphasis of production toward banjos. The Epiphone name was first used in 1928, a combination of the proprietor's nickname, "Epi," and "phone" (from the Greek word meaning sound or voice). Combined, the name was also a play on the word "epiphany."

From the early 1930s, Epi Stathopoulo changed the emphasis of production from banjos to the guitar, and throughout the decade Epiphone was responsible for some of the finest archtop guitars being produced in the United States. Indeed, models such as the Emperor from this period are now highly sought-after collectors' pieces.

In 1943, Stathopoulo died and control of the company passed to his younger brothers. The company was already foundering when, in 1951, the workforce fell into dispute with the Stathopoulo family. Relocating from New York to Philadelphia, Epiphone was now in dire financial straits. In 1957 the company was bought out by former rivals Gibson, which moved production to its main plant in Kalamazoo, Michigan.

Throughout the 1960s, Gibson allowed Epiphone its own identity, producing hollow-body electrics like the Casino, which was widely used by several members of The Beatles. By the end of the 1970s, however, the brand had become a vehicle for cheap, Korean-built instruments.

Epiphone was given a major brand overhaul in 1988, and has since become associated with the manufacture of high-quality, reasonably priced versions of classic Gibson models made in Asia. Some would argue, in fact, that there is little to choose between the high-end Epiphone Elitist guitars and their U.S.-produced counterparts.

**1903** Greek oud-maker Anastasios Stathopoulo moves to the U.S.

**1928** Epaminondas "Epi" Stathopoulo creates the Epiphone brand

**1935** Epiphone Emperor archtop model first appears

**1943** Company struggles following the death of Epi Stathopoulo

**1951** Production stops after New York workforce strikes

**1957** Epiphone brand sold to Gibson, its former rival

**1970** First Epiphones are built in Japan

# EPIPHONE: THE FAMILY TREE (PRE-1960 ARCHTOPS)

For more than fifty years, the Epiphone brand has been under the wing of the mighty Gibson empire. For much of that time it has been widely viewed as a Gibson diffusion label, enabling players to buy cheaper versions of classic designs such as the SG and Les Paul, normally built in the Far East. Indeed, Epiphone is now one of the world's biggest-selling brands with a reputation for producing fine instruments at affordable prices. Epiphone guitars are frequently seen in use by professional musicians.

Prior to Gibson's buy-out of the Epiphone company in 1957, however, the story was very different. Before the outbreak of World War II, the company founded in New York by Greek emigree "Epi" Stathopoulos was one of the finest makers of archtop guitars, and, being the only major leading archtop producers, Epiphone and Gibson were bitter rivals. This family tree covers the models produced by Epiphone before 1960, and includes some significant electric models built after the Gibson takeover.

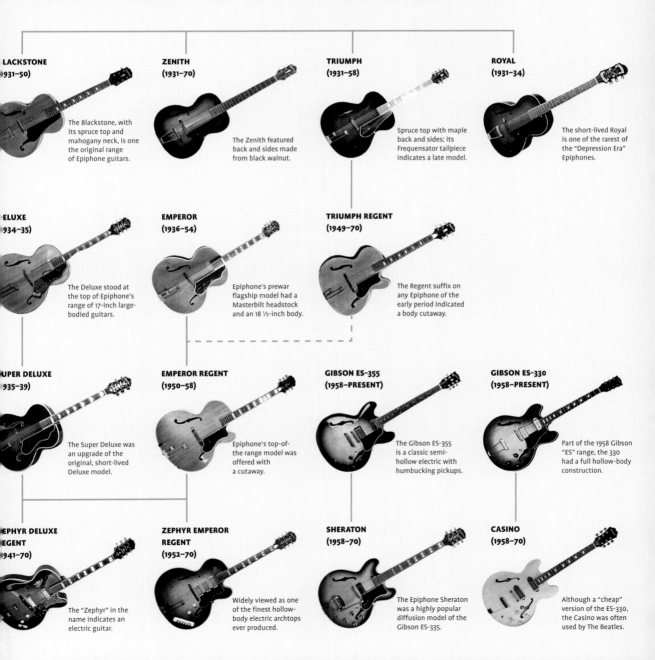

**LACKSTONE**
**1931–50)**

The Blackstone, with its spruce top and mahogany neck, is one the original range of Epiphone guitars.

**ZENITH**
**(1931–70)**

The Zenith featured back and sides made from black walnut.

**TRIUMPH**
**(1931–58)**

Spruce top with maple back and sides; its Frequensator tailpiece indicates a late model.

**ROYAL**
**(1931–34)**

The short-lived Royal is one of the rarest of the "Depression Era" Epiphones.

**ELUXE**
**1934–35)**

The Deluxe stood at the top of Epiphone's range of 17-inch large-bodied guitars.

**EMPEROR**
**(1936–54)**

Epiphone's prewar flagship model had a Masterbilt headstock and an 18 ½-inch body.

**TRIUMPH REGENT**
**(1949–70)**

The Regent suffix on any Epiphone of the early period indicated a body cutaway.

**UPER DELUXE**
**935–39)**

The Super Deluxe was an upgrade of the original, short-lived Deluxe model.

**EMPEROR REGENT**
**(1950–58)**

Epiphone's top-of-the range model was offered with a cutaway.

**GIBSON ES-355**
**(1958–PRESENT)**

The Gibson ES-355 is a classic semi-hollow electric with humbucking pickups.

**GIBSON ES-330**
**(1958–PRESENT)**

Part of the 1958 Gibson "ES" range, the 330 had a full hollow-body construction.

**EPHYR DELUXE**
**EGENT**
**941–70)**

The "Zephyr" in the name indicates an electric guitar.

**ZEPHYR EMPEROR**
**REGENT**
**(1952–70)**

Widely viewed as one of the finest hollow-body electric archtops ever produced.

**SHERATON**
**(1958–70)**

The Epiphone Sheraton was a highly popular diffusion model of the Gibson ES-335.

**CASINO**
**(1958–70)**

Although a "cheap" version of the ES-330, the Casino was often used by The Beatles.

# EPIPHONE DELUXE 1931

The 1930s was the decade in which, thanks in part to the Gibson L-5, the guitar was beginning to find an expanded role in popular music. The acoustic volume achievable with this new generation of guitars challenged the supremacy of the banjo in jazz groups, and consequently many banjo players were now beginning to switch to the guitar.

In 1931 Epiphone set out to challenge Gibson's dominance of the archtop market with its Masterbilt range of highly crafted guitars. The two principal Epiphone archtops of this period were the Deluxe and Emperor models. First built in 1931, the Epiphone Deluxe with its large body was a direct competitor to Gibson's L-5, but was considerably more ornate.

An interesting feature of early Epiphones is the famous Frequensator tailpiece, with which bass and treble strings of different lengths are used. Lengthening the bass strings causes greater tension, making for a tighter bass sound; the shorter top strings have a looser tension making it easier to play solos in the upper register.

The 1934 model (*see right*) appears to have been customized with the addition of a pickup, probably during the 1940s.

▲
Billy Bauer was one of the pioneers of "cool jazz." He used a number of different Epiphones, including the Deluxe.

▼
Bauer worked extensively with pianist Lennie Tristano. The 1949 track "Digression" has been cited as one of the first examples of "free improvisation."

| | |
|---|---|
| **Body style:** | Hollow body |
| **Materials:** | Maple back and sides; spruce top; maple neck |
| **Finish:** | Natural or sunburst |
| **Body width:** | 16 ⅜" (increased to 17 ⅜" in 1937) |
| **Fretboard:** | Rosewood |
| **Inlays:** | Mother-of-pearl "V" block; vine design on headstock |
| **Frets:** | 20 |
| **Scale:** | 25 ½" |
| **Width at nut:** | 1 ¹¹⁄₁₆" |
| **Bridge:** | Rosewood, fixed |
| **Machine heads:** | Gold-plated Grover Sta-Tite tuners with butterbean keys |

# EPIPHONE 6832 1971

the Epiphone name from Kalamazoo to Japan. Unsurprisingly, given the poor reputation that Japanese-built instruments enjoyed in the West (one it would very rapidly lose), the 1971 Epiphone catalog makes no mention of these changes, simply offering a range of basic, decent-quality guitars that wouldn't break the bank.

Although neither Gibson nor Epiphone had been well-known for their flat-top acoustic guitars—Martin had long conquered that area—this first generation of Japanese acoustic guitars proved to be extremely popular.

The full-bodied 6832, with its rosewood sides and spruce top, was equipped with a slim bolt-on neck that was particularly well suited to players who primarily played electric instruments. The guitar boasted a rich, mellow tone and the ability to project its sound. The 6832, and other guitars in the series, were produced until around 1981.

By the turn of the 1970s Gibson had all but buried Epiphone's illustrious past, the brand representing little more than a budget range. In an attempt to make that part of their business more profitable, Gibson took the momentous decision to move production of guitars bearing

▲
"This popular deluxe model produces a rich mellow tone, good response, and fine carrying power"—the 6832 described in the 1971 Epiphone catalog.

▼
The instrument shown at right once belonged to cult progressive rock artist Ramases. It is likely to have been played on his 1975 album *Glass Top Coffin*.

| | |
|---|---|
| **Body style:** | Hollow-body acoustic |
| **Materials:** | Rosewood back and sides; spruce top; with multiple binding; bolt-on maple neck |
| **Body dimensions:** | Length 19"; width 15 ¼"; depth 4" |
| **Finish:** | Natural; polyurethane gloss varnish |
| **Fretboard:** | Rosewood |
| **Sound hole:** | Features decorative purfling |
| **Inlays:** | Mother-of-pearl block |
| **Frets:** | 20 (not including zero fret) |
| **Scale:** | 24 ¾" |
| **Width at nut:** | 1 ¹³⁄₁₆" |
| **Bridge:** | Rosewood with adjustable saddle |
| **Machine heads:** | Closed design with mother-of-pearl handle |

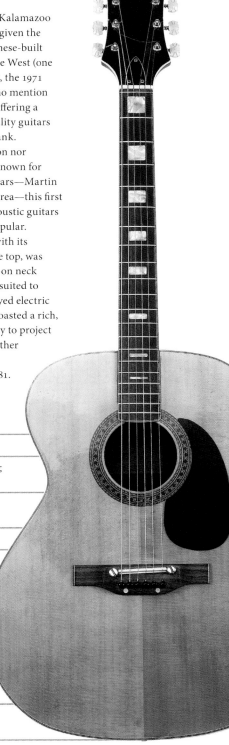

# EPIPHONE ZEPHYR EMPEROR REGENT 1952

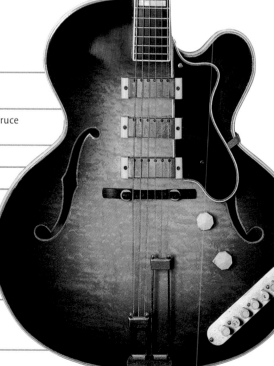

In 1950, the Emperor was offered with a Venetian cutaway, and was christened the Emperor Regent. Two years later, an electric version of this model was launched, the Zephyr Emperor Regent. It was the most luxurious instrument that Epiphone would ever make.

The Zephyr Emperor Regent has all the standard high-end features of its acoustic counterpart: maple back and sides, seven-ply binding on the top and back, three-ply binding around the f-holes, a single-bound fingerboard with a pair of inlaid white lines along edges, triple-bound peghead, vine-design inlay on the headstock, and gold-plating on the Frequensator tailpiece and other hardware.

The electrics are noteworthy in that the three single-coil New York pickups are engaged by pressing the six buttons on the control panel. Any combination of the three is possible (except, curiously, all three "on" at the same time).

The Emperor was one of Epiphone's most significant prewar archtop guitars. Launched in 1935 it was positioned in the market to compete with Gibson's flagship SJ-400. A large-bodied instrument, at 18½ inches, it was more than 2 inches wider than the Deluxe.

▲
"Dedicated to the best in fretted instruments and bass viols since 1873." Epiphone came up with this snappy slogan for their 1954 catalog, the cover of which proudly displays the flagship electric model, by then known more briefly as the Emperor Electric.

| | |
|---|---|
| **Body style:** | Hollow body with single Venetian cutaway |
| **Materials:** | Maple back and sides; laminated spruce top (laminated maple on later models) |
| **Finish:** | Sunburst or natural blonde |
| **Fretboard:** | Rosewood |
| **Inlays:** | Mother-of-pearl "V" block |
| **Frets:** | 20 |
| **Scale:** | 25½" |
| **Width at nut:** | 1 11/16" |
| **Bridge:** | Adjustable; Frequensator tailpiece |
| **Pickups:** | 3 single-coil Epiphone "New York" pickups; combinations selected by 6-switch control panel |
| **Electrics:** | Master volume and tone controls |

# EPIPHONE CASINO 1958

▲
**The Beatles give a legendary show on the rooftop of Apple headquarters in London's Mayfair. John Lennon can be seen wielding his Epiphone Casino.**

▼
**Lennon played his Casino on most of the sessions that made up 1970's *Let It Be*, the final album before The Beatles' breakup.**

B y the mid-1960s The Beatles were by any measure the most famous pop group in the world. Yet although they evidently took their musicianship seriously, they showed a surprising lack of snobbery when it came to choosing their instruments—look at the modest Hofner bass used throughout his career by Paul McCartney. And when it came to guitars, such wealthy young musicians might have been expected to choose the best that money could buy—yet all three of the band's guitar players bought Epiphone Casinos.

Issued in 1958, the Epiphone Casino was another of Gibson's early crossover models. A thinline, hollow body, twin-pickup electric guitar, it is essentially an Epiphone-branded version of the Gibson ES-330. However, the Casino's association with Harrison, Lennon, and McCartney has ensured a level of long-lasting fame overshadowing its high-end relative.

Soundwise, the Casino is a versatile instrument, equally capable of warm, jazzy tones and biting overdrive.

The Casino was temporarily discontinued in 1970. A 1965 Elitist model appeared in 2010, a replica of John Lennon's own pickguard-free Casino, shown here.

| | |
|---|---|
| **Body style:** | Semi-hollow body with double cutaway |
| **Materials:** | Solid maple center block with maple wings; set mahogany neck |
| **Finish:** | Sunburst, royal tan (other colors available later) |
| **Fretboard:** | Rosewood |
| **Inlays:** | Acrylic block |
| **Frets:** | 22 |
| **Scale:** | 24 ¾" |
| **Width at nut:** | 1 5⁄16" |
| **Bridge:** | Tune-o-matic |
| **Tailpiece:** | Frequensator (end block after 1961); optional Bigsby vibrato |
| **Pickups:** | 1 or 2 P-90 pickups; 3-way selector switch (on 2-pickup models) |
| **Electrics:** | Dedicated volume and tone controls for each pickup |

# EPIPHONE SHERATON 1958

W hen "Epi" Stathopoulos died from leukemia in 1943, the company lost its innovator and driving force. His brother Frixo jointly took the reins but the coming decade was fraught with difficulties, including a workers' strike that ended with the company moving from New York to Pennsylvania. When Frixo died in 1957, the company could no longer continue independently, and was sold to its erstwhile rivals, Gibson.

Gibson continued production of some of the most important Epiphones while adding new models based on Gibson designs. The Sheraton was a twin-humbucker, double-cutaway thinline that closely resembled the 335.

One immediate, fundamental change for Epiphone was the reduction in scale length from 25 ½ inches to the Gibson standard 24 ¾. Initially, the Epiphone was able to retain the brand's unique Frequensator tailpiece, but the later Sheraton II featured the standard Gibson endstop tailpiece. Both were offered with optional Bigsby vibrato.

Production of the Sheraton in its original form was discontinued in 1970, but later resumed in the Far East. In 2000, one of the guitar's best-known users, John Lee Hooker, was given his own signature model.

▲
**Ezra Koenig of Vampire Weekend is a prominent modern-day user of the Epiphone Sheraton. His "high-life" African-style guitar work is central to the band's sound.**

▼
**Ezra Koenig plays his Epiphone Sheraton II (the guitar lacks the Frequensator tailpiece of the original) on Vampire Weekend's eponymous debut album of 2008.**

| | |
|---|---|
| **Body style:** | Semi-hollow body with double cutaway |
| **Materials:** | Solid maple center block with maple wings; set mahogany neck |
| **Finish:** | Ebony, natural, vintage sunburst |
| **Fretboard:** | Rosewood |
| **Inlays:** | Acrylic block |
| **Frets:** | 22 |
| **Scale:** | 24 ¾" |
| **Width at nut:** | 1 $^5/_{16}$" |
| **Bridge:** | Tune-o-matic |
| **Tailpiece:** | Frequensator (end block after 1961); optional Bigsby vibrato |
| **Pickups:** | 2 "New York" humbuckers (mini-humbucker after 1961); 3-way selector switch |
| **Electrics:** | Dedicated volume and tone controls for each pickup |

# EPIPHONE G-310 "EMILY THE STRANGE" 2009

Emily the Strange, a figure who had begun life as a decoration on a range of skateboards in California.

Artist and skateboarder Rob Reger designed Emily in 1991. A moody, black-haired young girl with an interest in "dark themes," Emily started getting noticed on stickers given away at concerts advertising Cosmic Debris, a clothing label selling skate and surf wear. Her popularity spread on the Internet, spawning comics, books, and assorted merchandise, often featuring her catch phrases: "Get Lost!" and "Wish You Weren't Here."

The G-310 is a basic Epiphone SG model, priced to appeal to Emily the Strange's (mainly) teenage audience. And it reflects why the Epiphone brand represents such an important part of the Gibson operation: behind the cute decor is a more-than-decent-quality guitar, with a body shape that nods to Gibson's illustrious past, but presented at an affordable price.

Signature instruments have played a large part in the guitar world's marketing landscape since the 1950s. In 2009, rather than seeking out a cool young player to endorse a new model, Gibson hooked up their Epiphone brand with a cult counterculture cartoon girl named

▲
Guitarist and singer Machy of Latin female group La Conquista from Monterrey, Mexico, poses with her Epiphone G-310 "Emily the Strange."

▼
Dark Horse Comics have produced a series of *Emily the Strange* comics.

| | |
|---|---|
| **Body style:** | Solid-body double cutaway |
| **Materials:** | Basswood body with bolt-on mahogany neck |
| **Finish:** | Emily the Strange graphics |
| **Fretboard:** | Rosewood |
| **Inlays:** | Acrylic dot |
| **Frets:** | 22 |
| **Scale:** | 24 ¾" |
| **Width at nut:** | 1 ¹⁷/₂₅" |
| **Bridge:** | Chrome Tune-o-matic with separate block tailpiece. |
| **Pickups:** | 750T and 650R humbuckers, 3-way selector switch |
| **Electrics:** | Dedicated volume and tone control for each pickup |

# ERLEWINE CHIQUITA 1979

Mark Erlewine and his friend Billy Gibbons (guitarist/vocalist with ZZ Top) designed the Chiquita travel guitar in 1979. Despite being short scale—it's a full foot shorter than a typical guitar—the Chiquita was, unlike some similar instruments, no toy, but a highly playable electric guitar. With its mahogany body and humbucking pickup it was also capable of matching most electric guitars from a tonal perspective.

The Chiquita unexpectedly reached a worldwide cinema audience, appearing at the beginning of the 1985 film *Back To The Future*. Erlewine subsequently licensed production to the U.S. International Music Corporation, where they were manufactured in large numbers under the Hondo brand, including models with switchable double- and single-coil pickups. Mark Erlewine was unhappy with the quality of these instruments, however, and when the IMC deal ran out he resumed production himself from his base in Austin, Texas.

There have been many different approaches to the idea of a travel guitar, an instrument that can be stowed away easily on a journey. Some instruments have been developed to be easily dismantled or even folded at the neck, but a more common approach has been to experiment with dimensions, often reducing the scale length.

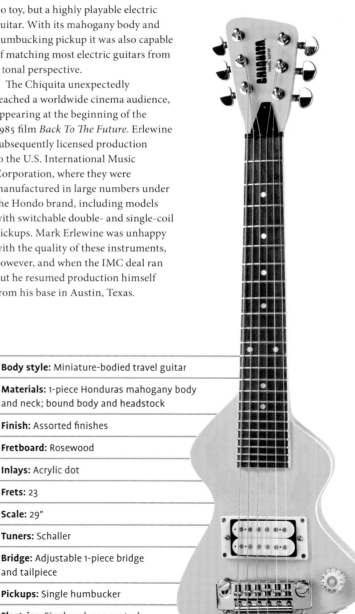

▲
**The *Back To The Future* guitar!** Marty McFly (Michael J. Fox) plays a chord on the Erlewine Chiquita he picks up in Doc Brown's garage at the start of the 1985 film . . . and is promptly thrown across the room as the amp explodes.

▶
**The Erlewine Chiquita, compared in size to a Fender Stratocaster.**

| | |
|---|---|
| **Body style:** | Miniature-bodied travel guitar |
| **Materials:** | 1-piece Honduras mahogany body and neck; bound body and headstock |
| **Finish:** | Assorted finishes |
| **Fretboard:** | Rosewood |
| **Inlays:** | Acrylic dot |
| **Frets:** | 23 |
| **Scale:** | 29" |
| **Tuners:** | Schaller |
| **Bridge:** | Adjustable 1-piece bridge and tailpiece |
| **Pickups:** | Single humbucker |
| **Electrics:** | Single volume control |

# ESTESO 1934

Domingo Esteso learned his trade under the great Spanish luthier Manuel Ramirez. Born in San Clemente in the province of Cuenca in 1882, Esteso joined Ramirez at his workshop in Madrid during the 1890s. When Ramirez died in 1916, in the tradition of the time Esteso continued working for the master's widow: for around a year he and fellow employee Santos Hernández (*see page 159*) produced instruments bearing the label "Viuda de Manuel Ramirez" (Widow of Manuel Ramirez).

In 1917, Esteso opened his own shop on Madrid's Calle Gravina, where he concentrated on the production of flamenco guitars. Already established through his former employer, he had few difficulties attracting customers. Among his clients was Ramón Montoya, the first virtuoso flamenco guitarist. His work in the 1930s all but defined the genre, and two decades later his nephew Carlos would further evolve the form.

In 1926, Esteso was joined by his nephew, Faustino Conde. In 1937, when Esteso died, Faustino and his two brothers, Mariano and Julio, continued building for Esteso's widow. Following her death in 1960, they renamed the workshop Hermanos Conde, Sobrinos de Domingo Esteso (Conde Brothers, Nephews of Domingo Esteso), producing some of the finest flamenco guitars of the past fifty years.

▲
**Ramón Montoya is widely considered the father of modern flamenco.**

▼
**Montoya's immaculate technique can be heard on the fifth volume of Chant du Monde's 2007 *Great Masters Of Flamenco*.**

| | |
|---|---|
| **Body style:** | Classical figure-eight |
| **Materials:** | Indian Rosewood back and sides; German spruce top |
| **Finish:** | French polish |
| **Fretboard:** | Rosewood |
| **Inlays:** | None |
| **Frets:** | 19 (including partial fret) |
| **Scale:** | 25 ³/₅" |
| **Width at nut:** | 2 ¹/₁₆" |
| **Bridge:** | Rosewood bridge; bone saddle |
| **Tuners:** | Friction pegs |

# FENDER: THE STORY

Leo Fender (1909–1991), arguably the most important single figure in the evolution of the electric guitar.

The story of Fender Electric Instrument Corporation is told at the Fullerton Museum Center.

Clayton "Doc" Kauffman designed guitars for Rickenbacker in the 1930s before going into business with Leo Fender.

Given the immeasurable influence he would have on the music of the second half of the twentieth century, it is perhaps surprising to learn that Clarence Leonidas (Leo) Fender, ① the founder of the company, had no musical grounding whatsoever.

Born on August 10, 1909, in Anaheim, California, Fender showed an early interest in tinkering with electronics. As a teenager, he visited an electrical shop in Santa Maria run by his uncle and became fascinated by a radio his relative had built from spare parts. He soon began repairing radios in a small shop in his parents' home. This remained a hobby while he qualified to be an accountant. In 1938, finding work hard to come by in post-Depression California, and with a loan of $600, he set up the Fender Radio Service shop in Fullerton. ② Quickly he carved a reputation for building PA systems and amplification for the "electric Spanish" and Hawaiian lap steel guitars that were beginning to appear in California. The shop proved to be a useful meeting place for people involved in the music or electronics businesses.

In 1940, Clayton "Doc" Kauffman, ③ an inventor and lap steel guitarist, took an amplifier into Fender's shop for repair. Kauffman had previously worked for Rickenbacker—the company that produced the first electrified instruments—and the two began working together. They were quickly disrupted by America's entry into World War II, when Kauffman was drafted into the Air Force. Fender was ineligible for combat, a childhood accident having left him blind in one eye. As he was left with few competitors he was able to expand.

On the cessation of hostilities in 1945, Fender and Kauffman resumed their activities and formed a business—the K&F Manufacturing Corporation—building amplified Hawaiian guitars and amplifiers. Kauffman designed the instruments, Fender the electronics, and the two products were sold paired together in kit form. The business would be short-lived: Kauffman realized that they would have to expand their business heavily if they were to get into large-scale production, and, having lived through the Depression, he feared the consequences of failure. Nor did he share Fender's dedication to long hours. In February 1946 Kauffman pulled out of the business.

**1909**
Birth of Leo Fender

**1938**
Opening of Fender Radio Service shop in Fullerton, California

**1945**
Fender opens K&F Manufacturing Corporation with "Doc" Kauffman

**1946**
Launch of the Fender Musical Instrument Company

**1949**
Prototype of Fender's first solid-body electric guitar completed

**1950**
Fewer than fifty single-pickup Esquire guitars are produced

**1950**
Twin-pickup Broadcaster goes into production

Leo Fender's entrepreneurial bent was undiminished by his experience with K&F. That same year he created the Fender Musical Instruments Corporation, expanding into new premises near his original workshop. He would continue to manufacture lap steels and amplifiers, but would also develop new products.

Fender was already well aware of the growing popularity of the amplified guitar, but his experience of providing PAs for musicians also enabled him to understand the shortcomings of the existing instruments—namely that a typical amplified archtop guitar would feedback, creating a howling sound. This unpleasant effect was created by the loud sounds emanating from the PA or speaker vibrating the guitar's acoustic chamber which, in turn, caused the strings to vibrate of their own accord.

A Fender catalog illustrates some of the "fine electric instruments" the company made available in 1955.

Like experimenting musician/inventors Les Paul and Paul Bigsby (who had already produced a workable solid-body instrument for country musician Merle Travis), Fender understood how the problem might be solved—by constructing a body using a denser material that would not vibrate to anything like the same degree as an acoustic chamber. In 1948, Fender and one of his employees, George Fullerton, set about creating an affordable production-line solid-body electric guitar.

The first prototypes of the design by Fender and Fullerton were created in 1949. A year later, fewer than fifty of the single-pickup instruments named the Esquire were displayed at music trade shows in the U.S. Later in 1950, with a number of design flaws identified and fixed and a second pickup added, the Fender Broadcaster came off the assembly line—it was the first ever mass-produced solid-body electric guitar.

Leo Fender (right) and George Fullerton, who succeeded in putting Fender guitars into mass production.

Fender salesmen of the time reported that the new instrument was treated with a mixture of amusement and suspicion at trade shows. But musicians who gave the Broadcaster a spin were quick to see its potential. The guitar offered all the excitement and volume of semi-acoustic guitars, without the unpredictable feedback that could spoil performances and musical events.

The Fender Broadcaster itself was to have a rather brief existence. In 1951, Fender received a communication from the large New York-based Gretsch company, which had already begun marketing a range of drum kits under the name Broadkaster. The feeling at Gretsch was that its copyright had been

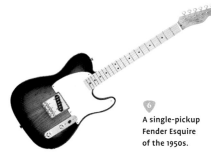

A single-pickup Fender Esquire of the 1950s.

**1951** Gretsch causes Broadcaster to be renamed Telecaster

**1951** Launch of Fender Precision—the first production-line bass guitar

**1952** Launch of Fender Twin amplifier

**1954** Fender launches the Stratocaster

**1957** Buddy Holly appears on Ed Sullivan playing a Stratocaster

**1960** Fender issues the Jazzmaster and an electric violin

**1963** Launch of the classic Fender Twin Reverb amplifier

infringed and, mindful that a lawsuit was not in the interests of his budding company, Fender agreed to a change of name. Overnight, the Broadcaster was rechristened the Telecaster. The guitar would quickly become a standard reference for countless generations of musicians.

The Telecaster was a basic instrument, with its design and manufacture kept deliberately simple. It was intended as an affordable working guitar for working musicians. Some converts to the solid-body concept, however, had other ideas. Country guitarist Bill Carson  was happy to act as a musical testing ground for the company in its early days. He gave Leo Fender a list detailing the areas in which he would like to see the Telecaster improved. As he would later recall, his dream guitar would feature, "six bridges that would adjust vertically and horizontally . . . The guitar should fit like a good shirt, with body contours, and stay balanced at all times."

Fender issued this image as an advertisement with the line "Billy Carson uses Fender fine electric instruments exclusively."

Leo Fender had the jump on the competition, but now there were other established guitar companies about to make their own mark. Gibson produced the Les Paul, a pointedly upscale instrument in quality and cost, and Gretsch came up with the cool-looking black Duo Jet. Fender knew it was time to produce an upscale alternative to the Telecaster, while continuing to manufacture that guitar for its unique sound. He and draughtsman Freddie Tavares worked on the prototype of a guitar that would take into account some of the preferences voiced by the Telecaster's critics, Bill Carson among them.

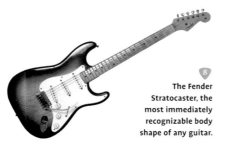

The Fender Stratocaster, the most immediately recognizable body shape of any guitar.

In 1954, the men at Fender surpassed themselves with only their second six-string electric guitar design, unleashing that magnificent icon of popular culture—the Stratocaster. This instrument—smooth, modern, and stylish—was arguably the most important electric guitar ever made. An immediate hit with musicians, the Stratocaster has remained a constant feature of the world's musical landscape ever since, spawning not only a plethora of cheap imitations but also innumerable variants from niche luthiers attempting to tap the guitars huge established market.

At a distance of over half a century we can look back at the 1950s and see that they really *were* an extraordinary decade for a company that had only been in existence since 1946. Not only was Fender the first to come up with a production-line solid-body electric guitar, but the company's first design,

The Telecaster is described in a 1973 Fender advert as "the world's favorite love machine."

**1964** Fender produces the company's first acoustic guitars

**1965** Leo Fender sells his company to CBS for $13 million

**1967** Jimi Hendrix plays (and sets fire to) his Stratocaster at Monterey

**1968** Fender launches the Thinline Telecaster Series

**1977** Five-way pickup selector switch becomes standard on Stratocaster

**1982** CBS hit by financial crisis; guitar production in U.S. curtailed

**1982** Launch of Fender Japan

the Telecaster,  was one that musicians, alien to this new idea, wanted to play—and are *still* playing well into the twenty-first century.

With two superb electric guitars in production Fender turned to the bass guitar, and within a year it had also introduced the Fender Precision. Although Leo Fender didn't invent the bass guitar, he saw its potential and introduced it to the masses. Sixty years later, it is impossible to imagine how modern music, from soul and the late jazz of Miles Davis to rock 'n' roll, The Beatles, progressive rock, and today's guitar bands, would have sounded without the existence of the electric bass guitar.

The Telecaster, Stratocaster, and Precision ranked among the most popular guitars of the second half of the twentieth century. All have remained in constant production, finding a place in any musical genre you care to mention. All have also been taken up by successive generations. And all look set to maintain their popularity over the decades to come.

But focusing overmuch on this trio would be to overlook some of the other great instruments carrying the Fender name during the company's first fifteen years of existence: the Jazzmaster 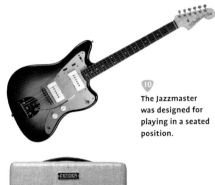 and Jaguar guitars—not so popular at the time, but evolving cult followings in the years since, and now back in production; the Fender Jazz bass, more highly rated than the Precision in some circles; and then there are the Fender valve amplifiers, such as the Champ,  the Bassman, and the ever-popular Twin Reverb. The list could be extended to cover the whole page. Unsurprisingly, for Fender it was a decade of innovation that would never again be matched.

By the mid-1960s Fender was the most successful musical instrument manufacturer in the United States, with sales worth in excess of $10 million a year. One of the factors behind this success was the effort the company put into achieving overseas sales. Photographs of Buddy Holly playing his Stratocaster  had reached the U.K. and Europe and ramped up the demand for Fender guitars. In those regions Gibson instruments, by contrast, were unfeasibly rare, exotic, and expensive at that time.

By 1965 it was said that Fender was so successful that they were exporting more American-made musical instruments than the rest of their competitors put together. Their market was growing, not only through adulation of American guitarists, but through emulation of homegrown Fender users.

The Jazzmaster was designed for playing in a seated position.

The Champ amplifier remained in production from 1948 until 1982.

Buddy Holly plays a Fender Stratocaster on the nationally broadcast *Ed Sullivan Show* in 1957.

**1983**
Fender launches Squier—the company's first imported range

**1985**
CBS sells Fender to management group; sale does not involve factory

**1987**
Opening of Fender Custom Shop in Corona, California

**1988**
Eric Clapton becomes Fender's first signature artist

**1989**
First guitars built at Fender's factory in Ensenada, Mexico

**1991**
Leo Fender dies at the age of 81 years

**1994**
Release of 40th-anniversary Stratocaster

Eric Clapton is seen here in 1978 playing "Blackie," his favorite Strat. Auctioned in 2004, the guitar raised almost a million dollars for his Crossroads charity.

Humorous contemporary fake advert from Romania that harks back to the days when owning a Fender electric guitar was close to a revolutionary act.

A display of vintage Fender guitars captured in 2008 at a music store on Sunset Boulevard, Los Angeles.

One famous Stratocaster of this later period was "Blackie," a guitar Eric Clapton built from the best parts of three black Stratocasters that he bought for $100 each in Nashville. ⑬ The Stratocaster was fast becoming the coolest possession a young player could hope for. ⑭

But change was afoot in the Fender company. Leo Fender was evidently something of a hypochondriac, and a sinus condition from which he had suffered for the previous decade had gradually worsened, leading him to believe he had a serious illness. In 1965, he decided to sell the Fender Electric Instrument Corporation. The eventual buyer was the mighty Columbia Broadcasting Systems group (CBS). The price was $13 million.

While at first the Fender company carried on in much the same way as it had before the sale, over time many of the original staff began to leave. Some critics believe corners were cut in production, finishes became inconsistent, and instruments were not set up to play as well. Leo Fender, who stayed on for a while as a consultant, was more charitable: "They weren't trying to cheapen the instrument . . . Maybe they were trying to accelerate production." Most agree that from 1969 past standards were eroded.

Throughout the 1960s and most of the 1970s, however, Fender continued to be a highly profitable company. Furthermore, it continued to attempt to develop new instruments, or significant variations on older themes.

During the early 1980s, Fender established a base in Japan, initially with the intention of killing off the market for copies of Fender guitars made in the Far East. In the late 1960s these had often been of laughably poor quality, but barely a decade later companies such as Tokai were producing copies of the Stratocaster, for example, that rivaled the original guitar.

In 1984, CBS decided to leave the musical instrument business and put Fender up for sale. This was a turbulent time for the firm. Finally, an investor group, led by Fender's now president Bill Schultz, bought the company for $12.5 million—less than the buying price of two decades earlier.

Fender has since concentrated its efforts on producing variations of its classic lines from the 1950s to the early 1970s; the originals now command high prices. ⑮ Now based in Scottsdale, Arizona, it has also taken control of some of the most significant names in the history of the guitar, including Gretsch, Guild, Jackson, Charvel, and Hamer.

# FENDER BROADCASTER 1950

L eo Fender developed the world's first production-line solid-body electric guitar in 1949. The following year he launched the single-pickup Fender Esquire. Fewer than fifty guitars were manufactured. Most of those were returned when serious neck-bending problems, arising from the lack of a truss rod, became evident.

This design flaw was amended, an extra pickup added, and, later that same year, the Broadcaster was born.

The production-line process was made as simple as possible: a single-cutaway slab of solid ash and a maple neck bolted on to the body. This was a far cry from the self-styled craftsmanship of traditional guitar makers such as Gibson and Martin. The electrics were also basic: a mellow-sounding neck pickup and a slanted "lead" pickup, heavily wound—and hence far higher in output—fixed into a steel bridge-plate.

Within a matter of months, the Gretsch company—at that time a well-established manufacturer of many different types of musical instruments—made a claim that Fender had violated the trademark for their "Broadkaster" line of drums. As a new company, Fender did not wish to engage anyone in legal action, so the guitar was relaunched with a brand-new name: the Telecaster.

▲
Guitar legend James Burton—seen here in the early 1950s accompanying Elvis Presley—has been playing Telecasters since he was thirteen.

▼
James Burton provided the cutting Telecaster solo on Dale Hawkins' 1957 swamp-rock classic "Susie Q."

| | |
|---|---|
| **Body style:** | Single cutaway solid body |
| **Materials:** | Ash body with maple neck |
| **Finish:** | Blonde |
| **Fretboard:** | Maple |
| **Inlays:** | Fiberboard dot |
| **Frets:** | 21 |
| **Scale:** | 25 ½" |
| **Width at nut:** | 1 ⅝" |
| **Bridge:** | Fixed; 3 saddles |
| **Tailpiece:** | Strings pass through body |
| **Pickups:** | 2 x single coil with different windings/outputs; 3-position switch |
| **Machine heads:** | Single-line Klusons |
| **Electrics:** | Master volume and tone controls |

# FENDER TELECASTER 1951

Having agreed to change the name of the Broadcaster, Don Randall, who handled Fender's early sales and distribution, came up with a name that reflected the cutting-edge modern era of television—hence the Telecaster. For the first half of 1951, Fender continued to use the same headstock decals with the word "Broadcaster" removed. These instruments are now highly prized by collectors, and are generally referred to as "Nocasters."

The first notable Telecaster user was jazz/country player Jimmy Bryant—the self-styled "Fastest Guitar In The Country." His regular appearances on the *Hometown Jamboree* TV show in the early 1950s created huge interest. As Fender's George Fullerton recalled: "Everybody wanted a guitar like Jimmy Bryant's . . . That was one of the starting points of that guitar."

The Telecaster was a deliberately basic instrument. As Fullerton went on to say: "You think of a cowboy and you think of Roy Rogers . . . fancy hats and shirts and boots . . . but did you ever see a working cowboy? He's dirty and got rough boots on and leather on his pants. So we looked at guitar players as being working cowboys."

Six decades later the iconic Fender Telecaster remains one the most popular "work" guitars.

▲
A powerfully energetic R&B guitarist, Dr. Feelgood's Wilko Johnson played his Telecaster without a pick, striking the strings aggressively with his fingernails.

▼
Johnson's percussive Telecaster playing is showcased on Dr. Feelgood's *Stupidity* (1976), one of rock's finest live albums.

| | |
|---|---|
| **Body style:** | Single cutaway solid body |
| **Materials:** | Ash, alder, or poplar; bolt-on maple neck |
| **Finish:** | Numerous finishes have been available over the past 60 years; nitrocellulose lacquer |
| **Fretboard:** | Maple or rosewood |
| **Inlays:** | Black fiberboard or (from 1959) acrylic dot on maple fingerboard; white clay or (from 1964) pearl dot on rosewood fingerboard |
| **Frets:** | 21 |
| **Scale:** | 25 1/2" |
| **Width at nut:** | 1 11/16" |
| **Bridge:** | Fixed; 3 saddles; "ashtray" cover |
| **Pickups:** | 2 single-coil pickups with different windings/outputs; 3-position switch |
| **Electrics:** | Master volume and tone controls |

# FENDER THINLINE TELECASTER 1968

A solution was put forward in 1968 by Fender's well-traveled German luthier Roger Rossmeisl. He designed a Telecaster with a series of cavities routed out from the rear and covered with a thin panel. Later that year, Fender launched the resulting guitar—the "semi-solid" Thinline Telecaster. It was around half the weight of the typical late-sixties Telecaster.

The most noteworthy differences from a standard Telecaster were visible in the body, where a violin-style f-shaped sound hole was carved. The redesigned pickguard bore resemblance to the Stratocaster in that it also held in place both the tone and volume controls and the pickup selector switch.

In 1972, the Thinline received a radical update when the standard Telecaster single-coil pickups were replaced by Wide Range humbuckers. That same year a similar configuration of pickups would be used on the Telecaster Deluxe.

As the 1960s progressed, the supply of the light ash that Fender had used to build many of their guitar bodies dwindled. Heavy ash was brought into use but, as a consequence, some Fender guitars became increasingly heavy and, for some, uncomfortable to play.

▲
**A 1968 advertisement for the new range of Fender Thinline Telecasters, initially available in two different natural finishes—ash and mahogany. A sunburst option was added in 1969.**

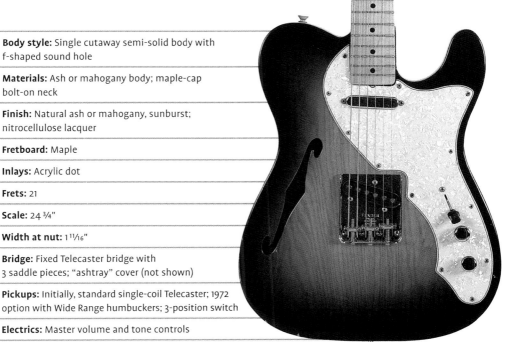

| | |
|---|---|
| **Body style:** Single cutaway semi-solid body with f-shaped sound hole | |
| **Materials:** Ash or mahogany body; maple-cap bolt-on neck | |
| **Finish:** Natural ash or mahogany, sunburst; nitrocellulose lacquer | |
| **Fretboard:** Maple | |
| **Inlays:** Acrylic dot | |
| **Frets:** 21 | |
| **Scale:** 24 ¾" | |
| **Width at nut:** 1 ¹¹⁄₁₆" | |
| **Bridge:** Fixed Telecaster bridge with 3 saddle pieces; "ashtray" cover (not shown) | |
| **Pickups:** Initially, standard single-coil Telecaster; 1972 option with Wide Range humbuckers; 3-position switch | |
| **Electrics:** Master volume and tone controls | |

# FENDER TELECASTER DELUXE 1972

B y the end of the 1960s, the Gibson Les Paul had completed its remarkable rebirth and was well en route to winning regard as the instrument of choice among the newly emerging heavy rock bands. Much of this appeal is down to the "thickness" in sound of the Gibson twin-coil

humbuckers, which came to life so perfectly when played through an overdriven valve amplifier.

Fender's response was a rethink of its single-coil strategy, hiring Seth Lover—the ex-Gibson man who had *invented* the humbucker! The result was the Fender Wide Range pickup, constructed using cunife magnets. The first model to be kitted out with the Wide Range pairs was the new top-of-the-range Telecaster Deluxe. It featured a number of further departures: an unusually enlarged headstock, a maple fingerboard with medium-jumbo sized frets, and a body shape that featured a Strat-style "belly contour," making the guitar more comfortable to play.

Discontinued in 1981, the Deluxe returned to production in 2004. However, the updated Wide Range pickups, with the cunife magnets replaced by an alnico bar, produced a significantly different sound.

▲
Scottish band Franz Ferdinand emerged in 2004 with the international hit single, "Take Me Out." Much of their sound revolves around the angular interplay of two guitars.

▼
You can hear the Telecaster Deluxe of Alex Kapranos on Franz Ferdinand's 2005 sophomore album, *You Could Have It So Much Better.*

| | |
|---|---|
| **Body style:** | Single cutaway solid body |
| **Materials:** | Alder or ash; 3-hole bolt-on maple neck |
| **Finish:** | Black, sunburst, cherry, Olympic white, walnut; polyester coating |
| **Fretboard:** | Maple |
| **Inlays:** | Acrylic dot |
| **Frets:** | 21 (medium-jumbo) |
| **Scale:** | 25 ½" |
| **Width at nut:** | 1 ¹¹⁄₁₆" |
| **Bridge:** | Vintage Strat-style, hardtail; strings through body; "ashtray" cover (not shown) |
| **Pickups:** | 2 Fender Wide Range humbuckers; 3-way selector switch |
| **Machine heads:** | Vintage F-style |
| **Electrics:** | Dedicated volume and tone controls for each pickup |

# FENDER JERRY DONAHUE TELECASTER 1990

I n 1984, the problematic CBS ownership of Fender came to an end. Three years later, CEO Bill Schultz launched Fender's Custom Shop, a specialist wing of the company in which master luthiers would once again be able to produce the kinds of instrument on which Leo Fender had forged his reputation. This was part of a general approach that would see the Fender brand concentrate on developing variations on classic designs customized to the demands of well-known players. Some of these would be released as limited-run "signature" editions, enabling the public to try out the instrumental modifications.

The first such model produced by Fender was the Eric Clapton Stratocaster. Clapton had requested a Strat with the V-shaped neck of his favorite 1930s Martin, and a heavily compressed pickup sound. The resulting guitar, with active circuitry and Lace Sensor pickups, went on sale in 1988. Fender has since honored many great guitarists, not all them necessarily household names, with signature models.

The Jerry Donahue signature model is a typical example—a more-or-less standard 1950s Telecaster with the neck pickup replaced by a single-coil from a Stratocaster, and a five-way switch with custom wiring.

▲
Although New York born and bred, Jerry Donahue forged his reputation on the U.K. folk-rock scene with the bands Fairport Convention and Fotheringay.

▼
The intricacies of Jerry Donahue's Telecaster work can be heard to the full on the 1975 Fairport Convention album *Rising For The Moon*.

| | |
|---|---|
| **Body style:** | Single cutaway solid body |
| **Materials:** | Basswood; bolt-on maple neck |
| **Finish:** | Custom finishes; nitrocellulose lacquer |
| **Fretboard:** | Maple |
| **Inlays:** | Black acrylic dot |
| **Frets:** | 21 |
| **Scale:** | 25 ½" |
| **Width at nut:** | 1 ¹¹⁄₁₆" |
| **Bridge:** | Fixed; 3 saddles; "ashtray" cover (not shown) |
| **Pickups:** | Custom Telecaster single-coil bridge pickup; Custom Stratocaster neck pickup; 5-position switch with unique circuitry |
| **Machine heads:** | Fender in-line |
| **Electrics:** | Master volume and tone controls |

# FENDER STRATOCASTER 1954

It is probably not too great an exaggeration to say that pretty much every notable guitarist (certainly in the fields of pop and rock music, at least) has at some time owned or played a Fender Stratocaster.

Several factors lay behind the development of the Stratocaster. One was Leo Fender's desire to understand the requirements of his customers—the working musicians who had been using his Telecasters night after night. A second factor was the launch in 1952 of the Gibson Les Paul, a shiny, exotic beast that contrasted markedly with the crude simplicity of the Telecaster. It was clear that Fender needed to produce an upmarket alternative.

Critical to the development was the input of western swing guitarist Bill Carson, a working musician who'd had several years' experience with the Telecaster. He provided a wish list for his dream instrument, which included individually adjustable saddles, at least three pickups, a vibrato arm that could work in both directions, and a body shape that could be played comfortably when both standing and sitting. Fender, along with George Fullerton and Freddie Tavares, turned Carson's inventory into a reality, and in doing so came up with an iconic design that would very soon alter the world's musical landscape.

▲
**Although he died at the age of twenty-seven with only a handful of albums to his name, Jimi Hendrix redefined the art of playing the electric guitar.**

▼
**Jimi Hendrix recorded the remarkable *Axis: Bold As Love* (1967) armed, as ever, with his Olympic white Fender Stratocaster.**

| | |
|---|---|
| **Body style:** | Double cutaway solid body |
| **Materials:** | Alder, ash, poplar (at times models have been available in basswood, mahogany, and koa); maple bolt-on neck |
| **Fretboard:** | Maple or rosewood |
| **Frets:** | 21 (22 on some models) |
| **Scale:** | 25 ½" (24 ¾" on some models) |
| **Width at nut:** | 1 ¹¹⁄₁₆" |
| **Bridge:** | Floating bridge with tremolo arm |
| **Tailpiece:** | Strings through body |
| **Pickups:** | 3 single-coil pickups; 3-position switch (5-position switch after 1977) |
| **Electrics:** | Master volume control; 2 tone controls that provide treble boost to various configurations of pickup selection |

# FENDER STRATOCASTER "ROCKY" 1967

I n their early days, George Harrison and John Lennon of The Beatles were usually seen sporting Rickenbacker guitars. In 1965, during the recording of the *Rubber Soul* album, the situation changed. As George Harrison would recall in the 1980s: "We sent our roadie out—Mal [Evans]. John and I had decided to get

a Strat. There was a pair of them and they were both pale blue. During that album I used it a lot—I suppose 'Nowhere Man' is the most noticeable . . . During '67 everybody started painting everything, so I decided to paint it . . . I got some DayGlo paint, which was quite a new invention in those days . . . and just sat up late one night and did it."

Harrison christened his psychedelic masterwork "Rocky," and would continue to use it on assorted Beatles recordings. It can be seen in the groundbreaking live satellite broadcast of "All You Need Is Love" on June 25, 1967, and later in the TV movie *Magical Mystery Tour*.

In 1969, following a conversation with guitarist Ry Cooder, Harrison decided to raise Rocky's bridge, equip it with thicker strings, and use it exclusively for slide playing—which he did until his death in 2001.

Rocky is undoubtedly the most famous of all celebrity guitars.

▲
George Harrison used a Stratocaster on most of The Beatles' recordings after 1965.

▼
In the movie *Magical Mystery Tour* (1967), Harrison plays Rocky in a performance of "I Am The Walrus." A soundtrack album (*below*) of the movie was released in the U.S. in November; in the U.K., an EP was released in December.

| | |
|---|---|
| **Body style:** | Double cutaway solid body |
| **Materials:** | Alder; maple bolt-on neck |
| **Finish:** | Hand-painted in DayGlo colors and nail varnish |
| **Fretboard:** | Rosewood |
| **Frets:** | 21 |
| **Scale:** | 25 ½" (24 ¾" on some models) |
| **Width at nut:** | 1 ¹¹⁄₁₆" |
| **Bridge:** | Floating bridge with tremolo mechanism (arm removed) |
| **Tailpiece:** | Strings through body |
| **Pickups:** | 3 single-coil pickups; 3-position switch |
| **Machine heads:** | Kluson Deluxe |
| **Electrics:** | Master volume control; 2 tone controls that provide treble boost to any pickup selection |

# FENDER STRATOCASTER PLUS 1987

One of Fender's most lucrative markets since the company was reborn as a private concern in 1984 has been in the area of vintage reissues. These are generally U.S.-built, high-performance, high-cost, limited-edition reworkings of classic models. Sometimes the aim is simply to recreate the specification of a particular instrument—for example, the American Vintage '62 Stratocaster Reissue. Sometimes, as is the case with the Vintage Hot Rod series, the aim is to take a classic specification and update it with modern features, such as custom-wound pickups or alternative fret sizes.

The guitar shown here belongs to British Stratocaster-wielding legend (and automobile enthusiast) Jeff Beck. It is a decorated Stratocaster Plus, which itself evolved from a design intended as a Jeff Beck signature model. Significant in its choice of pickup, it was the first Fender to feature the Lace Sensor pickup. A single-coil pickup designed by Don Lace, the Sensor was housed in a metal block that was intended to shield against electromagnetic interference, such as mains hum. Sensors were used on various Fender instruments up until 1996.

Beck has since been honored with his own signature models, the first, in 1991, featuring four Lace Sensors—one pair linked together at the bridge.

▲
Jeff Beck may not be very well known to the public, but he is worshipped by other players. During the 1980s he abandoned the use of picks in favor of his fingers.

▼
Jeff Beck's brilliant Stratocaster work can be heard on the 1975 album *Blow By Blow*, one of the finest rock instrumental albums.

| | |
|---|---|
| **Body style:** | Double cutaway solid body |
| **Materials:** | Alder; maple bolt-on neck |
| **Fretboard:** | Rosewood |
| **Frets:** | 22 |
| **Scale:** | 25½" |
| **Width at nut:** | 1 11/16" |
| **Nut:** | Wilkinson nut, with all 6 strings being fed between two roller pins |
| **Bridge:** | Fender Deluxe locking tremolo assembly |
| **Pickups:** | 3 Lace Sensor single-coil pickups; 5-position switch |
| **Electrics:** | Master volume control; 2 TBX tone controls providing treble boost to various configurations of pickup selection |
| **Machine heads:** | Sperzel locking |

# FENDER STRAT STEVIE RAY VAUGHAN 1992

successful *Let's Dance* album. Shortly after this, Vaughan turned his back on a career as a session side-man to concentrate on playing with his electric blues band Double Trouble. Steadily growing in popularity throughout the 1980s, the band looked set for major international success when Vaughan was tragically killed in a helicopter crash in 1990.

An exclusive Stratocaster user, Vaughan referred to his main guitar— a battered 1962/63 hybrid model— as "Number One" (and sometimes also as his "First Wife"). Vaughan was always happy to modify his instruments, the most interesting alteration being the application of a left-handed tremolo, so that he could imitate Jimi Hendrix—who played a right-handed guitar left handed. A few months before his death, he had begun discussing the idea of a signature model with Fender. The model that emerged two years later was a replica of Number One, complete with tremolo and "SRV" logo.

Born in Texas in 1954, the same year that the guitars that he would play for most of his life were launched, Stevie Ray Vaughan was inspired to take up the guitar by his elder brother, Jimmy—later the founder of the Fabulous Thunderbirds. Vaughan's name first reached an international audience in 1983 when he played on David Bowie's hugely

▲
**Stevie Ray Vaughan was viewed by many as the greatest guitarist of modern blues. He was at his artistic peak at the time of his death.**

▼
**Listen to the track "Say What!" from 1985's *Soul To Soul* album to hear Stevie Ray Vaughan's powerful Strat soloing at its very best.**

| | |
|---|---|
| **Body style:** Double cutaway solid body | |
| **Materials:** Alder body; maple bolt-on neck | |
| **Fretboard:** Pau Ferro | |
| **Frets:** 21 (medium-jumbo) | |
| **Scale:** 25½" | |
| **Width at nut:** 1¹¹⁄₁₆" | |
| **Bridge:** Floating bridge with left-handed tremolo arm assembly | |
| **Tailpiece:** Strings through body | |
| **Pickups:** 3 specially wound single-coil pickups (middle pickup reversed in polarity); 5-position switch | |
| **Electrics:** Master volume control; 2 tone controls that provide treble boost to various configurations of pickup selection | |

# FENDER JAZZMASTER 1958

Leo Fender announced the launch of the Jazzmaster at the 1958 NAMM trade show. The intention was to market this deluxe instrument, at the top of the Fender range as the name suggests, to jazz and blues musicians. The Jazzmaster was designed with what Fender called an "offset-waist" body, meaning the inward-sweeping curves were not aligned as they had been on the Stratocaster. This was to make playing more comfortable in the sitting position—the posture favored by most jazz musicians; the edges of the body were further gently contoured for maximum comfort.

The guitar's electrics also represented something of a departure for Fender. The wide soapbar pickups were unlike the company's usual single-coils. Wound flat and wide, they were able to provide the warmth of a Gibson humbucker without any loss of cutting single-coil clarity.

Although the Jazzmaster produced a smooth, mellow tone, the guitar was not particularly popular with jazz musicians—Joe Pass was the only one of any note to take an interest. Instead it found a home in many of the guitar instrumental bands of the period.

The Jazzmaster has remained a cult instrument, often popular with bands of an experimental leaning.

▲

**Although primarily a singer-songwriter, Elvis Costello was also sole guitarist on early albums. In 2008 Fender issued an Elvis Costello signature Jazzmaster.**

▼

**The eerie twang of Elvis Costello's Jazzmaster can be heard on the intro to his 1977 hit single, "Watching The Detectives."**

| | |
|---|---|
| **Body style:** | Offset waist, contoured edges |
| **Materials:** | Alder or ash body (basswood on later models); maple bolt-on neck |
| **Finish:** | Standard Fender color options; nitrocellulose lacquer |
| **Fretboard:** | Rosewood or maple |
| **Inlays:** | Acrylic dot (replaced by pearloid block in 1966) |
| **Frets:** | 21 |
| **Scale:** | 25 1/2" |
| **Width at nut:** | 1 5/8" |
| **Bridge:** | Floating tremolo |
| **Pickups:** | 2 single-coil soapbar pickups |
| **Machine heads:** | Fender/Gotoh |
| **Electrics:** | Master volume and tone controls; 3-position pickup switching; "rhythm circuit" filter switch |

# FENDER JAGUAR 1962

It also featured smaller single-coil pickups that were fitted with notched side plates to improve electromagnetic shielding, which made the Jaguar less likely to suffer electrical interference than other single-coil guitars. The circuit switching was considerably more complex than the Jazzmaster's with many players never *fully* understanding its functionality.

A particularly curious feature was the spring-loaded mute, which brought a series of rubber pads into contact from beneath the strings at the touch of the lever. This was intended to have the same sort of impact as muting the strings with the palm of the hand, which was difficult to perform with the Jaguar's floating bridge system. Many players disliked the mute for its tendency to put the guitar out of tune.

Like the Jazzmaster, the top-of-the-range Jaguar was never a mainstream hit, but found niches in the world of surf music and later on the thrash and grunge scenes.

The Fender Jaguar was based closely on the Jazzmaster, sharing the same offset-waist, floating tremolo bridge, and the same dual-circuit electrics. At 24 inches, the Jaguar was shorter in scale than the Jazzmaster and was also notable as the first production Fender guitar to feature a twenty-two-fret fingerboard.

▲
Johnny Marr, formerly guitarist of 1980s band The Smiths, often selects one of his Fender Jaguars for performances with current bands Modest Mouse and The Cribs.

▼
A 1965 Jaguar was Kurt Cobain's main instrument at the time of Nirvana's groundbreaking 1991 *Nevermind* album.

| | |
|---|---|
| **Body style:** | Offset waist, contoured edges |
| **Materials:** | Alder or ash body; maple bolt-on neck |
| **Finish:** | Standard Fender color options |
| **Fretboard:** | Rosewood or maple |
| **Inlays:** | Acrylic dot (replaced by pearloid block in 1966) |
| **Frets:** | 22 |
| **Scale:** | 24" |
| **Width at nut:** | 1 5/8" |
| **Bridge:** | Floating tremolo |
| **Pickups:** | 2 single-coil pickups |
| **Machine heads:** | Fender/Gotoh |
| **Electrics:** | Master volume and tone controls; individual on/off switches to each pickup; 3 dual-circuit tone switches |

# FENDER MUSTANG 1964

its "three-quarter" scale length and twenty-one-fret neck. The Musicmaster and Duo-Sonics were later updated to take the new Mustang body and neck shapes, and given a "II" suffix. All three models were also made available in twenty-one-fret/22 ½-inch or twenty-two-fret/24-inch scales.

The Mustang has slightly unusual electrics: two angled single-coil pickups, each with its own three-way switch operating in "on-off-on" mode, rather than a conventional selector switch. These switches also offered unusual options for their time in that the second "on" position reversed the phase of the selected pickup. The Mustang was also notable in its use of the Dynamic Vibrato tailpiece, which was more sensitive than the Stratocaster Synchronized Tremolo.

Fender reissued the Mustang in 1990. Modern interest in the guitar stems largely from the cult status it achieved in the 1990s through use by well-known alternative rock bands.

Fender had always produced what they termed "student" guitars—budget models such as the Musicmaster and Duo-Sonic launched in the 1950s. The Fender Mustang was created in 1964 with an offset-waist body reminiscent of the Jazzmaster. However, it retained the general dimensions of its predecessors, with

▲

**Thurston Moore of Sonic Youth** plays a Fender Mustang customized with a third pickup. Because they were cheap instruments, owners often performed their own modifications.

▼

Listen to *Goo* (1990) by Sonic Youth to hear some unusual uses of vintage Fenders, such as the Mustang and Jazzmaster.

| | |
|---|---|
| **Body style:** | Offset waist double cutaway solid body |
| **Materials:** | Poplar, alder, ash, basswood; bolt-on maple neck |
| **Finish:** | Standard Fender color options |
| **Fretboard:** | Rosewood; maple |
| **Inlays:** | Acrylic dot |
| **Frets:** | 21 (22 optional on updated models) |
| **Scale:** | 22 ½" (24" optional on updated models) |
| **Width at nut:** | 1 ¹¹⁄₁₆" |
| **Bridge:** | Fender Dynamic Vibrato |
| **Pickups:** | 2 single-coil pickups; individual "on-off-on" switch with polarity reversed in second "on" |
| **Machine heads:** | Kluson (Fender "F" on later models) |
| **Electrics:** | Master volume and tone controls |

# FENDER ELECTRIC XII 1965

In June 1965, when The Byrds unleashed their cover of Bob Dylan's "Mr. Tambourine Man," a new genre was born. U.S. music journalists coined the term "folk rock," at its heart a jangling electric twelve-string guitar sound. Leo Fender wanted to produce an instrument to tap into this new market. Unlike Rickenbacker and other electric twelve-string manufacturers, who did little more than add an extra set of machine heads and a new bridge to existing six-string models, Fender decided to go for bottom-up, purpose-built design.

Launched at the end of 1965, the Electric XII took a Jazzmaster/Jaguar style body and added a neck with a unique headstock, a downward curving droop that quickly acquired the nickname "the hockey stick." The bridge was notable in that it had an individual saddle for each string, enabling extremely precise intonation, but it nonetheless retained the Telecaster's string-through-body design to increase sustain. The Electric XII's electrics were also unusual: the newly designed split pickups were brought into action by a four-way selector switch, the two central positions engaging both pickups either in or out of phase. The Electric XII didn't enjoy great success and was discontinued in 1969.

▲
Trevor Burton of The Move originally played a Fender Electric XII, later turning to a white Fender Precision for bass duties.

▼
The Electric XII can be heard on The Who's 1969 rock "opera" *Tommy* and was used by Jimmy Page on the 1972 studio version of Led Zeppelin's "Stairway To Heaven."

| | |
|---|---|
| **Body style:** | Offset waist solid body |
| **Materials:** | Alder body with bolt-on maple neck |
| **Finish:** | Candy apple red, lake placid blue, Olympic white |
| **Fretboard:** | Rosewood |
| **Inlays:** | Acrylic dot |
| **Frets:** | 21 |
| **Scale:** | 25 ½" |
| **Width at nut:** | 1 11/16" |
| **Bridge:** | Fixed, individual saddles |
| **Pickups:** | 2 split single-coil pickups; 4-position selector switch (1 neck; 2 neck + bridge [in series]; 3 neck + bridge [in parallel]; 4 bridge) |
| **Machine heads:** | Kluson Deluxe |
| **Electrics:** | Master volume and tone controls |

# FENDER CORONADO 1966

GREAT **NEW** SOUND
SAME **OLD** QUALITY

the vogue for semi-acoustic guitars.

A true hollow-body guitar, the Coronado *wasn't* constructed using a central solid wooded block through the middle with hollow attached "wings," like the famous Gibson ES-335s. The sides and back of the body were constructed from laminated beechwood, the top being slightly arched—another departure for Fender. There were a number of different Coronados produced between 1966 and 1972. The model shown here is a Coronado II in what was known as a "Wildwood" finish. This unique process involved injecting a chemical dye into the growing beech tree prior to harvesting, creating a uniquely stained grain pattern of the wood. A thin laminate of the wood was then used on the top of the body. Also unusual for Fender at that time, the Coronado used pickups made by DeArmond and a Tune-o-matic-style bridge with a suspended tailpiece.

D esigned by Roger Rossmeisl, the Coronado was a double-cutaway, thin-line, hollow-body electric guitar that bore very little resemblance to other Fender models. Rossmeisl, who had previously designed hollow-body electrics for Rickenbacker, was given the task of producing a guitar that capitalized on

▲
Fender's 1967 advertisement for the Coronado promised a "Great New Sound" with the "Same Old Quality." The Coronado was an excellent instrument, but showed, once again, that the guitar fraternity was not wholly convinced by the idea of a non-solid Fender.

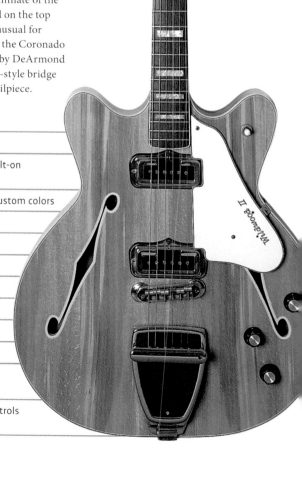

| | |
|---|---|
| **Body style:** | Double cutaway hollow body |
| **Materials:** | Maple and beech body with bolt-on maple neck |
| **Finish:** | Sunburst, cherry, wildwood, and custom colors |
| **Fretboard:** | Rosewood |
| **Inlays:** | Mother-of-pearl block |
| **Frets:** | 22 |
| **Scale:** | 25 ½" |
| **Width at nut:** | 1 ¹¹⁄₁₆" |
| **Bridge:** | Tune-o-matic style |
| **Tailpiece:** | Suspended |
| **Pickups:** | 2 DeArmond single-coil pickups; 3-position switch |
| **Electrics:** | Dedicated volume and tone controls for each pickup |

# FENDER STARCASTER 1976

T he market for semi-solid electric guitars had long been dominated by Gibson, in particular with its ES-335 model. Fender had made a number of attempts to tap into this area of the market—notably with the Fender Thinline series. This may have yielded some interesting instruments, but they largely failed to capture the imagination of the guitar fraternity.

Designed in 1975 by Gene Fields, the Starcaster was a high-end semiacoustic instrument, even if it did appear in the middle of Fender's CBS period, when manufacturing standards had been heavily compromised by economic considerations.

Unlike all of Gibson's famous "semis," which featured their necks set in the bodies, the Starcaster retained Fender's bolt-on neck design—at that time using a three-bolt joint. The guitar's most curious design feature is in the headstock, with its painted lower edge. The use of an asymmetric offset-waist body was also unusual in non-solid-body instruments.

The Starcaster made an unheralded debut during 1976 and was in production for just six years. It also seems unlamented by Fender, who rather than offering vintage reissues have instead given the name over to a budget line of instruments.

▲
**One of the few guitar "heroes" to emerge from the "alt rock" scene, Radiohead's Jonny Greenwood makes extensive use of a Fender Starcaster both in the studio and on stage.**

▼
**Touted by critics as *the* album of the 1990s, Radiohead's *OK Computer* (1997) has Greenwood's Fender Starcaster to the fore.**

| | |
|---|---|
| **Body style:** | Double cutaway semi-solid body |
| **Materials:** | Maple body with 3-hole bolt-on maple neck |
| **Finish:** | White, natural (blonde), sunburst, tobacco, and mocha brown |
| **Fretboard:** | Maple |
| **Inlays:** | Acrylic dot |
| **Frets:** | 22 |
| **Scale:** | 25 ½" |
| **Width at nut:** | 1 ¹¹⁄₁₆" |
| **Bridge:** | Fixed, string-through-body |
| **Pickups:** | 2 Fender Wide Range humbuckers; 3-position switch |
| **Electrics:** | Dedicated volume and tone controls for each pickup; master volume control |

# FENDER KATANA 1985

Fender's stock in the eyes of many musicians, as a producer of classic guitars, had slowly diminished throughout the 1970s. Corner-cutting exercises brought about by CBS gradually compromised the quality of output. A new generation of American guitar makers was also beginning to make its mark with companies like Kramer and Jackson drawing plaudits and attracting celebrity rock guitarists. By the start of the 1980s, Fender had become a brand in crisis. What's more, CBS was facing financial difficulties, in the end agreeing to a sellout that resulted in the creation of the Fender Musical Instruments Corporation. The period of transition in the mid-1980s was a traumatic one for the company. This is the background in which the Katana—by a country mile the most unorthodox design to come off the Fender production line—came into being.

Proof that Fender had lost some of its vision can be seen by the fact that the demand for the Katana came from pressure applied by dealers to create an instrument that looked as if it came from the same generation as unusual, angular shaped competitors like the Jackson Randy Rhoads or anything produced by B.C. Rich.

The Katana was designed under duress by marketing director Dan Smith in 1985. He was thoroughly unconvinced by the new fashion in guitars: "These things are revolting . . . but to pacify the dealers we needed something. So I sat down with the art program on the Macintosh and screwed around."

In spite of its seemingly half-hearted origins, the Katana—named after a Japanese broadsword—is a highly playable rock guitar, kitted out with much the same kind of hardware found on any superstrat—low action, locking tremolo, and humbucking pickups. Sales, however, were miserable and the guitar dropped from the production line within a year.

▼
**The Jackson Randy Rhoads model was a clear influence on Fender's Katana.**

| | |
|---|---|
| **Body style:** | Scalene triangle, no cutaways |
| **Materials:** | Ash body with maple glued-in neck |
| **Finish:** | Black or white; nitrocellulose lacquer |
| **Fretboard:** | Rosewood |
| **Inlays:** | Acrylic triangle |
| **Frets:** | 22 |
| **Scale:** | 24 ¾" |
| **Width at nut:** | 1 ¹¹⁄₁₆" |
| **Bridge:** | Fender "System One" locking tremolo bridge with locking nut |
| **Pickups:** | 2 coverless humbuckers; 3-position selector switch |
| **Electrics:** | Master volume and tone controls |
| **Output Socket:** | Inset |

# FENDER PERFORMER 1985

body. Conceived in the early 1980s by designer John Page, the Performer was intended as the "elite" edition of the Jazz bass, but eventually appeared with a new identity in both six-string and bass guises.

The Performer was a high-end rock guitar, the equal of any fashionable superstrat. It featured a two-octave fingerboard, locking nut, and floating tremolo. Unusual for a Fender, the Performer featured humbucking pickups with a coil-tap switch that disabled one coil of each humbucker. This enabled the guitar to produce fat humbucker sounds as well as crisp, sharp, single-coil Strat-like tones.

The Performer, arguably Fender's last attempt at designing an original instrument, was given little chance to succeed during a turbulent time in the company's history, and was produced for just a year. Fender has since concentrated on producing subtly different variations on designs first seen four decades ago.

With the transition from corporate to private ownership in full swing, Fender launched a second Japanese-built model—the Performer. Nothing like as alienating as the Katana in appearance, the Performer resembled a Stratocaster with pointed, angular horns reminiscent of a B.C. Rich

▲
Kele Okereke, the singer and rhythm player with British rock band Bloc Party, provides a rare glimpse of the Fender Performer in action.

▼
Bloc Party's twin-guitar lineup is in force on the band's award-winning 2005 debut, *Silent Alarm*.

BLOC PARTY.

| | |
|---|---|
| **Body style:** | Double cutaway with offset waist |
| **Materials:** | Alder or birch with 4-screw bolt-on maple neck |
| **Finish:** | Assorted solid metallic and sunburst finishes |
| **Fretboard:** | Rosewood |
| **Inlays:** | Acrylic dot |
| **Frets:** | 24 |
| **Scale:** | 25½" |
| **Width at nut:** | 1¹¹⁄₁₆" |
| **Bridge:** | Fender "System One" locking tremolobridge with locking nut |
| **Pickups:** | 2 covered humbuckers; 3-position selector switch |
| **Electrics:** | Master volume; tone control uses stacked 250k and 1M potentiometers with a center detent. |

# LEO FENDER : BASS PIONEER

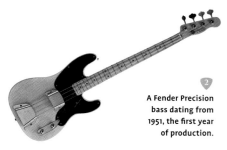

**Paul Tutmarc Jr. stands alongside his bass guitar in the 1940s.**

**A Fender Precision bass dating from 1951, the first year of production.**

**In a mid-1950s Fender catalog the Precision is partnered with the Bassman amplifier.**

With the creation of the Broadcaster, the first mass-produced solid-body electric guitar, in 1949, Leo Fender's position in the history and development of modern music would have been assured. Barely two years later, however, he would bring his revolution to a different area of music with the Fender Precision, the first production-line bass guitar. Fender was not, however, the originator of the bass guitar concept. The bass guitar is a descendant of the double bass, which dates back to the seventeenth century. It underwent little evolution until the 1920s, when Gibson's Lloyd Loar, experimenting with magnetic pickups, created a prototype for an electric double bass.

It could be argued that the true father of the bass guitar was Paul Tutmarc, a musician and inventor from Seattle, Washington, who began experimenting with the size of the double bass during the 1930s, eventually producing an electric instrument, the Model 736 Bass Fiddle. In 1947, Tutmarc's son, Paul Tutmarc Jr., ① adapted this idea when he built a compact fretted bass instrument designed to be played horizontally. Around a hundred of them were built, marketed as The Serenader, but the invention was a commercial failure.

The path was left clear for Leo Fender and his associate George Fullerton to take the same manufacturing principles they had conceived for the Broadcaster/Telecaster and apply them to a larger four-stringed "guitar."

The Fender Precision was a revolutionary instrument. ② Unlike the bulky double bass, it could be transported to a gig without difficulty, and, coupled with the Bassman amplifier, it could be amplified to high volumes without feeding back. ③ Since the fingerboard was fretted, it could be played easily by an electric guitarist. The first professional to adopt the Fender Precision was Monk Montgomery, who toured widely during the early 1950s with Lionel Hampton's jazz orchestra.

Other guitar manufacturers were quick to follow Fender's lead, with Gibson's 1953 violin-shaped EB (Electric Bass) covering all eventualities with an extendable pin that enabled it to be played upright or horizontally. Fender, however, extended its grip on the market in 1960 when it introduced the Jazz model. The Precision and the Jazz have remained the most popular bass guitars in production ever since.

**c. 1924**
Gibson's Lloyd Loar creates an electric upright bass

**1930s**
Gibson, Lyon & Healy, and others market electric upright basses

**1947**
Paul Tutmarc Jr. markets a horizontally-played electric bass

**1951**
Fender launches the Precision, styled on the Telecaster guitar

**1952**
Fender launches the Bassman amplifier for the Precision

**1957**
The Precision is redesigned with Stratocaster stylings

**1960**
Fender introduces the twin-pickup Jazz bass

# FENDER BASSES : THE FAMILY TREE (1951–PRESENT)

As was certainly the case with the solid-body electric guitar, Leo Fender may not have actually invented the electric bass, but he was absolutely integral to its emergence as an instrument in its own right.

Launched in 1951, the first production-line electric bass was the Fender Precision. Its name was well considered: the role had traditionally been fulfilled by the upright bass, an instrument with an evolutionary line from the violin and cello rather than the guitar. The upright acoustic bass is

not a fretted instrument, which means that the player has to use skill and experience to play notes at a precise pitch. The Fender Precision reduced this necessity, and throughout the 1950s a new breed of bass player emerged—one that had learned to play the guitar before switching to the bass.

Since its arrival, the electric bass guitar has largely dominated all forms of popular music, with jazz being the only field to see a widespread return to the upright bass over the past two decades.

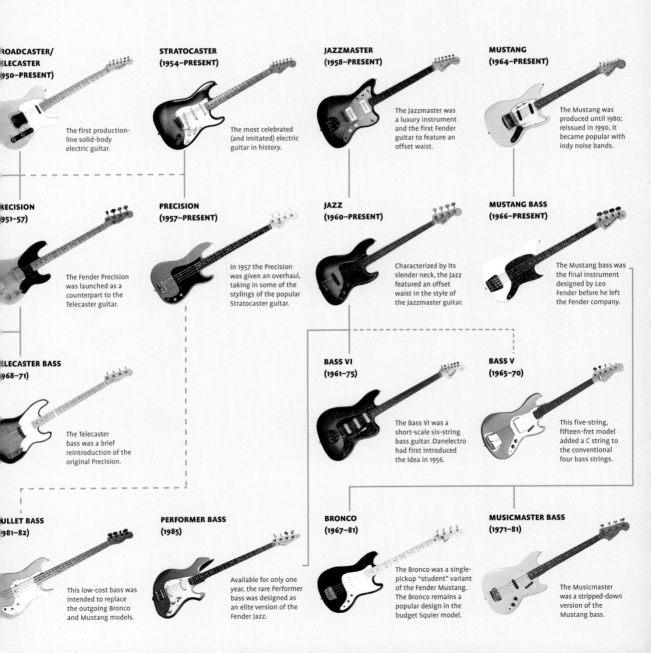

**BROADCASTER/ TELECASTER (1950–PRESENT)**

The first production-line solid-body electric guitar.

**STRATOCASTER (1954–PRESENT)**

The most celebrated (and imitated) electric guitar in history.

**JAZZMASTER (1958–PRESENT)**

The Jazzmaster was a luxury instrument and the first Fender guitar to feature an offset waist.

**MUSTANG (1964–PRESENT)**

The Mustang was produced until 1980; reissued in 1990, it became popular with indy noise bands.

**PRECISION (1951–57)**

The Fender Precision was launched as a counterpart to the Telecaster guitar.

**PRECISION (1957–PRESENT)**

In 1957 the Precision was given an overhaul, taking in some of the stylings of the popular Stratocaster guitar.

**JAZZ (1960–PRESENT)**

Characterized by its slender neck, the Jazz featured an offset waist in the style of the Jazzmaster guitar.

**MUSTANG BASS (1966–PRESENT)**

The Mustang bass was the final instrument designed by Leo Fender before he left the Fender company.

**TELECASTER BASS (1968–71)**

The Telecaster bass was a brief reintroduction of the original Precision.

**BASS VI (1961–75)**

The Bass VI was a short-scale six-string bass guitar. Danelectro had first introduced the idea in 1956.

**BASS V (1965–70)**

This five-string, fifteen-fret model added a C string to the conventional four bass strings.

**BULLET BASS (1981–82)**

This low-cost bass was intended to replace the outgoing Bronco and Mustang models.

**PERFORMER BASS (1985)**

Available for only one year, the rare Performer bass was designed as an elite version of the Fender Jazz.

**BRONCO (1967–81)**

The Bronco was a single-pickup "student" variant of the Fender Mustang. The Bronco remains a popular design in the budget Squier model.

**MUSICMASTER BASS (1971–81)**

The Musicmaster was a stripped-down version of the Mustang bass.

# FENDER PRECISION 1951

Leo Fender's original Precision bass was clearly intended as a counterpart to the six-string Telecaster, with which it clearly shared a number of design features. As with all Fender production-line guitars, its construction process was unashamedly simple—a slab of ash to which a neck was bolted. However, the Precision (or "P Bass" as it is often called) underwent a number of early revisions, gradually evolving a personality of its own. The first major upgrade came in 1953 when the body was given contoured edges, making it considerably more comfortable to play. This was followed in 1957 with a more dramatic restyling, as the headstock was altered to reflect the modern line of Fender's successful "deluxe" guitar—the Stratocaster. More significantly, at the same time the original basic single-coil pickup was replaced with a new split-coil version incorporating staggered polepieces and wired, to all intents and purposes, as a humbucker. Fender was careful not to make too much of this feature since Gibson still held the patent on the idea.

The Precision has never left the production line, over the years having been offered in a variety of vintage reissued editions. It remains one of the most iconic of bass guitars.

▲
Jean-Jacques Burnel of The Stranglers created a unique sound by playing the strings of his Fender Precision extremely close to the bridge, and using overdrive from a valve amplifier.

▼
Burnel's powerful and melodic bass can be heard throughout The Stranglers' early albums, such as 1977's *Rattus Norvegicus*.

| | |
|---|---|
| **Body style:** | Double cutaway solid body |
| **Materials:** | Ash or alder (poplar and basswood on Mexican-made diffusion range); bolt-on maple neck |
| **Finish:** | Assorted color options; nitrocellulose lacquer |
| **Fretboard:** | Maple, rosewood, ebony, pao ferro |
| **Inlays:** | Acrylic dot |
| **Frets:** | 20 (22 on later "special" models) |
| **Scale:** | 34" |
| **Width at nut:** | 1 ⅝" |
| **Bridge:** | Fixed |
| **Pickups:** | 1 single-coil pickup (1951–57); 1 split "P" pickup, wired as humbucker (1957–present); some later 2-pickup models exist combining "P" pickup with a second from a Fender Jazz |
| **Electrics:** | Dedicated volume and tone controls for each pickup |
| **Machine heads:** | Fender bass |

# Fender Jazz 1960

Just as the Precision had first been modeled on the Telecaster (and after 1957, the Stratocaster), the Jazz was, with its offset-waist shape, quite clearly a stablemate of the new Jazzmaster guitar. One notable departure in design from the Precision was the narrow width of the neck, which Fender believed would appeal to jazz musicians. Fender's intention had been to encourage acoustic bass players to switch over to an instrument viewed with suspicion within the jazz fraternity. To further this end, the instrument featured two single-coil "J" pickups with two pole pieces per string, giving the bass a stronger treble, richer midrange, and less emphasis on the fundamental harmonic.

The Fender Jazz has remained an immensely popular instrument, and is still widely used by musicians with a melodic playing style. Its unique sound can be heard at the heart of many music genres, including jazz and funk.

Introduced in 1960 as the "Deluxe Model," the Jazz was Leo Fender's second bass guitar. Like other early Fenders, the Jazz was designed to compete with a specific rival product; the Rickenbacker electric bass, launched in 1957, with its bright, treble sound, was seen as a significant threat to Fender's market position.

▲
Canadian trio Rush emerged in the mid-1970s, their sound driven by the vocals and intricate bass work of Geddy Lee. The Fender Jazz remains his instrument of choice.

▼
Lee used a Fender Jazz on *Permanent Waves* (1980). Previously his favored instrument was a custom-made Rickenbacker.

| | |
|---|---|
| **Body style:** | Double cutaway solid body |
| **Materials:** | Ash or alder body with C-shaped maple neck |
| **Finish:** | Many color finishes; nitrocellulose lacquer |
| **Fretboard:** | Rosewood, ebony, maple, or pao ferro |
| **Inlays:** | Acrylic dot |
| **Frets:** | 20 |
| **Scale:** | 34" |
| **Width at nut:** | 1½" |
| **Bridge:** | American Vintage 4-saddle bass, removable cover |
| **Pickups:** | 2 single-coil "J" pickups |
| **Machine heads:** | Vintage reverse-tuning |
| **Electrics:** | Originally master volume and tone control; after 1961, dedicated volume control and master tone for each pickup |

# FENDER JAZZ PASTORIUS TRIBUTE 1999

veterans Wayne Shorter and Joe Zawinul, he was invited to join Weather Report, a band that would achieve levels of commercial success unprecedented in the jazz field. By the end of the decade—and based on a relatively slim body of work—Pastorius had established himself as arguably the greatest ever exponent of the bass guitar. His triumph was tragically brief: plagued by health and drug problems, he died in 1987 at the age of thirty-five.

Pastorius inspired a generation to take up the fretless bass. Curiously, his own instrument was a standard 1962 Fender Jazz with the frets removed and the fingerboard protected by a marine resin. What he called his "Bass of Doom" was stolen in 1986, shortly before his death, but reappeared in 2008. It was bought by Metallica's Robert Trujillo, who is keeping it in trust for the Pastorius family.

Fender have kept the Pastorius legacy alive by issuing a faithfully "distressed" recreation of this instrument.

The world of the bass guitar at the end of the 1970s was dominated by one figure, Jaco Pastorius, whose emergence on the jazz scene was as sudden as it was startling. His 1976 debut album (*see below*) heralded a fully formed talent of extraordinary proportions. Capturing the attention of fusion

▲
Jaco Pastorius, whose trademark "Jaco growl" was achieved by switching off the neck pickup and plucking the strings directly above the bridge pickup.

▼
Pastorius set a new benchmark for the bass guitar with his 1976 debut album, which included the startling "Portrait of Tracy," a track played using only harmonics.

| | |
|---|---|
| **Body style:** | Double cutaway solid body |
| **Materials:** | Alder body with C-shaped maple neck |
| **Finish:** | Cosmetically "aged" sunburst; nitrocellulose lacquer |
| **Fretboard:** | Epoxy-coated round laminate rosewood |
| **Inlays:** | Center-side dot position markers |
| **Frets:** | Fretless, with frets replaced by inlays |
| **Scale:** | 34" |
| **Width at nut:** | 1½" |
| **String Nut:** | Synthetic bone |
| **Bridge:** | American Vintage 4-saddle bass |
| **Pickups:** | 2 single-coil "J" pickups |
| **Machine heads:** | Vintage reverse-tuning |
| **Electrics:** | Dedicated volume controls for each pickup; master tone control |

# FENDER BASS VI 1961

Not *exactly* a bass, but certainly no regular guitar, the curious Fender Bass VI first appeared in 1961. Like the 1956 Danelectro six-string bass, the Bass VI was designed to be strung and tuned in the same way as a standard Spanish guitar—E to E—only one octave lower in pitch.

The Bass VI owes much of its styling

and technology to Fender's earlier Jazzmaster guitar, but in appearance it most closely resembles an oversized version of the Jaguar, which wouldn't go into production for another year.

Unusual for a bass instrument, the Bass VI featured a tremolo arm, three pickups, and, a few years later, a bass cut switch. All of which suggested that it was designed to cater for the soloing bass guitarist—of which there were seemingly very few in the early 1960s.

The Bass VI was not a commercial success, players finding that the instrument's tight string spacing required greater playing accuracy. It is therefore no great surprise that the two names most closely associated with the Bass VI—Cream's Jack Bruce and John Entwistle of The Who—were also two of the most progressive and nimble-fingered bass players in rock music.

The Bass VI remained in small-scale production until 1975 and was made available as a vintage reissue in 1995.

▲
A former jazz player, Jack Bruce of British heavy rock trio Cream performed some of his finest work using a Fender Bass VI.

▼
Bruce's free-flowing Bass VI playing can be heard on Cream's *Disraeli Gears* (1967)—in particular, the rock classic "Sunshine of Your Love."

| | |
|---|---|
| **Body style:** | Single cutaway solid body |
| **Materials:** | Alder body; quartersawn maple C-shaped bolt-on neck |
| **Finish:** | Three-tone sunburst; nitrocellulose lacquer |
| **Fretboard:** | Rosewood |
| **Frets:** | 21 |
| **Scale:** | 30" (30⅓" on 1995 Japanese models) |
| **Width at nut:** | 1½" |
| **Bridge:** | Vintage Jazzmaster-style floating tremolo with tremolo lock button; adjustable saddles; removable cover |
| **Tailpiece:** | Built into bridge |
| **Pickups:** | 3 Jaguar single-coil pickups |
| **Electrics:** | Master volume and tone controls; on/off switch for each pickup; bass filter switch added on later models |

# FLETA CLASSICAL 1955

n his early life, Ignacio Fleta (1897–1977) established himself as a maker of a wide range of stringed instruments—cellos and violins, as well as the occasional classical or jazz guitar. In 1955, Fleta attended a recital by the master guitarist Andrés Segovia (1893–1987) which changed his life. Following the concert he devoted himself exclusively to building guitars.

In 1957, Segovia played one of Fleta's guitars for the first time, and immediately declared him to be Spain's finest luthier. Segovia would own three Fletas, and would use them exclusively in concert and in the recording studio over the remainder of his life.

Fleta's construction methods were unusual in that the body was built first, initially from Brazilian rosewood, and the neck fixed in place by a kind of dovetail joint. The body's spruce top was also unusually thin, creating a unique tone but limiting the volume of the instrument. Fleta later made guitars from Indian rosewood with a cedar top. Unlike the bright and crisp tone of the spruce-top guitars, these had a dark tone; they were also favored by recording artists such as Segovia, John Williams, and Eric Hill.

During the 1960s, Fleta brought his sons into the business, which has remained one of the preeminent names in classical guitar making. However, the models built by Ignacio himself during the 1950s are among the most collectible classical instruments, fetching up to $40,000 on the rare occasions they appear on the open market.

Segovia's first Fleta now may be found in New York's Metropolitan Museum of Art.

▲
**Andrés Segovia plays his Fleta guitar in a rare U.S. television appearance in 1960.**

▼
**Segovia's Deutsche Grammophon (2003) recordings feature his Fleta guitar.**

| | |
|---|---|
| **Body style:** | Figure-eight "Spanish" style |
| **Materials:** | Spruce top, rosewood back and sides |
| **Fretboard:** | Ebony |
| **Inlays:** | None |
| **Frets:** | 19 |
| **Scale:** | 25 2/3" |
| **Width at nut:** | 2" |
| **Bridge:** | Classical bridge and saddler |
| **Tuners:** | Geared |

# FODERA ANTHONY JACKSON 1988

W hy do bass guitars only have four strings? That was a question jazz player Anthony Jackson asked himself in the early 1970s. He would later respond: "The only reason . . . was because Leo Fender was thinking in application terms of an upright bass, but he built it along guitar lines because that was his training. The logical conception for the bass guitar encompasses six strings." Rather than regard the bass as low-register underpinning for musical compositions, Jackson sees its potential as a virtuoso instrument.

During the 1970s Jackson sought a luthier to build the model he had in mind—a "contrabass guitar" that added a low B and a high C to the standard four strings (resulting in strings tuned to B-E-A-D-G-C). By the early 1980s Jackson was using his custom-made six-string basses exclusively both in performance and for recordings.

In 1988 he approached Vinnie Fodera to make a new instrument. The result was his own signature model, a monster of an instrument with a 34–36-inch scale and an extraordinary twenty-eight-fret fingerboard. The electrics are unusually spartan, a single humbucking pickup wired directly to the output socket, with no tone or volume controls to be seen on the body.

Fodera bass guitars are squarely aimed at the professional player, versions of this model costing around $20,000. Fodera endorsees number among the elite of the modern jazz world.

▲
Anthony Jackson is highly respected on the U.S. jazz/fusion scene. He has worked with Pat Metheny, Billy Cobham, and Chick Corea.

▼
Jackson's bass work can be heard on Donald Fagen's 1982 masterpiece, *The Nightfly.*

| Body style: | Single cutaway chambered body |
|---|---|
| Materials: | Western red alder body; quilted mahogany top; three-piece maple neck |
| Finish: | Natural |
| Fretboard: | Brazilian rosewood |
| Inlays: | None |
| Frets: | 28 |
| Scale: | 34–36" |
| Width at nut: | 1 9/10" |
| Bridge: | Fixed; six saddles |
| Pickups: | Single humbucker |
| Electrics: | None |

# FRAMUS STRATO DE LUXE 1965

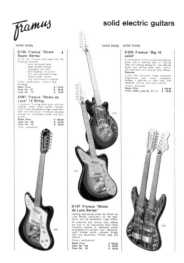

Between 1946 and 1975, the Framus company was among the largest guitar manufacturers on mainland Europe. It was formed in Bavaria immediately after the end of World War II, and founder Fred Wilfer was able to take advantage of his official status as an "anti-fascist" while Germany was still an occupied nation. Initially producing violins, Wilfer began manufacturing acoustic guitars in the 1950s and electric guitars at the start of the 1960s.

Framus guitars don't enjoy a particularly high reputation, but have their place in history as an affordable first guitar for many young musicians, among them Paul McCartney and John Lennon. Furthermore, the company's "Star" bass range was one of the first to be imported to the U.K. and so was widely used at a time when its Fender counterparts were very hard to secure. Indeed, Bill Wyman was to play a Framus bass for much of the Rolling Stones' 1960s heyday.

The Fender Jaguar-inspired Strato series came in many different varieties, including those fitted with "Orgeleffekt" circuitry, designed to transform the guitar into what Framus claimed was "an excitingly different instrument—smooth organ tones at the touch of a fingertip!" Shown here is the unusual three-pickup Strato De Luxe. A twelve-string variant was also made.

▲
The 1966 Framus catalog boasted a number of different "Strato" models, including a rather unusual nine-string instrument, on which the top three strings were doubled up in the manner of a regular twelve-string guitar.

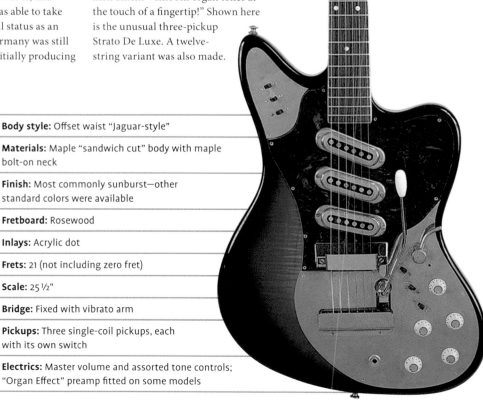

| | |
|---|---|
| **Body style:** | Offset waist "Jaguar-style" |
| **Materials:** | Maple "sandwich cut" body with maple bolt-on neck |
| **Finish:** | Most commonly sunburst—other standard colors were available |
| **Fretboard:** | Rosewood |
| **Inlays:** | Acrylic dot |
| **Frets:** | 21 (not including zero fret) |
| **Scale:** | 25 ½" |
| **Bridge:** | Fixed with vibrato arm |
| **Pickups:** | Three single-coil pickups, each with its own switch |
| **Electrics:** | Master volume and assorted tone controls; "Organ Effect" preamp fitted on some models |

# FRAMUS SUPER YOB 1974

S lade was a band full of odd contradictions. They were Britain's biggest-selling "singles" band during the the first half of the 1970s, with such classic hits as "Cum On Feel The Noize" and the perennial "Merry X'mas Everybody" (both 1973). Yet there was nothing at all "teenybop" about Slade. This was a band who, a few years earlier, had presented

themselves as a troublesome bunch of suede-headed boot boys. Their sound also contrasted with that of other teen idols of the time, with its hard-edged, raucous energy. Yet at its heart was an irresistible pop sensibility, full of memorable tunes and catchy football-terrace chants.

The band were often tagged as "Glam Rockers," but this only really applied to guitarist Dave Hill, whose sparkly stage persona contrasted with the "building site" sensibilities of his colleagues.

In 1974, Hill commissioned British luthier John Birch to produce the "Super Yob," an instrument styled after a 1950s-style sci-fi ray gun. Hill used the guitar on stage and on many TV shows, but found it to be neck-heavy and the action too high. Hill then had a copy built for him by the German guitar manfucturer Framus.

The original model was later owned by Marco Pirroni, guitarist with Adam and the Ants and Siouxsie and the Banshees, as part of a collection that has numbered some 400 instruments.

▲
**Slade's Dave Hill** on stage at the Hammersmith Odeon, London, in 1974, playing the original Super Yob.

▼
In 1975, Slade starred in the movie *Flame*, a surprisingly gritty and pensive piece of pop cinema.

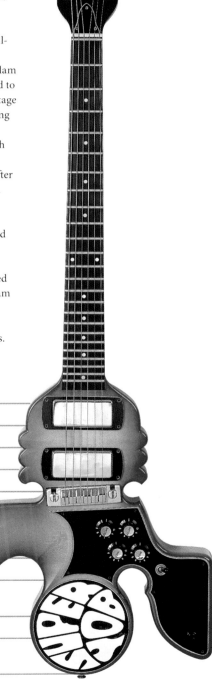

| | |
|---|---|
| **Body style:** | Sci-fi "ray gun" shape |
| **Materials:** | Alder, bolt-on maple neck |
| **Finish:** | Orange sunburst |
| **Fretboard:** | Maple |
| **Inlays:** | Acrylic dot |
| **Frets:** | 24 (not including zero fret) |
| **Scale:** | 25 ½" |
| **Bridge:** | Fixed, individual saddles |
| **Pickups:** | 2 x humbuckers; 3-way selector switch |
| **Machine heads:** | Framus |
| **Electrics:** | Dedicated volume and tone controls for each pickup |

# FUTURAMA RESONET 1958

Futurama was a brand name applied to a series of guitars imported by Selmer UK, a British semi-independent branch of the famed French musical instrument company. It was the Resonet that launched Selmer's guitar range.

The story of the Resonet begins in the city of Blatná in what is now the Czech Republic. At the end of World War II, Czechoslovakia once again became a communist state and the Drevokov Co-operative, a nationalized company specializing in wooden furniture, was also tasked with guitar production. The guitars were released under the name of Rezonet. In 1955, a Fender Stratocaster was brought to the factory for careful examination, but what emerged—the Resonet Grazioso—was not a cheap copy, but an instrument that in a number of ways improved on the Fender. To begin with, each of the three pickups had its own on/off switch, allowing for every possible pickup configuration. Furthermore, the vibrato unit was completely re-engineered and was considerably more advanced in design and performance than those found on mid-1950s Stratocasters.

Britain's trade embargo on American goods made original Fender guitars almost impossible to acquire, and the Resonet made for a popular substitute. At first Selmer's imported guitars continued to be called the Resonet Grazioso, but the name was soon changed to Futurama Resonet. But at £55 (the equivalent of $1,000 in today's currency) it was also one of the most expensive electric guitars on the U.K. market.

A young George Harrison seen playing his Resonet in 1959.

George Harrison played a Futurama Resonet on early recording sessions, such as "My Bonnie" by Tony Sheridan.

| | |
|---|---|
| **Body style:** | Double cutaway solid body |
| **Materials:** | Beech, with a beech bolt-on neck |
| **Fretboard:** | No separate fretboard; frets fitted directly into the beech neck |
| **Frets:** | 21 |
| **Scale:** | 25 ½" |
| **Width at nut:** | 1 $^{11}/_{16}$" |
| **Bridge:** | Floating bridge with vibrato arm |
| **Pickups:** | 3 single-coil pickups; individual on/off switches for each pickup |
| **Electrics:** | Master volume and tone controls |

# G&L COMANCHE 1989

Having sold the company that bore his name six years earlier, in 1971 Leo Fender formed a new alliance with two of his former employees. MusicMan guitars would thrive until later in the decade when, following disagreements, Fender teamed up with another figure from his early days—George Fullerton, the man with whom he had designed the Telecaster. Using their Christian names as their brand, G&L guitars was born.

In appearance, the G&L models gave clear clues to their heritage. Leaning heavily on the Fender classics, the only major difference was a shift away from single-coil to humbucking pickups. But the agenda was self-evident: to produce the kind of instruments on which the Fender reputation had been built— but which throughout the 1970s had gradually diminished.

Produced near the end of the superstrat era, the Comanche was a slim, spiky take on the classic Strat body, with three split humbucking pickups geared strongly to the rock and metal markets.

Both nearing what for most people would have been retirement age when G&L was formed, Fender and Fullerton have both since passed on, but the company has continued its quest to produce fine guitars in the traditions of its founders.

▲
Grammy award-winning guitarist John Jorgenson, using a customized G&L Comanche. Alongside his solo work he has also been a member of the Desert Rose Band and the Hellecasters.

▼
Formed by Chris Hillman of The Byrds, the Desert Rose Band enjoyed a number of country crossover hits during the 1980s.

| Body style: | Double cutaway solid body |
|---|---|
| **Materials:** | Alder (swamp ash available on newer models); maple 3-hole bolt-on neck |
| **Nut:** | Graph-Tech |
| **Fretboard:** | Rosewood |
| **Frets:** | 22 |
| **Scale:** | 25 ½" |
| **Width at nut:** | 1 ⅝" |
| **Bridge:** | G&L Dual Fulcrum vibrato with chrome-plated brass saddles |
| **Pickups:** | 5-position pickup selector plus mini-toggle switch enabling additional pickup combinations of neck plus bridge or all 3 pickups together |
| **Electrics:** | Master volume control; 2 tone controls that give treble boost to various configurations of pickup selection |

# GIBSON : THE STORY

① Orville Gibson had little involvement in the company founded on his instrument-building ideas.

② By the late 1950s the Gibson factory in Kalamazoo had expanded into a major concern.

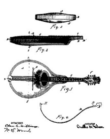

③ Orville Gibson's flat-bodied design for a mandolin earned him a patent in 1898.

It was Charles Frederick Martin and his descendents who, in nineteenth-century America, established many of the most important innovations in the "folk" guitar. In a number of ways their achievement mirrored the progress being made in Spain by Antonio de Torres Jurado ("Torres") in the evolution of the classical instrument. There was, however, another name that would not only provide an important alternative to Martin's superlative flat-top instruments but also play a critical role in the evolution of the electric guitar. That name is Orville Gibson. ①

Born in 1856 in Chateaugay, New York, the son of a British immigrant, Orville Gibson was both an accomplished musician, especially on the mandolin, and a skilled woodcarver. With no formal training as a builder of musical instruments, in 1894 he set up a workshop at his home in Kalamazoo, Michigan. ② A few years earlier he had begun experimenting with a new approach to the design and construction of the mandolin, an approach more closely associated with the violin.

Traditionally mandolins had a flat solid-wood top and a bowl-like back, much the same as a classical lute. Gibson disliked the shape, which reminded him of "potato bugs." Furthermore, the bowled backs made the instruments unstable and vulnerable to damage. Gibson's alternative mandolin, which he named the F-style, featured a distinctively carved, arched solid wood top and back with bent wooden sides, with the bridge and saddles positioned on the highest point. This innovation created an instrument richer in tone, louder and better able to project than traditional mandolins. Furthermore, the design was also more straightforward to manufacture in large quantities. Gibson's design was so radical that in 1898 he was finally awarded his first (and only) patent. ③ Having established the principle of the arch-top with the mandolin, Gibson was not slow to apply it elsewhere, going on to produce the first arch-top guitars.

Orville Gibson's one-man workshop in Kalamazoo gradually established a reputation with local musicians, and he was soon struggling to keep up with demand. On the strength of his local success, five Kalamazoo businessmen grouped together in 1902 to form the Gibson Mandolin-Guitar Manufacturing Company, ④ exclusively producing instruments according to Orville's revolutionary designs, such as the Style O mandolin. ⑤

**1856** Orville Gibson born in Chateaugay, New York

**1894** The earliest documented instrument made by Gibson

**1898** Orville Gibson granted his first and only patent

**1902** Gibson company formed in Kalamazoo, Michigan

**1918** Orville Gibson dies in Ogdensburg, New York

**1921** Ted McHugh invents the adjustable truss rod and the height-adjustable bridge

Although Gibson received royalties based on his patented designs, he evidently had little to do with the operation of the business that bore his name. He only worked on a consultative basis—the board even passed a motion that "Orville H. Gibson be paid only for the actual time he works for the Company." Gibson was variously viewed as an eccentric or difficult figure. Some of his reputation may even have been attributable to mental illness—in 1918 he died at a psychiatric center in Ogdensburg, New York.

In 1902, the year of its foundation, the Gibson company introduced its first range of guitars. Based on Orville's designs, naturally, the Style O and Style L series went into production at the Kalamazoo factory. The instruments were symmetrical figure-eight-shaped archtops. Six years later, Gibson took the unusual step of remodeling the Style O along the lines of his F-style mandolin,  adding an intricately carved scroll on the bass side of the upper bout—a move that presaged the "horn" often found on solid-body electric guitars five decades later.

Orville Gibson's designs remained the staple of the factory's output long after his association with the company had ended. But inevitably it became clear that if Gibson as a business was to move forward, it would need a fresh input of ideas. Fresh ideas came in abundance when, in 1919, musician, engineer, and luthier Lloyd Allayre Loar joined the company. Loar was an unorthodox figure—a theosophist and vegetarian—who brought an experimental attitude to the company. Although he was employed by the company for only five years, his work yielded results that would have a sizeable impact on the future of the guitar. His most public achievement was the creation of the L-5 guitar.

Just as Orville Gibson had studied the design and construction of the violin in order to create a new type of mandolin, Loar reexamined the traditional guitar, replacing the central sound hole on an archtop guitar with a pair of f-holes. These allowed for a balanced tone to be projected at a greater volume. The Gibson L-5 is arguably the single most important acoustic guitar in the instrument's history, and enabled the guitar to take over from the tenor banjo in the jazz orchestras of the period.

There is evidence to suggest that Loar's experiments went considerably further. Loar believed that the future lay squarely in the development of

**4**

A sticker of the Gibson Mandolin-Guitar Manufacturing Company.

**5**

Gibson Style O mandolin.

**6**

The F-style mandolin is distinguished by the curlicue on its upper bout.

**1922** Gibson introduces revolutionary L-5 archtop acoustic guitar

**1934** Gibson launches the Super 400 archtop acoustic

**1935** Gibson enters the electric market with a Hawaiian guitar

**1936** Gibson launches first electric guitar—the ES-150

**1938** Super Jumbo (later the SJ-200/J-200) is launched

**1939** Gibson introduces first cutaways—the updated Super 400 Premier and L-5 Premier

**1946** P-90 Pickup introduced

electric instruments. Walter Fuller, head of Gibson's electric department in the 1930s, claimed that Loar developed a type of electrostatic pickup during his time with the company, and also built a prototype for a solid electric bass. Sadly, no evidence of his work in this area has been preserved. Loar left Gibson in 1924, having fallen out with the company's management, and immediately founded the Vivi-Tone company.

In 1931, the Ro-Pat-In Corporation—formed in 1931 by Adolph Rickenbacker and George Beauchamp—produced the world's first electric stringed instrument, a Hawaiian lap steel guitar known, because of its shape, as the "Frying Pan." In the years that immediately followed this innovation a number of electric guitars emerged. At first little more than basic acoustic instruments with pickups fitted, these new guitars were viewed initially more as novelty items than as serious instruments.

Once again, it was left to Gibson to introduce a perception-altering model of a new concept. In 1936, the ES-150 **(7)** made its debut: the "ES" denoted that it was an "Electric Spanish" guitar—Gibson's first in the genre—and the "150" denoted the price at which it retailed: $150. Since the electric guitar was still a new concept, the ES-150 was supplied with its own amplifier **(8)** and a cable—a complete kit, and everything the player needed to get started.

The guitar itself was not simply an archtop acoustic with a pickup fitted: the construction beneath its soundboard was designed to minimize the instrument's potential for transforming the energy from the strings into sound. This made it less effective as an acoustic instrument, but reduced the problem of feedback that plagued many early electric guitar players.

It is no exaggeration to say that the ES-150 was largely responsible for establishing the electric guitar as a serious musical proposition. This elevation was in no small measure due to the work of jazz guitar virtuoso Charlie Christian. **(9)** Although by no means the first ES-150 player, Christian, in a career that lasted barely five years before his untimely death in 1942 at the age of 25, created a blueprint for the jazz guitar soloist. The warmth of his tone, and deftly executed runs, would exert a inestimable influence on *every* jazz guitarist over the decades that followed. **(10)** During his lifetime, Christian became so closely linked with the instrument that the hexagonal bar pickup became known as the "Charlie Christian Pickup,"

**(7)**
Gibson ES-150
"Electric Spanish."

**(8)**
The Gibson
EH-150 amplifier
was sold with the
ES-150 guitar.

**(9)**
Charlie Christian
plays a Gibson
ES-150—the first
commercially
successful electric
guitar in the world.

**1946**
Les Paul visits Gibson with his solid "Log" guitar

**1949**
ES-175 launched—it becomes a "standard" jazz guitar

**1952**
Gibson introduces its first solid-body—the Les Paul

**1954**
Gibson president Ted McCarty, invents the tune-o-matic bridge

**1957**
Gibson's Seth Lover invents the humbucking pickup

**1957**
Gibson acquires Epiphone—its foremost rival in the 1930s

**1958**
"Modernistic" models debut at the annual NAMM show

a remarkable association and accolade considering that no commercial relationship between player and manufacturer ever existed.

During the 1940s, a number of musicians, luthiers, and engineers sought to address the problem of feedback in amplified electric guitars. The solution appeared to be a matter of replacing the vibrating sound chamber with a body made from a dense material, such as a hard wood. Nobody can say with any certainty who actually *invented* the solid-body electric guitar, although a popular claimant to this title is guitarist/inventor Les Paul.

During the late 1930s, Les Paul was an up-and-coming country/jazz picker who had developed a friendship with "Epi" Stathopoulos, the man behind the Epiphone company, at that time Gibson's fiercest rivals. Les Paul was given access to the Epiphone factory at weekends when it was closed. Paul took a standard Epiphone acoustic guitar, removed its neck and bolted it to a four-by-four block of pine. The wings from the disassembled acoustic guitar were fitted to the sides of the pine block, although he did this for no other reason that to make his instrument look like a normal guitar. Finally, he fitted a hand-made pickup. The resulting guitar became known as "The Log." Paul made a number of refinements to his design and in 1946 demonstrated it to Gibson president Maurice Berlin and his colleaugues. As Paul later recalled, "They laughed at the guitar."

Over the four years that followed, two critical factors altered the company viewpoint: first, Fender successfully launched the Telecaster, the first production-line solid-body electric guitar; second, Les Paul and his wife, Mary Ford, became huge stars in their own right. Gibson recalled Paul with the offer of a collaboration and endorsement on a new solid-body electric guitar.

The result, launched in 1952, was the Gibson Les Paul. Although it was initially unsuccessful and dropped from the production line eight years later, its reputation thrived among the blues-rockers of the 1960s and it was reintroduced in 1968. It remains, along with Fender's Telecaster and Stratocaster models, one of the "holy trinity" of the electric guitar world, and the massive popularity of all three models remains undiminished.

From the onset of the 1950s, the Gibson story was dominated by its fierce rivalry with Fender, with each new Gibson product invariably geared toward

Gibson's 1954 catalog boasts an impressive array of endorsees, including jazzmen Tal Farlow, Herb Ellis, and Barney Kessel.

Les Paul's prototype solid-body electric guitar was dubbed "The Log."

Les Paul and wife Mary Ford pose with Gibson guitars bearing Les's name.

**1958** Launch of the ES-335 semi-hollow electric guitar

**1960** Production of the original Les Paul models abandoned

**1961** Release of revamped Les Paul—later named the SG

**1965** Gibson production exceeds 100,000 US-built instruments

**1968** Relaunch of the original Les Paul model

**1969** Gibson bought out by conglomerate Norlin

**1974** Nashville plant opens—production is split between Nashville and Kalamazoo

restraining the seemingly unstoppable success of the Stratocaster. At the end of the decade, under a new president, Ted McCarty, Gibson was continuing to experiment with new designs. As with the Les Paul, these were not always accepted at the time. Its so-called "modernistic" range of instruments, which included the Flying V  and Explorer, were intended to show that in the battle with Fender, their new upstart rivals, Gibson could produce a cutting-edge design. But these space-age instruments were far too strange for the marketplace and were dropped within a year. However, like the Les Paul itself, the futuristic designs would resurface during the following decade and are now considered classics.

Although Gibson produced some outstanding solid-body guitars, some of which—like the SG—were hugely successful from the outset, there was always a sense that they were playing catch-up with Fender. The reverse was true, however, when it came to hollow-body electrics. In 1958, Gibson launched the ES-335, a revolutionary semi-solid guitar that successfully combined the benefits of a solid-body instrument with the warmth and tonal depth of a hollow-body model. Over the past five decades, this kind of guitar has proved to be surprisingly versatile across many musical genres.

During the 1970s both Gibson and Fender began to lose their way, having undergone corporate takeovers, and over the decade that followed their instruments began to look jaded and outdated as a new generation of American luthiers began to make high-powered instruments, often based, ironically, on classic Fender and Gibson designs.

In 1986, having been bought out by Henry Juszkiewicz and David Berryman, Gibson began a period of huge expansion, buying out established musical instrument brands such as Baldwin, Steinberger, and Kramer. At the same time, like its rivals at Fender, Gibson began to see the marketing value of signature models, and began producing variants on existing designs in collaboration with celebrity players, such as B.B. King, Larry Carlton, Scotty Moore, Johnny A., Tony Iommi, and Zakk Wylde.

Like Fender, Gibson now trades on its rich history and concentrates on the production of its classic models. This is not to say that the company has ceased experimentation, as evidenced by the technologically stunning computerized Les Paul Robot guitars produced from 2007.

**13**

The Flying V, a classic Gibson electric guitar that initially failed commercially.

**14**

Influential metal star Zakk Wylde of Black Label Society plays his signature "bullseye" Les Paul. Wylde is a major artist for Gibson and Epiphone.

**15**

The Gibson Dark Fire Les Paul, launched in 2008, was a second-generation "Robot" guitar.

**1984**
Kalamazoo plant is closed after sixty-five years—headquarters moved to Nashville

**1986**
Gibson bought by Henry Juszkiewicz and David Berryman

**2001**
Gibson acquires Baldwin Pianos, among other well-known brands

**2002**
Gibson celebrates the fiftieth anniversary of the Les Paul

**2002**
Gibson opens plant in China dedicated to making Epiphones

**2007**
Gibson introduces the world's first guitar with robotic technology

**2009**
Les Paul dies in White Plains, New York

# GIBSON
## FAMILY TREE

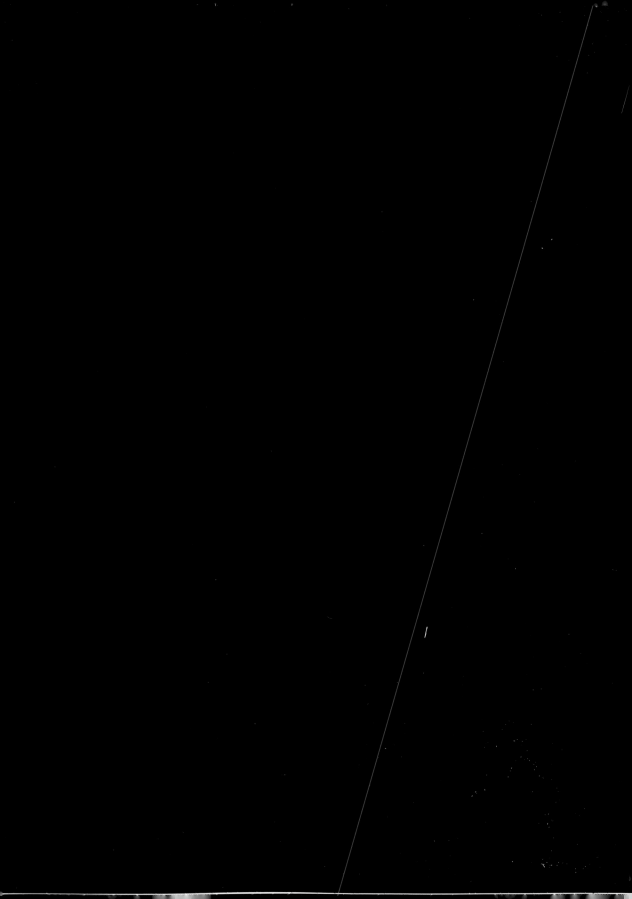

# GIBSON STYLE O 1903

In 1903, the Gibson company published its first catalog, featuring two ranges of revolutionary archtop guitars. Those prefixed with an "O" featured an oval sound hole; the "L" range of instruments with a conventional round hole. Both ranges were offered in varying degrees of ornamentation—the Style O, for example, was a plain and simple instrument; the O-3 featured an intricate binding that alternated blocks of green and white pearl, and consequently was a costly guitar.

The Style O issued in 1903 was straightforward in appearance. However, in 1908 it was given a radical overhaul. Reflecting Gibson's heritage, and based around Orville's original design for the F-Style mandolin, the new Style O (shown) was given an exotic carved scroll on the upper bass bout. The guitar, later known as the Style O Artist, was produced until 1923.

The Gibson Mandolin-Guitar Manufacturing Company was founded in 1902 by five Kalamazoo businessmen, with a view to the large-scale manufacture of Orville Gibson's unusual archtop designs. However, Gibson's personal involvement with the company was thereafter limited by mental ill-health.

▲
**Big Bill Broonzy used a Gibson Style O in the 1920s. His rediscovery and U.K. tour in the 1950s was an important influence on the British blues boom.**

▼
**Big Bill Broonzy's early "78s" have been gathered on the 1973 compilation *Do That Guitar Rag: 1928–1935*.**

| | |
|---|---|
| **Body style:** Figure-eight hollow body; after 1908 F-style mandolin scroll on bass bout and cutaway on treble bout | |
| **Materials:** Mahogany top, back and sides, set mahogany neck | |
| **Finish:** Ornamentation dependent on model | |
| **Fretboard:** Rosewood | |
| **Inlays:** Pearl dot | |
| **Frets:** 22 (including partial frets) | |
| **Scale:** 25" | |
| **Width at nut:** 1 7⁄8" | |
| **Bridge:** Fixed, pyramid ends; after 1908 trapeze tailpiece with pins anchored in tortoise grain celluloid plate | |
| **Tuners:** Friction pegs (right-angled after 1908) | |

# GIBSON L-4 1912

**STYLE L-4 GUITAR**
CARVED TOP AND BACK MODEL
$100.00
CASES
No. 514 Flannel Lining    $20.00
No. 515 Felt Lining        27.00
**FEATURES**
**Wood:** Eastern spruce top;
maple back and rim; mahogany neck with rosewood fingerboard.
**Finish and Decorations:** Choc-
olate brown with sunburst at
bridge; pearl position dots and
pearl peghead inlay; white ivoroid
binding on top and bottom of
body and sides of fingerboard;
ivoroid side position dots
purfling around sound-hole.
**Fittings:** Elevated fin-
gerrest; individual ma-
chine heads; white end
pin; extension tailpiece;
adjustable bridge; nickel
plating.
**Body Size:** Grand Audi-
torium; 16" wide and
20" long.

RUDY VALLEE
FRANK STAFFA
Rudy Vallee Orchestra

**GIBSON
INSTRUMENTS
ARE ACCURATE**

A guitar has six
strings and nineteen
frets—making an in-
strument that is true
on every string in
every position isn't
just luck—it is infi-
nite care and expe-
rience.

Gibson instruments
are noted for their
accuracy—from the
lowest in price to
the most expensive.

ntroduced in 1912, the L-4 guitar would undergo many changes in design before full-scale production ended in 1956.

An archtop guitar with a standard symmetrical body, unlike the three L models launched in 1903 (L-1, L-2, and L-3), the L-4 was produced initially with an oval sound hole.

The body of the L-4 was 16 inches wide and 20 inches long, and was built using maple for the back and sides, and Eastern spruce for the top. The neck construction was made from mahogany and was set into the body. The oval sound hole featured three rings inlaid with a diamond pattern in the center. The strings were held in place at the body with a trapeze tailpiece. Models also featured an elevated pickguard with two supports (not shown here). In 1928, the L-4 was given a round sound hole.

The L-4 was Gibson's most important guitar during the period leading up to the birth of the revolutionary L-5 in 1922, finding a place for itself in the ensembles of the time, which, in the era of large dance bands, had been dominated hitherto by the tenor banjo.

Although production of the Gibson L-4 ended in 1956, a number of related instruments were still made: the L4-C, for example, launched in 1949, was an acoustic version of the ES-175 jazz guitar, and was built until 1971.

▲
**The Gibson L-4 cost $100 in 1930, or more than $1,000 today—an expensive item in the Depression years.**

▼
**Guitarist Frank Staffa endorsed the Gibson L-4. Staffa appears on *The Vagabond Lover*, a CD compilation of Rudy Vallée's prewar recordings.**

| | |
|---|---|
| **Body style:** | Symmetrical, archtop hollow body with oval sound hole (round after 1928) |
| **Materials:** | Maple back and sides, eastern spruce top; set mahogany neck |
| **Finish:** | Black, natural "orange," mahogany sunburst |
| **Fretboard:** | Rosewood |
| **Inlays:** | Pearl dot |
| **Frets:** | 20 |
| **Scale:** | 24 ¾" |
| **Width at nut:** | 1 ¾" |
| **Bridge:** | Fixed, trapeze tailpiece |

# GIBSON L-5 1922

One of the difficulties facing the early jazz guitarist was the instrument's lack of projection within a large band. For this reason, in the early jazz dance groups many players had switched over to the tenor banjo, its fierce treble "attack" considerably more capable of penetrating to the dancefloor.

In 1919, Gibson had been joined by young musician/engineer Lloyd Loar. During the first few years of his time at the company he conceived a number of significant technological advances to the design and construction of the guitar. One of the first of his projects to reach the marketplace was the Gibson L-5 archtop acoustic guitar. Loar looked at ways in which the volume of the instrument could be boosted without a massive increase in the body size. One of his best innovations was in creating f-holes in the body of an archtop guitar, thus boosting the volume. Loar also experimented with increasing the length of the neck, thus allowing the bridge to move to a more central position on the guitar body.

In 1934 the design of the L-5 was enhanced in two significant ways: the 16-inch body was expanded to 17 inches, and cross-bracing was applied to the underside of the soundboard. This "advanced" edition of the L-5 would become the premier guitar of the big band era.

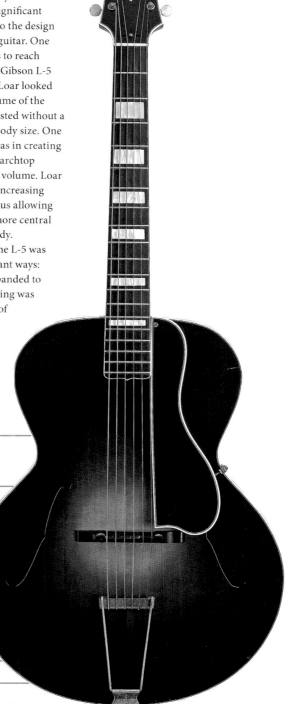

▲
Eddie Lang was the first great jazz guitar soloist. Unfortunately he did not live to enjoy the advent of the electric guitar.

▼
Between 1925 and his death eight years later, Eddie Lang made a large number of recordings. Most featured him playing a Gibson L-5.

| | |
|---|---|
| **Body style:** | 16" symmetrical, archtop hollow body with violin-style f-holes. (Body size increased to 17" in 1934) |
| **Materials:** | Maple back and rim, Adirondack spruce top; set mahogany neck |
| **Finish:** | Black, natural "orange," mahogany sunburst |
| **Fretboard:** | Madagascan ebony |
| **Inlays:** | Pearloid block |
| **Frets:** | 19 |
| **Scale:** | 24 ¾" |
| **Width at nut:** | 1 ¾" |
| **Bridge:** | Fixed, trapeze tailpiece |

# GIBSON SUPER 400 1934

▲
**Jazz star Kenny
Burrell is seen here
playing a "Florentine"
variant of the Gibson
Super 400.**

▼
**Burrell recorded
his 1963 jazz classic
*Midnight Blue* for the
legendary Blue Note
label. On the record
he can be heard
playing a Super 400.**

The Gibson Super 400 archtop acoustic guitar was launched in 1934. The name was derived—like many Gibson models—from its retail price. At $400, in the aftermath of the Great Depression, this was the most expensive production guitar on the market. Furthermore, with its 18-inch "auditorium" body, the Super 400 was also the largest guitar that Gibson would produce.

Befitting of such an instrument, Gibson spared no expense on either functionality or detailing. The single cutaway body featured intricate binding, as well as the f-holes that had been applied so successfully to the L-5. The bridge was adjustable with triangular designs at either end, and the strings were held in place by a gold-plated Y-shaped tailpiece. The inlays were similarly detailed, with a double-split block on the fingerboard and diamond headstock design. A sleek pearloid pickguard completed the look.

In 1951, having noticed that players were beginning to fit pickups to their acoustic guitars, Gibson decided to launch an electric archtop version—the Super 400 CES. Still in production, this model has been offered in a number of variants, the most visually distinct being those featuring an ES-175-style Florentine cutaway.

| | |
|---|---|
| **Body style:** | 18" single cutaway hollow body with f-shaped sound holes ("sharp" Florentine cutaway available on some later models) |
| **Materials:** | Figured maple back and sides with cross-braced top; set mahogany neck |
| **Finish:** | Cremona sunburst |
| **Fretboard:** | Ebony |
| **Inlays:** | Pearloid double-split block |
| **Frets:** | 20 |
| **Scale:** | 24 ¾" |
| **Width at nut:** | 1 ¹¹⁄₁₆" |
| **Bridge:** | Adjustable with trapeze tailpiece |
| **Tuners:** | Grover ("stairstep" buttons added in 1938) |

# GIBSON SJ-200 1938

When it came to archtop acoustic guitars, Gibson was unrivaled—indeed, it had all but invented the genre. But even though the company had produced its first flat-top steel-string acoustic guitar in 1926, the serious professionals tended to go for models made by Martin.

In 1938, the company launched a new flat-top guitar aimed at the professional player. Called the Super Jumbo, it was named after its large 16⅞-inch body, and featured a double-braced spruce top, rosewood back and sides, and sunburst finish. The Super Jumbo's most visually distinctive feature is its "mustache" bridge carved from ebony. The guitar retailed at the considerable cost of $200; for an extra $50 you could have your name inlaid in the fingerboard! A year after it was launched it was rechristened the SJ-200.

During the 1950s, the SJ-200 became strongly associated with country music, and has remained so to the present day. However the name most strongly linked to the guitar is Elvis Presley, who used many different J-200s (the name was changed again in 1955) throughout his career.

Gibson prewar Super Jumbos are now among the most highly collectible acoustic guitars.

▲
Elvis Presley's SJ-200 featured a customized pickguard and his name inlaid in the fingerboard.

▼
After obtaining his first Gibson J-200 in 1956, Presley played one in his 1958 movie, *King Creole*. The J-200 can be heard on the movie soundtrack.

**Body style:** 16 ⅞" symmetrical flat-top hollow body

**Materials:** Spruce top, rosewood back and sides, set mahogany neck (maple back and sides used after 1947)

**Finish:** Sunburst

**Fretboard:** Single-bound ebony

**Inlays:** Mother-of-pearl block

**Frets:** 20

**Scale:** 24 ¾"

**Width at nut:** 1 ¾"

**Bridge:** Fixed "mustache" with height-adjustable saddle bearings

**Tuners:** Grover with "stairstep" buttons

# GIBSON HUMMINGBIRD 1960

Introduced in 1960, the Hummingbird was Gibson's first square-shouldered "dreadnought" instrument. This term was coined by the Martin Company in 1916 to describe a guitar that had a larger and deeper body shape than usual, and was named after the enormous battleships of the period, the first of which was the British HMS *Dreadnought*, launched in 1906. Dreadnought guitars were typically square-shouldered, meaning the upper bout was horizontal, joining the neck at a 90-degree angle, and usually around the fourteenth fret.

The Hummingbird was another of Gibson's high-end instruments, its back and sides initially constructed from mahogany, which gives a warmer tone than the maple used on cheaper models; Sitka spruce was used to make the Hummingbird's top. The guitar in its standard form may be recognized by its ornately carved scratchplate.

The Hummingbird has been through many modifications since its introduction. In 1969 the bracing was altered, which some claim has adversely affected the tone; it was further altered two years later. Alternative woods have also been used in the body construction at various times.

A versatile guitar used in different musical genres, the Hummingbird now exists in a range of variants, including an electro-acoustic version.

▲
**Sheryl Crow uses a 1962 Hummingbird as her main guitar. She has been honored by Gibson with her own signature model.**

▼
**The Hummingbird can be heard on Crow's Grammy-nominated fifth album, *Wildflower* (2005).**

**Body style:** Square-shouldered hollow-body dreadnought

**Materials:** Sitka spruce top, mahogany back and sides (models have been available with maple, cherry, and koa back and sides); mahogany neck set within dovetail joint

**Fretboard:** Ebony

**Frets:** 20

**Scale:** 24 ¾"

**Width at nut:** 1 ¾"

**Bridge:** Rosewood

**Pickups:** L.R. Baggs Element Active pickup on electro-acoustic models

# GIBSON EVERLY BROTHERS 1962

The often feuding Phil and Don Everly were among the top-selling pop stars of the early 1960s.

A pair of Gibson Everly Brothers acoustic guitars can be heard throughout *The Everly Brothers Sing Great Country Hits* (1963).

The Everly Brothers, Phil and Don, recorded numerous international hits from the late 1950s onward—such pop classics as "All I Have To Do Is Dream," and "Bye Bye Love." On stage they dressed identically and played the same guitars—Gibson J-200s customized with dual white pickguards.

In 1962, they collaborated with Gibson to produce their own signature flat-top guitar—the Gibson Everly Brothers. Based on the narrow-waisted J-185, but with a slimmer body, the Gibson Everly Brothers was distinctive not only for the intricate star inlays on the fingerboard and headstock, but also for the unorthodox pickguard design. Although the top of the guitar was finished in black, with smart white binding around the sides, the double-grain tortoiseshell pickguard was cut symmetrically to cover the area both above and below the sound hole. The double pickguard made for an attractive instrument but the pickguard, by covering half the soundboard, reduced the natural vibration of the spruce, resulting in a guitar with reduced volume.

Gibson ended the original production run in 1972, by which time the Everlys, notorious for their difficult relationship, had split. But many well-known artists have used their guitar model, among them Paul McCartney, Bob Dylan, Cat Stevens, Jimmy Page, and Albert Lee.

**Body style:** 16" "jumbo" hollow body, single white binding, top and back

**Materials:** Maple back and sides, spruce top; set mahogany neck

**Finish:** Black (natural offered from 1963)

**Fretboard:** Rosewood

**Inlays:** Pearloid star

**Frets:** 20

**Scale:** 24 ¾"

**Width at nut:** 1 ¹¹⁄₁₆"

**Bridge:** "Belly" bridge with adjustable saddle; strings thread through bridge

# GIBSON ES-150 1936

U ntil Gibson launched the ES-150 model, the electric guitar had been treated as a novelty by many musicians, most of whom had seen only the amplified Hawaiian lap-steel models produced by Rickenbacker.

Launched in 1936, the ES-150 was an "Electric Spanish" model with a retail price of $150—hence its name. In with

the price came an EH-150 amplifier and a guitar cable—everything the buyer needed to get up and running.

As the first commercially successful electric guitar, the importance of the ES-150 cannot be overestimated. Until that time, the guitar could only be played as a rhythm instrument in all but the smallest of ensembles. It simply wasn't loud enough to compete with the horn sections in the popular jazz orchestras of the day, and amplifying an acoustic guitar with a microphone all too often ended in howling feedback. For the first time, the guitarist could step up and take a solo.

Although jazz guitarist Eddie Durham is thought to have performed the first recorded solo on an ES-150, it was Charlie Christian who popularized the instrument. In the briefest of careers, his fluid solos and warm tone all but created the jazz guitar sound that we know today, and influenced every player of note who followed.

**Charlie Christian's electric guitar work with the Benny Goodman Sextet would influence many successive jazz musicians.**

▼

**Although Christian's recording career lasted barely four years, his ES-150 can be heard on numerous compilations.**

| | |
|---|---|
| **Body style:** | "Electric Spanish" hollow body with two f-holes |
| **Materials:** | Maple back and sides, solid spruce arched top; set mahogany neck |
| **Fretboard:** | Rosewood |
| **Inlays:** | Pearl dot |
| **Frets:** | 19 |
| **Scale:** | 24 ¾" |
| **Width at nut:** | 1 ¹¹⁄₁₆" |
| **Bridge:** | Ebony archtop-style, height-adjustable bridge with trapeze tailpiece |
| **Pickups:** | 1 single-coil steel-magnet blade pickup in the neck position (replaced with P-90 in 1946) |
| **Electrics:** | 1 volume control, 1 tone control |

# GIBSON ES-175 1949

The Gibson ES-5 may have been intended to set the benchmark for an electric jazz guitar, but it would be the less expensive ES-175—the electric version of the mid-level L-4 acoustic guitar—that assumed the position. Indeed, it remains the most famous jazz guitar of all, and is still widely used today.

The most striking visual feature of the ES-175 is the sharp "Florentine" cutaway—the first to feature on a Gibson electric guitar—which offered greater access to the upper register, making playing between the eighteenth and twentieth frets much easier.

The first ES-175 models produced in 1949 featured one single-coil P90 pickup in the neck position. In 1953 a two-pickup model was made available, and, four years later, the single-coil P90 was replaced by a humbucker. It is this configuration, invariably played from the neck pickup, which has provided more than six decades of the warm, smooth sound we now associate with classic jazz guitar.

Yet the ES-175 has greater versatility than its reputation suggests, appearing in some unlikely scenarios: Steve Howe, guitarist with prog-rock pioneers Yes, became so closely associated with the instrument that in 2002 Gibson honored him with a signature model.

▲
Joe Pass is revered as one of the most influential exponents of unaccompanied jazz guitar. He played a Gibson ES-175 during most of his career.

▼
Recorded in 1973, *Virtuoso* by Joe Pass is widely considered to be one of the finest jazz guitar albums ever recorded.

**Body style:** 16 ¼" single Florentine cutaway hollow body with 2 f-holes

**Materials:** Maple back and sides, maple laminate top; set mahogany neck

**Fretboard:** Rosewood

**Inlays:** Double parallelogram

**Frets:** 20

**Scale:** 24 ¾"

**Width at nut:** 1 ¹¹⁄₁₆"

**Bridge:** Tune-o-matic bridge with trapeze tailpiece

**Pickups:** 1 P90 pickup; 2 P90s from 1953; 2 humbuckers from 1957; 3-way switching on 2-pickup models

**Electrics:** Dedicated volume and tone controls for each pickup

# GIBSON ES-295 1952

The ES-175 was available in sunburst and natural finishes, its costlier counterpart dazzled in its shimmering gold-paint finish, with matching gold-plated hardware and a back-painted white pickguard with ornate golden floral pattern. Even the pickups—regular P90s—were given a matching gleaming white cover.

The ES-295 was not a commercial success and was discontinued in 1958. Curiously, it is now more likely to be remembered as a "rockabilly" instrument—a reputation almost entirely derived from the patronage of Scotty Moore, who used one on Elvis Presley's celebrated debut sessions for Sun Records in 1953. Moore was honored by Gibson with a signature model when the guitar was reissued in the 1990s. Yet the ES-295 would be a footnote in history had it not been the template for Gibson's most famous electric guitar— the Les Paul.

The ES-175 proved to be a popular guitar, its retail price of $175 representing good value for an instrument bearing the Gibson marque. In 1952, a high-end version was introduced—the ES-295. There was very little *real* difference between the two guitars, but the ES-295 represented something of a cosmetic departure.

▲
**Scotty Moore (*left*) played electric guitar on most of Elvis Presley's "pre-army" recordings.**

▼
***The Sun Sessions*, released in 1976, compiles Presley's singles and other recordings made for the label in 1954 and 1955. Scotty Moore's ES-295 can be heard on such tracks as "That's All Right."**

| | |
|---|---|
| **Body style:** 16 ¼" single Florentine cutaway hollow body with 2 f-holes | |
| **Materials:** Maple back and sides, gold maple laminate top; set mahogany neck | |
| **Fretboard:** Rosewood | |
| **Inlays:** Double parallelogram | |
| **Frets:** 20 | |
| **Scale:** 24 ¾" | |
| **Width at nut:** 1 ¹¹⁄₁₆" | |
| **Bridge:** Tune-o-matic bridge with trapeze tailpiece | |
| **Pickups:** 2 P90 pickups with 3-way switching on bass bout | |
| **Electrics:** Dedicated volume and tone controls for each pickup | |

# GIBSON ES-5 SWITCHMASTER 1955

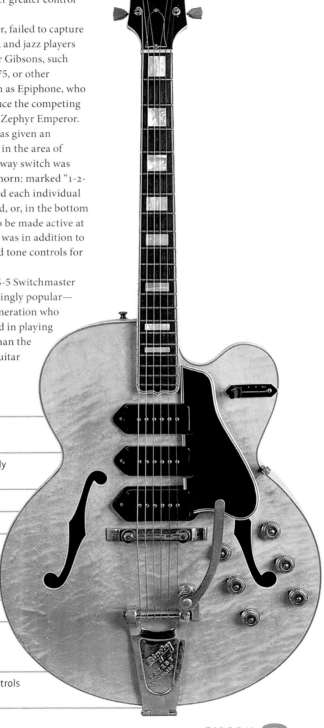

Launched in 1949, the ES-5 had been intended as "the supreme electronic version" of Gibson's influential top-end L-5 acoustic jazz guitar. The ES-5 was the first Gibson model to offer three pickups. It took a novel approach to controlling the sound: instead of the standard three-way switching system, it featured four individual volume controls—one for each pickup and one overall control—which gave the player greater control over the tone.

The ES-5, however, failed to capture its intended market, and jazz players drifted toward other Gibsons, such as the cheaper ES-175, or other manufacturers, such as Epiphone, who had rushed to produce the competing (and more popular) Zephyr Emperor.

In 1955 the L-5 was given an overhaul, primarily in the area of its electrics. A four-way switch was added to the treble horn: marked "1-2-3-ALL." This enabled each individual pickup to be selected, or, in the bottom position, all three to be made active at the same time. This was in addition to a pair of volume and tone controls for each pickup.

In the end, the ES-5 Switchmaster proved to be surprisingly popular— but with the new generation who were more interested in playing rock 'n' roll music than the jazz for which the guitar was conceived.

▲
In the mid-1950s, Carl Perkins was one Elvis Presley's biggest rivals. He also wrote his own songs; John Lennon and Paul McCartney cited him as an early influence.

▼
Many compilations exist on which "The King Of Rockabilly" and his Switchmaster can be heard. Listen to classic hits such as "Blue Suede Shoes."

| | |
|---|---|
| **Body style:** | 17" single cutaway hollow body with two f-holes |
| **Materials:** | Maple back and sides, maple ply top; 3-piece maple neck |
| **Fretboard:** | Rosewood |
| **Inlays:** | Pearl dot |
| **Frets:** | 20 |
| **Scale:** | 24 ¾" |
| **Width at nut:** | 1 ¹¹⁄₁₆" |
| **Bridge:** | Gold-plated Tune-o-matic |
| **Pickups:** | 3 P90 pickups with 4-way switching (one for each pickup; one that switches on all three at the same time) |
| **Electrics:** | Dedicated volume and tone controls for each pickup |

# GIBSON ES-335 1958

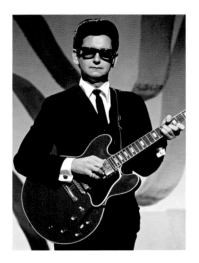

The drive to eliminate the feedback problems of amplified acoustic guitars led directly to the development of the solid-body guitar. Some players, however, felt that these guitars lacked the warmth of tone associated with hollow-body instruments. Launched in 1958, the

Gibson ES-335 was an attempt to find a middle ground.

It was an landmark in guitar body design technology, and could be described as neither hollow nor solid; instead, a solid wood block ran through the center of its body. The side "wings," however, *are* hollow; the maple plywood top features two f-holes at the top of each of the hollow chambers. The thinline body was complemented by a slim, comfortable neck, and a cutaway that gave easy access to the twenty-second fret. The ES-335 quickly became a bestseller, and has been in continuous production ever since.

The ES-335 has proved to be a versatile instrument at home in any musical genre, finding favor with rock musicians Eric Clapton, Paul Kossoff, Alvin Lee, and Eddie Van Halen; bluesmen B.B. King and T-Bone Walker; and jazz players John McLaughlin and Larry Carlton ("Mr. 335").

▲
**Roy Orbison used a cherry Gibson ES-335 for much of his career.**

▼
**For much of the time he spent touring with supergroup The Traveling Wilburys, Orbison used a black Gibson ES-335.**

| | |
|---|---|
| **Body style:** Semi-hollow double cutaway | |
| **Materials:** Maple center block, maple ply top; set mahogany neck (maple in some instances) | |
| **Finish:** Initially sunburst or natural; cherry red added in 1959; other colors available on reissues | |
| **Fretboard:** Rosewood (ebony on some models) | |
| **Frets:** 22 | |
| **Scale:** 24 ¾" | |
| **Width at nut:** 1 11⁄16" | |
| **Bridge:** Tune-o-matic bridge with stop tailpiece or Bigsby vibrato | |
| **Pickups:** 2 humbucking pickups; 3-way switching | |
| **Electrics:** Dedicated volume and tone controls for each pickup | |

# GIBSON ES-355 1958

The ES-355 came in several models, the best known of which was the ES-355TD-SV which featured stereo circuitry and a six-way varitone control enabling different preset notch filters to be switched in. Although it featured the same basic construction as the ES-335, the hardware was gold-plated throughout, making it substantially more costly than other ES guitars.

Although Gibson's advertising referred to it as a "jazz guitar," the ES-355 is best-known for its use by bluesmen—in particular by B.B. King. King's relationship with the black ES-355 he called "Lucille" is one of the most famous in music. Indeed, in 1968 he named an album in "her" honor. In 1980 Gibson paid the ultimate tribute with the launch of the B.B. King Lucille model. Apart from the "Lucille" script on the headstock, the main difference from King's original ES-355TD-SV models was the lack of the F-shaped soundholes, removed at King's request.

Launched after the ES-335, the ES-355 was its high-performance counterpart. A 1958 advert introduced the guitar by celebrating the "wonder-thin silhouette" that would fit "so close and comfortably to your body, it'll let you reach many chords easily you've never played before."

▲

B.B. King has often spoken of Lucille, his black ES-355: "Lucille is real, when I play her it's almost like hearing words."

▼

B.B. King's ES-355s can be heard on all of his recordings after the late 1950s. *Live At The Regal* (1965) is hailed as one of the best live blues albums ever.

| | |
|---|---|
| **Body style:** | Semi-hollow double cutaway |
| **Materials:** | Maple center block, maple ply top; set mahogany neck (maple in some intances) |
| **Finish:** | Initially sunburst, natural, cherry red, black, walnut; other colors available on reissues |
| **Fretboard:** | Single-bound ebony |
| **Frets:** | 22 |
| **Scale:** | 24 ¾" |
| **Width at nut:** | 1 ¹¹⁄₁₆" |
| **Bridge:** | Tune-o-matic bridge with Bigsby vibrato |
| **Pickups:** | 2 humbucking pickups; 3-way switching |
| **Electrics:** | Dedicated volume and tone controls for each pickup; Varitone notch filter switch |

# GIBSON BYRDLAND 1955

S ome guitarists didn't enjoy playing Gibson's bulky traditional archtops, such as the top-of-the-range L-5. Company president Ted McCarty had always sought ideas from musicians for new products, or refinements to existing models, and suggestions made by two guitarists, Billy Byrd and country/jazz picker Hank Garland, led to the development of Gibson's first thinline model—the Byrdland.

First built in 1955, the Gibson Byrdland is essentially a slimmer version of the L-5CES ("Cutaway-Electric-Spanish"): with an overall depth of 2 ¼ inches, the Byrdland was notably thinner than the L-5's 3 ⅜-inch depth. Byrd and Garland also specified a reduced neck length: the 23 ½-inch scale was over an inch shorter than most other Gibsons and enabled jazz players especially to finger intricate single-note patterns and unusual stretched chord voicings.

The Byrdland, a luxury instrument with gold-plated hardware and exquisite detailing, unsurprisingly went into production as one of Gibson's most expensive models. Later, the ES-350T, with standard hardware and a "no frills" finish, was offered as a cheaper option.

▲

**Hank Garland was one the guitarists who gave his name to the Gibson Byrdland. He started out as a session player in Nashville but made his name on the New York scene.**

▼

**Released in 1961, *Jazz Winds From A New Direction* was Garland's defining musical statement.**

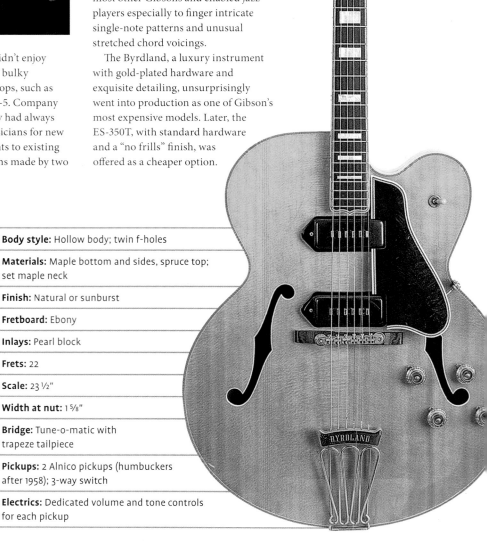

| | |
|---|---|
| **Body style:** | Hollow body; twin f-holes |
| **Materials:** | Maple bottom and sides, spruce top; set maple neck |
| **Finish:** | Natural or sunburst |
| **Fretboard:** | Ebony |
| **Inlays:** | Pearl block |
| **Frets:** | 22 |
| **Scale:** | 23 ½" |
| **Width at nut:** | 1 ⅝" |
| **Bridge:** | Tune-o-matic with trapeze tailpiece |
| **Pickups:** | 2 Alnico pickups (humbuckers after 1958); 3-way switch |
| **Electrics:** | Dedicated volume and tone controls for each pickup |

# GIBSON TRINI LOPEZ 1964

▲
Dave Grohl first found fame as drummer in Nirvana. After Kurt Cobain's death he formed Foo Fighters, taking lead vocal and guitar duties with enormous success.

The Gibson ES-335 proved popular with a wide variety of musicians from its first appearance. This led to the introduction of a number of variants. The first to appear was the ES-345 in 1959. Similar in design to the original, the ES-345 featured the same Varitone circuitry as found on the ES-355.

In 1964, Gibson issued a new version of the ES-335, the Trini Lopez Standard. Acknowledged as the first major Chicano popstar, in 1963 Lopez had recorded a version of the folk song "If I Had A Hammer" that topped the charts in thirty countries across the world. Gibson's adverts of the time claimed the guitar was "as exciting as the young performer who helped create it." In truth it was a cosmetically modifed ES-335, the most noticeable difference being the replacement of the violin-shaped f-holes with elongated diamond slits. The headstock, too, differed, using Fender-style six-in-row machine heads.

The ES-335 has remained in production, Gibson continuing to issue recent variants, among them the ES-333 (with alternative pickups); ES-340 (phase switching); ES-347 (coil tap and fine-tuning tailpiece); and the smaller-bodied CS-336. Gibson has also issued a number of limited-edition signature models of the guitar.

▼
Dave Grohl plays a Gibson Trini Lopez Standard throughout the 2005 album *In Your Honor*.

**Body style:** Semi-hollow double cutaway with diamond-shaped sound holes

**Materials:** Maple center block, maple ply top; set mahogany neck (maple in some instances)

**Finish:** Cherry, sparkling burgundy, pelham blue

**Fretboard:** Rosewood

**Frets:** 22

**Scale:** 24 ¾"

**Width at nut:** 1 ¹¹⁄₁₆"

**Bridge:** Tune-o-matic bridge with engraved trapeze tailpiece

**Pickups:** 2 humbucking pickups; 3-way switching

**Electrics:** Dedicated volume and tone controls for each pickup

# GIBSON LES PAUL "GOLDTOP" 1952

A guitar of endless myths and mysteries, the Gibson Les Paul first appeared in 1952. We know that guitarist and inventor Les Paul paid a visit to Gibson after the end of World War II to show him his idea for an electric guitar with a solid body that would not feed back like hollow-body electrics. Gibson saw no commercial value in the idea until Leo Fender's 1950 Broadcaster/Telecaster models began to catch on. By this time, Les Paul had become part of a hugely successful duo with his wife, Mary Ford. As America's best-known guitarist, Paul was asked to collaborate on, and give his name to, Gibson's first solid-body offering.

Paul's role in the guitar's design has always been a subject of dispute: the resulting guitar was too clearly in the ES-175 lineage for it to have been overly significant. It has been reported that he conceived the idea for the opulent gold paint finish, but the guitar's cosmetic resemblance to the ES-295, launched the same year, suggests Gibson already had such a plan in mind. More credible are the suggestions that Paul was behind the bridge/tailpiece design.

The first incarnation of the legendary Gibson Les Paul was not a success. And even after the instrument's legendary 1960s rehabilitation, the "Goldtop" remained unpopular.

▲
The Allman Brothers Band was one of the most influential groups of the early 1970s. Duane Allman played on their first three albums before his death in a motorcycle accident in 1971.

▼
Allman's best-known playing is with Eric Clapton on Derek and the Dominos' "Layla" (1971), on which he used a 1957 "Goldtop."

**Body style:** Single cutaway solid body in gold finish (back and sides natural brown)

**Materials:** Mahogany with maple top; set mahogany neck

**Fretboard:** Rosewood

**Inlays:** Trapezoid

**Frets:** 22

**Scale:** 24 ¾"

**Width at nut:** 1 ¹¹⁄₁₆"

**Bridge:** 1-piece trapeze-style bridge and "wrap-under" tailpiece ("wrap-over" tailpiece introduced in 1953; Tune-o-matic bridge and stop tailpiece introduced in 1955

**Pickups:** 2 P90 pickups (replaced by humbuckers in 1957); 3-way selector switch

**Electrics:** Dedicated volume and tone controls for each pickup

# GIBSON LES PAUL CUSTOM 1954

The first Les Pauls were not to everyone's taste. The neck shape was thinner than other Gibsons and the trapeze tailpiece made strings difficult to thread and was easy to knock accidentally from side to side, putting the guitar out of tune. And then there was the color itself: Leo Fender had created the simple Telecaster to mirror the average working musician—the garish Les Paul "Goldtop" was not for these players.

Thus, in 1954, a second issue of the Les Paul was introduced, the all-black Custom, dubbed the "Black Beauty." Featuring an all-mahogany body and the same hardware refinements that had been made to the "Goldtop," there was little obvious difference between the two models. The pickups were not quite the same, however, with a new, high-output Alnico V magnet placed in the neck position.

In 1957, the Custom was given its biggest refinement when the two single-coil pickups were replaced by a set of three of Gibson's new humbuckers. Retained, however, was Gibson's three-way switching—in the central position, both middle and bridge pickups became active. Consequently many of the original post-1957 Customs have undergone modification.

With Delaney and Bonnie, Eric Clapton played a black 1958 Les Paul Custom, which he gave to Albert Lee.

▲
Peter Frampton's main guitar *seems* to be a 1960 Les Paul Custom; in fact it is a 1954 model converted at the Gibson factory.

▼
*Frampton Comes Alive!* (1976) is one of the biggest-selling concert albums ever. The "customized" Custom can be heard throughout.

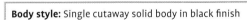

| | |
|---|---|
| **Body style:** | Single cutaway solid body in black finish |
| **Materials:** | Mahogany with set mahogany neck |
| **Fretboard:** | Ebony |
| **Inlays:** | Mother-of-pearl block |
| **Frets:** | 22 |
| **Scale:** | 24 ¾" |
| **Width at nut:** | 1 ¹¹⁄₁₆" |
| **Bridge:** | Tune-o-matic bridge and stop tailpiece |
| **Pickups:** | P-90 pickup in the bridge position; Alnico V pickup in the neck position; (replaced by 3 humbuckers in 1957); 3-way selector switch (bridge; bridge and center; neck) |
| **Electrics:** | Dedicated volume and tone controls |

# GIBSON LES PAUL JUNIOR 1954

A t the same time as the Custom was introduced, Gibson further widened the Les Paul range with the Junior. As the name suggests, this was a basic instrument aimed at the beginner. Over the years, however, it has proved itself to be a popular instrument even among professional players.

Initially, at least, the Junior took the same body shape as the other Les Paul models, but instead of having an arched top it was cut from a flat, thin slab of mahogany. A single P90 pickup was positioned alongside the bridge and the electrics comprised a single volume and tone control.

The first Les Paul Juniors were available in a sunburst finish. A year later, the Les Paul TV appeared—this was identical to the Junior but with a natural "mustard" finish. (Gibson had been surprised at the number of Juniors appearing on television, and it was thought that the yellow finish of the TV would not cast a glare when it appeared on a black and white screen.)

In 1958, the Junior/TV range was given a major cosmetic overhaul, and the classic Les Paul shape was replaced by a new double cutaway and a range of alternative colors.

The Les Paul Junior remained in production until 1963, reappearing once again in 2001.

▲
**The Replacements were among the most influential cult bands of the 1980s. Leader Paul Westerberg here plays an early 1960s Les Paul Junior with a double cutaway.**

▼
**The Replacements' album *Tim* (1985) features in *Rolling Stone* magazine's list of the 500 greatest albums of all time.**

| | |
|---|---|
| **Body style:** | Single cutaway solid body (double cutaway from 1958) |
| **Materials:** | Mahogany body with set mahogany neck |
| **Finish:** | Sunburst, cherry red, white, ebony, "TV" yellow |
| **Fretboard:** | Rosewood; ebony |
| **Inlays:** | Acrylic dot |
| **Frets:** | 22 |
| **Scale:** | 24 ¾" |
| **Width at nut:** | 1 ¹¹⁄₁₆" |
| **Bridge:** | Stud tailpiece bridge |
| **Pickups:** | 1 P90 pickup |
| **Electrics:** | Volume and tone controls |

# GIBSON LES PAUL STANDARD 1958

between 1958 and 1960, only around 1,700 of these instruments (referred to as the Standard) were built before the production line switched to the twin-cutaway Les Paul—shortly to be renamed the SG.

The Les Paul's fortunes began to turn posthumously in the mid-1960s when a new generation of young blues-based rock musicians, mostly based in the U.K., began to see the potential of the Les Paul—in particular the Standards built between 1958 and 1960. As Britain's blues-rock aristocracy—Eric Clapton, Peter Green, Keith Richards, Jeff Beck, and Jimmy Page—turned to the Les Paul Standard, second-hand prices began to accelerate. In 1968 the Les Paul was reintroduced and it has remained in production in numerous variants ever since.

The original Les Paul Standards have since taken on a mythological status, and, on the rare occasions they come up for auction, can easily draw bids in excess of $250,000.

T he first chapter in the story of the Les Paul ended in 1960 with the redesign that would see Gibson's problem child morph into the SG. Two years previously, the "regular" Les Paul was given one final makeover, as its gold top was replaced with an altogether more sober sunburst finish. Produced

▲
**Peter Green came to fame in the late 1960s as the guitarist with the first incarnation of Fleetwood Mac. He is widely viewed as one of the best electric blues players outside of the U.S.**

▼
**Peter Green's Les Paul Standard can be heard on Fleetwood Mac's 1968 debut album.**

| | |
|---|---|
| **Body style:** | Single cutaway solid body |
| **Materials:** | Mahogany with maple top; set mahogany neck |
| **Finish:** | Sunburst |
| **Fretboard:** | Rosewood |
| **Inlays:** | Trapezoid |
| **Frets:** | 22 |
| **Scale:** | 24 3/4" |
| **Width at nut:** | 1 11/16" |
| **Bridge:** | Tune-o-matic bridge and stop tailpiece |
| **Pickups:** | 2 humbucker pickups; three-way selector switch |
| **Electrics:** | Dedicated volume and tone controls for each pickup |

# GIBSON LES PAUL RECORDING 1971

Les Pauls. The first to appear was the somewhat controversial Les Paul Recording model.

In many ways a radical instrument, the Recording featured a complex—baffling to some—array of knobs and switches that gave the kind of on-board control that could only otherwise be achieved by an amplifier with a wide selection of equalization parameters. The most unusual of these controls was the eleven-way "decade" switch which allowed for the alteration of treble harmonics.

Also highly unusual were the low-impedance humbucking pickups. "The frequency response, tonalities, and range of harmonics will exceed any electric guitar on the market to date," boasted the 1971 Gibson brochure. Such was their sensitivity that the pickup height had to be set at the factory for optimum performance.

The Recording was clearly aimed at the "techno-savvy" guitarist, and as such, demand was never great.

A t the end of 1969, Gibson was bought by Norlin Industries, a conglomerate with interests in brewing, technology, and music. By this time, the Gibson Les Paul had established itself as being among the finest solid-body electric guitars on the market. The new owners immediately set about introducing a series of new

▲
Les Paul was precisely the kind of musician to make good use of the complexities of the Gibson Recording. Indeed, he further customized the guitar shown above.

▼
Paul used his Recording model on *Chester and Lester* (1976)—an album of duets recorded with country guitar legend Chet Atkins.

| | |
|---|---|
| **Body style:** Single cutaway solid body in natural finish | |
| **Materials:** Clear Honduras mahogany with center band; 3-piece set mahogany neck | |
| **Fretboard:** Rosewood | |
| **Inlays:** Mother-of-pearl block | |
| **Frets:** 22 (including partial fret) | |
| **Scale:** 24 ¾" | |
| **Width at nut:** 1 ¹¹⁄₁₆" | |
| **Bridge:** Tune-o-matic-style bridge with stop tailpiece | |
| **Pickups:** 2 low-impedance pickups; assorted switching combinations | |
| **Electrics:** Separate bass, treble, and volume controls; impedance switch; 11-way "decade control" switch; phase switch | |

# GIBSON LES PAUL ROBOT 2007

Over the years we have seen many attempts at bringing additional functionality to the electric guitar. The 1971 Les Paul Recording model was complex to use, but offered useful features. Similarly, MIDI guitar synthesizers have found a small but thriving niche community. The "organ guitars" of the 1960s, on the other hand, seem rather silly in retrospect. For most players, it seems, volume and tone controls are all that matter—and those are often set on "full" and left untouched. Musicians may not have been interested in on-board sonic innovations, but German guitarist Chris Adams brought his own technology to one area that concerns *every* player—tuning.

Adams spent ten years developing the Powertune system—an impressive device built into the guitar that takes care of the intonation of each string. The technology includes a computer system built into the underside of the stop bar that continually checks the

note. The player chooses the desired tuning system using the Master Control Knob (MCK). The sensor checks the intonation of each string against its internal tuner and sends messages to each machine head, causing it to turn automatically.

The system caters for a variety of different tunings, enabling the guitarist to switch from, for example, standard tuning to Drop D in a matter of seconds simply by turning the MCK.

In 2007, Gibson launched a range of "robot" guitars—classic Gibson designs fitted with the Powertune system. A year later, Gibson launched the Dark Fire, integrating the Powertune system with Chameleon Tone Technology, a system comprising onboard electronics designed to simulate various guitar tones. The Dark Fire also features an audio interface, making it possible to plug the guitar directly into a computer. The Firebird X, Gibson's most sophisticated robot guitar to date, was released in 2011.

▼
The Powertune's computer system is fitted into the guitar body below the stop bar. The player can switch tuning systems in seconds by rotating the Master Control Knob. Previously, guitarists wishing to switch tunings during a performance had no real option but to swap guitars.

| | |
|---|---|
| **Body style:** | Single cutaway chambered body |
| **Materials:** | Mahogany with maple top; set mahogany neck |
| **Fretboard:** | Ebony |
| **Inlays:** | Trapezoid |
| **Frets:** | 22 |
| **Scale:** | 24 ¾" |
| **Width at nut:** | 1 ¹¹⁄₁₆" |
| **Bridge:** | Tune-o-matic bridge and "Robot" stop tailpiece |
| **Pickups:** | 2 humbuckers; 3-way selector switch |
| **Electrics:** | Volume control for each pickup; Master Control Knob (MCK); full-color LED "control center" for dialing-in tuning settings, sound, and pickup coil selection |

# GIBSON EXPLORER 1958

prototype even existed—making the Moderne a kind of "holy grail" of the electric guitar.

The other instrument was originally named the Futura, but rechristened the Explorer prior to production. Almost as radical in appearance as the Flying V, the Explorer shared a broadly similar specification. Initial models were produced with a "split" headstock, containing three machine heads on each side; the redesign provided perhaps the guitar's most striking feature, its drooping "hockey stick" headstock. The headstock styling would influence many of the superstrat luthiers of the 1980s, such as Grover Jackson.

The Explorer was a spectacular failure, Gibson's rather vague production records suggesting that fewer than fifty were ever built. Yet, once again, McCarty's design was seen to be several decades ahead of his time. Growing appreciation of the design led to a reissue in 1976 that has since enjoyed long-lasting success.

Along with the Flying V, Ted McCarty filed patents for two other designs in 1957 that would make up this new range. The Moderne—a Flying V shape with an inwardly curving lower body—was never originally put into production. Indeed, conflicting accounts by those involved at the time have made it impossible to ascertain whether any

▲
David Evans—better known to U2 fans as The Edge—has made extensive use of the Gibson Explorer both on stage and in the recording studio.

▼
Released in 2000, *All That You Can't Leave Behind* saw U2 return to a conventional rock sound. Much of The Edge's guitar work features an Explorer.

| | |
|---|---|
| **Body style:** | Single cutaway solid body |
| **Materials:** | Korina body (mahogany, maple, alder, or korina on 1976 reissues); with set-in korina/mahogany/maple neck |
| **Finish:** | Natural, cherry, ebony, classic white on 1976 reissues |
| **Fretboard:** | Rosewood (ebony on classic white models) |
| **Inlays:** | Acrylic dot |
| **Frets:** | 22 |
| **Scale:** | 24 ¾" |
| **Width at nut:** | 1 ½" |
| **Bridge:** | Tune-o-matic |
| **Pickups:** | 2 humbuckers |
| **Electrics:** | Separate volume control for each pickup; master tone control |

# GIBSON FLYING V 1958

▲
**Blues master Albert King, seen with his personalized Flying V.**

T he first Flying Vs came off the production line in 1958. The first of Gibson President Ted McCarty's new "modernist" line of instruments, their *raison d'être* was simple—to stem the runaway success of Fender's Stratocaster. With the Flying V's Space-Age looks, McCarty certainly succeeded in producing a distinctive,

futuristic instrument—indeed, visually, nothing quite like it had existed before.

As with the Les Paul, the body of the Flying V prototype had been built from mahogany. This not only resulted in a weighty and poorly balanced instrument but also made it more expensive than its Fender rival. Gibson realized that the solution lay in selecting the lighter and more readily available korina wood.

Blues star Albert King quickly adopted the Flying V, and it remained his signature instrument throughout an illustrious career. Other guitarists were less convinced, however, and demand was extremely poor—dealers apparently ordered less than one hundred Flying Vs in total during 1958. Production was ended a year later.

Like the Les Paul, the Flying V enjoyed a renaissance in the 1960s, played by the likes of Jimi Hendrix and The Kinks. Production resumed in 1967 and it has since retained a niche position in the guitar market.

▼
**Albert King rarely used any guitar other than a Flying V. It can be heard to spectacular effect on 1969's boldly titled *King Of The Blues Guitar*.**

| | |
|---|---|
| **Body style:** Arrow shape | |
| **Materials:** Korina body (mahogany on reissues); with set-inkorina/mahogany neck | |
| **Finish:** Dark/light brown (original models); natural, cherry, ebony, classic white on reissues | |
| **Fretboard:** Rosewood or ebony | |
| **Inlays:** Acrylic dot | |
| **Frets:** 22 | |
| **Scale:** 24 ¾" | |
| **Width at nut:** 1 ½" | |
| **Bridge:** Tune-o-matic; Short Lyre Vibrola on some models | |
| **Pickups:** 2 humbuckers | |
| **Electrics:** Separate volume control for each pickup; master tone control | |

# GIBSON SG STANDARD 1961

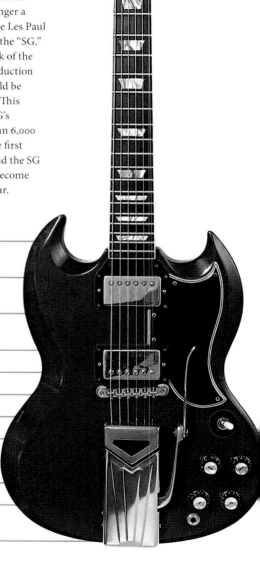

With sales of the Les Paul dropping significantly toward the end of the 1950s, a decision was taken to give the guitar a major overhaul. For a start, the thick mahogany archtop of the original Les Paul gave way to a thinner flat-topped body with a double cutaway, providing improved access to the upper frets. The neck also altered substantially. Both slimmer in profile and narrower at the nut, it was advertised as the "fastest neck in the world." The electrics that had helped to give the Les Paul its unique tone remained identical.

With its new look came a new identity. Les Paul claimed that he hadn't liked the new model and requested that his name be removed; other sources at Gibson recalled that, with the rock 'n' roll revolution now in full swing, Paul was no longer a relevant endorsee. In 1961 the Les Paul became the "Solid Guitar"—the "SG."

The thinner body and neck of the new design also enabled production costs to be reduced, so it could be priced closer to the Fenders. This contributed to the Gibson SG's immediate success. More than 6,000 units were sold in each of the first three years of production, and the SG Standard would ultimately become Gibson's biggest-selling guitar.

**▲**
Jim Morrison may have been the face of The Doors, but it was guitarist Robby Krieger who wrote many of their best-remembered songs.

**▼**
The Doors' 1967 debut album yielded the rock classic "Light My Fire," written by Robby Krieger and featuring a powerful SG Standard solo.

| | |
|---|---|
| **Body style:** | Double-pointed cutaway scalloped solid body |
| **Materials:** | Mahogany body (maple and birch laminate on some later models); mahogany neck |
| **Fretboard:** | Rosewood (ebony or maple on some later models) |
| **Inlays:** | Pearloid trapezoid |
| **Frets:** | 22 |
| **Scale:** | 24" |
| **Width at nut:** | 1 11/16" |
| **Bridge:** | Gibson Vibrato |
| **Pickups:** | 2 P.A.F. humbucking pickups |
| **Machine heads:** | Gibson nickel-plated |
| **Electrics:** | Dedicated volume and tone controls for each pickup |

# GIBSON SG SPECIAL 1961

Following the pattern set by the Les Paul range in the 1950s, the Gibson "Solid Guitar" was initially launched in four variants: the Standard, the Junior, the Special, and the Custom. The Junior, as its name suggested, was a pared-down budget version of the Standard, with a single pickup. The Custom *(see page 136)* was the luxury instrument of the SG range. The Special shared many of the features of the Standard but was fitted instead with a pair of Gibson's P90 "Soapbar" pickups. The P90 had been introduced in 1946 as a replacement for the hexagonal "Charlie Christian" model. A high-ouput, single-coil pickup, the P90 was largely superseded by Seth Lover's P.A.F. humbuckers from 1957. Many players, however—as evidenced by the enduring popularity of Fender guitars—continued to show a preference for the treble "bite" of a single coil. Indeed, some notable SG players, such as Pete Townshend of The Who, and Tony Iommi of Black Sabbath, chose the SG Special as their principal instrument.

Like all SGs, the Special has been known to suffer cracking between the body and the neck. This is due to the stress placed on the joint exacerbated by the thin body.

▲
In spite of having lost two fingertips on his fretting hand in a teenage workplace accident, Tony Iommi went on to form Black Sabbath and become one of the most influential heavy metal guitarists.

▼
Iommi played an SG Special nicknamed "Monkey" on *Paranoid* and all of the early Black Sabbath albums.

| | |
|---|---|
| **Body style:** | Double-pointed cutaway scalloped solid body |
| **Materials:** | Mahogany body (maple and birch laminate on some later models); mahogany neck |
| **Fretboard:** | Rosewood (ebony or maple on some later models) |
| **Inlays:** | Pearloid dot |
| **Frets:** | 22 |
| **Scale:** | 24" |
| **Width at nut:** | 1 11/16" |
| **Bridge:** | Wraparound "stairstep" tailpiece (Maestro vibrato optional from 1963) |
| **Pickups:** | 2 P90 "Soapbar" pickups |
| **Machine heads:** | Gibson nickel-plated |
| **Electrics:** | Dedicated volume and tone controls for each pickup |

# GIBSON SG CUSTOM 1961

turned out, the Custom was initially available only in an alpine white finish, providing a startling visual contrast with the opulent gold-plated hardware.

The most significant difference between the Custom and the other SG variants was the addition of a third P.A.F. humbucking pickup, creating a wider range of sonic possibilities. The control options remained the same as for two-pickup models, with a pair of volume and tone pots: this makes sense when you understand the way the three-way switching was wired: front pickup only, middle and back pickups together, or back pickup only.

Several tailpieces have existed throughout the life of the Custom SG. Early examples were fitted with Gibson "side-to-side" vibrato, followed by the Gibson Deluxe Lyre—probably the most commonly seen tailpiece on 1960s models. From 1973, Gibson offered the Custom with a Bigsby vibrato or an optional stop tailpiece.

The Gibson SG Custom was the deluxe model of the line. As the company's 1961 advert boasted: "Beauty in gleaming white or cherry red that must be seen. Wonderfully clear, bell-like tone that must be heard. Fast action that should be tried . . . soon. By Gibson, of course." As it

▲
**Ollie Halsall (*right*), British guitarist of 1970s bands Patto and Boxer, is a shoo-in for the award of "Greatest Guitar Player You've Never Heard Of."**

▼
**Halsall's incredible legato solo on "Give It All Away" from Patto's 1971 album *Hold Your Fire* was played on his white Gibson SG Custom.**

| | |
|---|---|
| **Body style:** | Double-pointed cutaway scalloped solid body |
| **Materials:** | Mahogany body (maple and birch laminate on some later models); mahogany neck |
| **Fretboard:** | Ebony |
| **Inlays:** | Mother-of-pearl block |
| **Frets:** | 22 |
| **Scale:** | 24 ¾" |
| **Width at nut:** | 1 ¹¹⁄₁₆" |
| **Bridge:** | Gibson Vibrato/Deluxe Lyre (Bigsby after 1973) |
| **Pickups:** | 3 P.A.F. humbucking pickups |
| **Machine heads:** | Gibson nickel-plated |
| **Electrics:** | 2 volume controls; 2 tone controls; 3-way switching (front only; middle and back together; back only) |

# GIBSON EDS-1275 1958

1963 produced the first popular model. The EDS-1275 was, in effect, a double-necked SG, combining a six-string lower neck with a twelve-string upper neck. The standard Les Paul/SG electrics applied to both sets of humbucking pickups; a switch between the two tailpieces activated either set.

The player that music fans overwhelmingly associate with the EDS-1275 is Led Zeppelin's Jimmy Page. In the 1976 film *The Song Remains The Same* we see it being used on the band's anthem, "Stairway To Heaven," as Page picks out the delicate opening sequence on the lower neck before switching to the twelve-string; he then reverts to the six-string for the extended solo, then completes the song with a chorus on the twelve-string.

The idea of producing a guitar with more than one neck is not new, with acoustic experiments known to have taken place in the 1800s. Even in the 1930s there were a number steel-string double-necked guitars being played in dance bands. It was, however, the Gibson corporation that in

▲
Jimmy Page tended to use the EDS-1275 on stage, where he was able to switch between six- and twelve-string necks, rather than on Led Zeppelin's studio recordings.

▼
You can hear Page play the EDS-1275 on many of the tracks on *The Song Remains The Same* (1976), soundtrack of the eponymous movie.

| | |
|---|---|
| **Body style:** | Double cutaway solid body |
| **Materials:** | Mahogany body with two set mahogany necks (maple neck on modern-day models |
| **Finish:** | Alpine white, cherry red |
| **Fretboard:** | Rosewood |
| **Inlays:** | Pearloid parallelogram |
| **Frets:** | 20 |
| **Scale:** | 24" |
| **Width at nut:** | 1 11/16" |
| **Bridge:** | Tune-o-matic |
| **Pickups:** | 2 pairs of humbuckers; 3-way switching |
| **Electrics:** | 2 volume controls; 2 tone controls; 3-way switching; 6/12-string switch |

# GIBSON FIREBIRD I 1963

At the start of the 1960s Gibson may have still dominated the worlds of the acoustic and semi-hollow guitars, but the company was engaged in a losing battle with Fender for the solid-body electric guitar market. The "modernist" experiment to turn around Gibson's reputation for dull conservatism

had failed dismally, as the Flying V and Explorer lasted barely a year on the production line. Meanwhile, the "Strat," "Tele," and other new Fender models seemed to be thriving.

Gibson responded by hiring noted U.S. automobile designer Ray Dietrich to create a luxury guitar that would have the same popular appeal, similar to the famed Chrysler and Lincoln cars he had designed. Dietrich came up with the Firebird, which clearly takes the lines of a 1950s tailfin. The Firebird also bore a resemblance to the abandoned Explorer, but with the spiked shape now given gently curved edges. From a visual perspective, the most unusual aspect is what became known as its "reverse" shape, in that the lower (treble) horn of the body extends further than the other side of the fingerboard.

The Firebird was offered in a number of variations in pickup and bridge style. These were denoted by Roman numerals.

▲
Bluesman Johnny Winter performs on a Gibson Firebird in 1973; his album of that year, *Still Alive And Well*, alluded to his recovery from heroin addiction.

▼
Rolling Stone Ronnie Wood's playing on the Gibson Firebird can be heard to good effect on the band's 1994 album *Voodoo Lounge*.

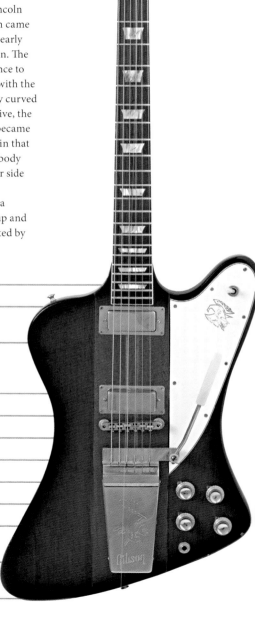

| | |
|---|---|
| **Body style:** | Single "reverse" cutaway solid body |
| **Materials:** | Mahogany body with mahogany "neck thru" construction |
| **Finish:** | Classic white, ebony, pelham blue, cherry, heritage cherry, vintage sunburst, antique brown, natural, wine red |
| **Fretboard:** | Rosewood or ebony |
| **Inlays:** | Mother-of-pearl trapezoid, block, or dot |
| **Frets:** | 22 |
| **Scale:** | 24 ¾" |
| **Width at nut:** | 1 ¹¹⁄₁₆" |
| **Bridge:** | Tune-o-matic |
| **Pickups:** | 1, 2, or 3 mini-humbuckers, full-size humbuckers, or P90s |
| **Electrics:** | Originally master volume and tone controls for each pickup |

# GIBSON FIREBIRD III "NON-REVERSE" 1965

The original Firebird was an outstanding guitar. It was Gibson's first to use a "neck-thru" technique, where the neck and the central block of the body are carved from a single piece of wood—in the Firebird's case, mahogany; the upper and lower "wings" of the body are glued in place separately. This production technique is thought by some to produce greater note sustain and an improved tone. It is, however, costly and generally only used on the most upmarket guitars.

During the first two years of its life, sales of the Firebird were disappointing. At the same time, Gibson had received complaints that the Firebird's body shape violated Fender design patents for the Jazzmaster and a lawsuit was threatened. So in 1965 Gibson redesigned the Firebird to take on a more conventional apperance. The result was the so-called "non-reverse" body—a more standard double-cutaway design. Gibson also reverted to "set" neck production.

The Firebird remained in production until 1969. Subsequent reissues have largely been of the now hugely sought-after "non-reverse" originals.

▲
From the mid-1960s, R&B guitarist Clarence "Gatemouth" Brown chose a "reverse" Firebird as his trademark guitar, personalizing it with an embossed leather covering.

▼
Although active during the 1940s, Brown wouldn't achieve recognition for another three decades. All of his 1970s albums feature the Firebird.

| | |
|---|---|
| **Body style:** | Single reverse double cutaway solid body |
| **Materials:** | Mahogany body with mahogany "set" neck |
| **Finish:** | Classic white, ebony, pelham blue, heritage cherry, cherry, vintage sunburst, antique brown, natural, wine red |
| **Fretboard:** | Rosewood or ebony |
| **Inlays:** | Mother-of-pearl trapezoid, block, or dot |
| **Frets:** | 22 |
| **Scale:** | 24 ¾" |
| **Width at nut:** | 1 ¹¹⁄₁₆" |
| **Bridge:** | Tune-o-matic |
| **Pickups:** | 1, 2, or 3 mini-humbuckers, full-size humbuckers, or P90s |
| **Electrics:** | Originally master volume and tone controls for each pickup. This arrangement was superseded by dedicated volume controls for each pickup plus a master tone control |

# GIBSON S-1 1975

Like Fender, the Gibson corporation arrived at the realization that musicians have no expectation of innovation from the global guitar market's two major players. And now many of the Gibson models that originally failed to stem the popularity of the Fender Stratocaster—the Flying V, Explorer, Firebird—are regarded as classic designs in their own right. As such, modern guitarists are prepared to pay a premium for faithful recreations of these originals. In the 1970s, however, Gibson still seemed to be perpetually chasing Fender's tail, never *quite* getting there.

The beginning of the 1970s saw the company trying its hand at the Fender-dominated single-coil market. Buoyed by the modest success of its first attempt, the Marauder—remembered now for its connection with the band Kiss—in 1975 Gibson produced a second single-coil instrument, the

S-1. Consisting of a flat Les Paul-style body, unusual for a Gibson instrument, the S-1 was produced with a bolt-on neck, in this instance based on that of a Flying V.

The unique feature of the S-1's design was in its electrics. A set of three see-through single-coil pickups specially created by Bill Lawrence—at that time among the world's most respected pickup designers. Backed with some unusually elaborate circuitry for a non-active guitar, a two-way toggle switch, and a four-position "chicken-head" rotary switch, the S-1 was capable of generating a wide range of single- and twin-coil sounds.

Gibson managed to entice a number of big names to endorse the S-1, including Carlos Santana and Rolling Stones Ronnie Wood and Keith Richards. Nevertheless it was not a success and production ended in 1980. Unlike other Gibson "failures," the S-1 is yet to reemerge as a classic reissue.

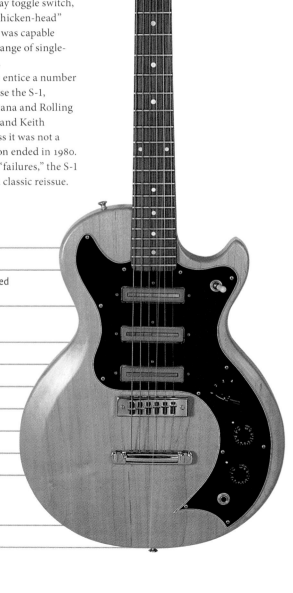

▼
**A Gibson S1 lends its voice to the sound of Washington, D.C.-based psychedelic band Dead Meadow, as attested by the cover portrait of *Feathers* (2005), their fifth album.**

| | |
|---|---|
| **Body style:** | Single cutaway solid body |
| **Materials:** | Alder body with bolt-on laminated maple neck |
| **Finish:** | Natural satin, lustrous ebony, lustrous sunburst |
| **Fretboard:** | Rosewood |
| **Inlays:** | Acrylic dot |
| **Frets:** | 22 |
| **Scale:** | 24 ¾" |
| **Width at nut:** | 1 ¹¹⁄₁₆" |
| **Bridge:** | Tune-o-matic |
| **Pickups:** | 1, 2, or 3 see-thru single coil pickups; 4-position "chicken-head" phase switch; backpickup bypass switch |
| **Electrics:** | Master volume and tone control |

# GIBSON CORVUS 1982

metal player. Displaying an uncanny ability to misread the current market, Gibson came up with a guitar that had none of the sharp angular body shapes popular at the time. The Corvus was heralded in the 1983 American Series catalog as: ". . . an instrument with a look as daring as it sounds." In truth, it bore more than a passing resemblance to Ovation's Breadwinner, a guitar that had first appeared in the early 1970s.

The early 1980s was a curious time for the guitar world. The fortunes of both Fender and Gibson had been in decline, and bold, newer U.S. manufacturers such as B.C. Rich, Kramer, and Jackson were producing unusually shaped instruments, often geared to the heavy

The Corvus came in three different models: I and II were armed with single or double high-output Alnico 5 humbuckers; the Corvus III featured three single-coil pickups. Like the S-1, the Corvus models featured bolt-on maple necks. (An upscale variant, the rarely seen Futura, was also available with a "set" neck.)

Now something of a cult guitar, the poorly received Corvus was only produced until 1984, and probably represents Gibson's last attempt at producing an "original" instrument.

Largely forgotten, the Corvus made a surprising comeback in the *Guitar Hero* video game series.

▼

The Breadwinner "ax" design from Ovation, produced from 1971, is echoed by the Corvus series.

| | |
|---|---|
| **Body style:** | Contoured offset V-shaped solid body |
| **Materials:** | Select American Hardwood with bolt-on maple neck |
| **Finish:** | Natural |
| **Fretboard:** | Rosewood |
| **Inlays:** | Acrylic dot |
| **Frets:** | 22 |
| **Scale:** | 24 ¾" |
| **Width at nut:** | 1 ¹¹⁄₁₆" |
| **Bridge:** | Top-adjusting bridge and tailpiece unit |
| **Pickups:** | Corvus I, single Alnico 5 humbucker; Corvus II, Alnico 5 humbucker (back), regular humbucker (front) with 3-way selector switch; Corvus III, 3 single coil pickups with 5-way selector switch |
| **Electrics:** | Master volume and tone control |

# GIBSON BASSES : THE FAMILY TREE (1950s-1980s)

In 1953 Gibson placed a series of adverts in the U.S. music press: "Leading combos, western and country groups are featuring a 'new sound' . . . the Gibson Electric Bass." Fender had, of course, arrived there two years earlier, and their Precision had been runaway success. Unlike Fender, the Gibson Electric Bass was not modeled on a guitar, but appeared rather as a miniature upright bass—it even featured painted f-holes on its solid mahogany body.

Gibson have continued to produce excellent basses, although none has been anything like as popular as the two principal Fender models.

**EB-0**
(1959–79)

The single-pickup EB-0 is the bass version of the Les Paul Junior.

**THUNDERBIRD**
(1963–PRESENT)

The bass counter of the Gibson Fi six-string guita Thunderbird wa launched in 196

**EB-1**
(1953–58)

The original Gibson bass was named the "Electric Bass" or EB; it was designated EB-1 later in the 1950s.

**EB-3**
(1961–79)

The EB-3 emerged in 1961 as part of the new SG range.

**GRABBER**
(1973–83)

Unusual for a Gibson, the Grabber featured a bolt-on neck. The headstock was taken from a Flying V guitar.

**RIPPER**
(1973–83)

The sister to the Grabber, the Rip featured a Les P style headstock set neck constr

**EB-2**
(1958–72)

The EB-2 was launched at the same time as the ES-335 guitar, on which it is based.

## A Matter of Taste

Gibson bass guitars differed from the more popular Fender instruments that dominated the bass market—and still do today. Whereas the Fender Precision and Jazz models featured single-coil pickups that produced a cutting sound, Gibson bass guitars were, until the 1970s, fitted with humbucking pickups. The Gibsons' thick, "murky" sound was preferred by progressive groups such as The Who and Cream, whose early recordings are characterized by the dense Gibson bass sound.

**G3**
(1975–83)

Descending fro Grabber, the G3 the bass partne S-1 guitar.

**"SB" RANGE**
(1971–73)

Of the "SB" range, the SB-300 and 350 featured single-coil pickups; the 400 and 450 had humbuckers.

**MELODY MAKER BASS**
(1967–71)

The Melody Maker was a single-pickup, budget, SG-style bass. It was replaced by the "SB" series.

**EB-4**
(1972–79)

This 1970s update of the EB-0 featured an SG-style body. Most of the EB-4s were built in 1973.

**RD ARTIST BASS**
(1977–81)

Gibson's first ac bass guitar deve over two years, w the aid of Moog John Entwistle.

**LES PAUL BASS**
(1969–71)

The 1969 Les Paul bass was the first to feature the guitar's single cutaway body style.

**LES PAUL TRIUMPH BASS**
(1971–79)

With its advanced circuitry, the Les Paul Triumph was Gibson's flagship bass of the 1970s period.

**LES PAUL SIGNATURE BASS**
(1973–79)

The Les Paul Signature was a thinline, hollow-body bass with one single-coil pickup.

**VICTORY**
(1981–86)

Victory options passive single-p Standard; activ pickup Artist; pa twin-pickup Cus

# GIBSON THUNDERBIRD IV 1963

creative talents could make a transition to the guitar. The two products he developed were the Gibson "Birds"— the Firebird guitar and the visually similar Thunderbird bass.

Gibson had achieved limited success in the bass guitar market, earlier models from the "EB" range being the less popular short-scale instruments. The Thunderbird bass, drawing on the design of increasingly popular Rickenbacker 4000s, featured a full 34-inch scale (like the Fenders) and, unusual for the time, a "neck-thru" construction. The Thunderbird was available in two different models: the "II" had a single pickup; the "IV" featured two pickups.

In 1966, following a lawsuit brought by Fender, who claimed that the Thunderbird's design had copied its Jazzmaster guitar, Gibson changed the design to a non-reverse body shape, where the lower extending horn was moved to the upper body.

From the moment that Fender introduced the Precision bass in 1951, it had been the unrivaled leader in the electric bass market. In the early 1960s, Gibson had engaged the noted U.S. car designer Raymond H. Dietrich—who had worked for Chrysler and Lincoln—to see if his

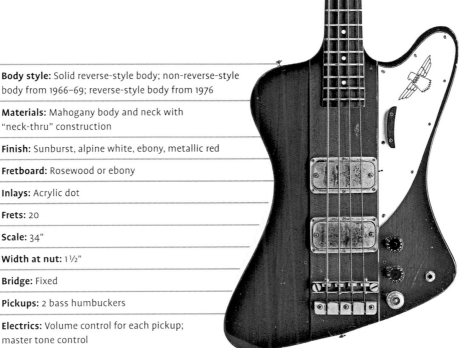

▲
The Who's John Entwistle was seen playing a Gibson Thunderbird IV during much of the 1960s.

▼
The Thunderbird IV was one of many bass guitars used by Entwistle at the time of 1967's *The Who Sell Out*.

| | |
|---|---|
| **Body style:** | Solid reverse-style body; non-reverse-style body from 1966–69; reverse-style body from 1976 |
| **Materials:** | Mahogany body and neck with "neck-thru" construction |
| **Finish:** | Sunburst, alpine white, ebony, metallic red |
| **Fretboard:** | Rosewood or ebony |
| **Inlays:** | Acrylic dot |
| **Frets:** | 20 |
| **Scale:** | 34" |
| **Width at nut:** | 1½" |
| **Bridge:** | Fixed |
| **Pickups:** | 2 bass humbuckers |
| **Electrics:** | Volume control for each pickup; master tone control |

# GITTLER "FISHBONE" 1975

Across the decades we have seen many bold attempts to reinvent the electric guitar, most of which have foundered and are now viewed as little more than period curiosities. Few innovators, however, have torn up the template quite so thoroughly as New York artist and inventor Allan Gittler, whose radical redesign began by questioning the necessity for almost every component of a conventional electric guitar.

The modern electric guitar clearly evolved from its acoustic counterpart. Gittler, however, felt that most of the traditional design references to an acoustic guitar were irrelevant to an electric instrument. What emerged in 1975 appeared to be the skeleton of a guitar constructed wholly from stainless steel. The neck was a thin bar that ran the full length of the instrument on which thirty-one frets were pressure-fitted. Pre-empting the later Steinberger models, Gittler's "Fishbone" had no headstock, tuning taking place behind the bridge. Equally

unusual was the guitar's individual pickup for each string.

Gittler built around sixty of these guitars while in New York, most of which have now found their way into museum collections—including the Museum of Modern Art. The only notable public sighting of the "Fishbone" was in the hands of Andy Summers of The Police, who had bought the instrument directly from Gittler, and used it in the video of the 1983 single "Synchronicity 2."

In the early 1980s Gittler evidently underwent some form of spiritual experience. Changing his name to Avraham Bar Rashi and relocating to Israel, he had 300 new computer-machined instruments built. These models (like the one shown here) featured a plastic body covering the electrics. Although this had no impact on the sound or playability, it undoubtedly compromised the design ethic of the original.

▼
**The Gittler guitar in New York's Museum of Modern Art.**

**Body style:** No body; plastic covering on models from 1982

**Materials:** Stainless steel

**Finish:** Stainless steel

**Fretboard:** None

**Frets:** 31

**Scale:** 25 ½"

**Bridge:** Fixed

**Pickups:** 6 individual single-coil pickups with combined output or 6 individual outputs (via D-sub-9-pin) for feeding into a mixing board

**Electrics:** Master volume and tone controls; built-in pre-amplifier powered by 9-volt battery or via D-sub connector

# Gordon-Smith Gypsy 60 ss 1986

the working musician. The company mantra is appropriately pragmatic: "Guitars, not furniture."

Although Gordon-Smith does produce original guitar designs, most of the 11,000 instruments built over the past three decades have been based on the American classics of the 1950s, among them the Les Paul Junior-inspired Gypsy series.

The flagship Gypsy range comprises both solid and semi-solid models that are offered with either single or double cutaways. Both body and neck are made from mahogany with a rosewood fingerboard. For comfort and playability the neck is set into the body at an angle of around 80 degrees. The semi-solid Gypsy 60 shown here is curious in that the visually distinctive f-holes are unusually large.

Gordon-Smith also designs its own humbucking pickups and was one of the first makers to offer a coil-tap feature, switching to a single-coil mode.

**B**ritain's largest modern-day guitar manfacturer, Gordon-Smith was established in 1979 in Partington, a small town near Manchester. Founders Gordon Whitham and John Smith set out with the aim of producing affordable high-quality hand-made instruments for

▲
Emerging in 2004, The Futureheads were influenced by the European post-punk scene of the early 1980s. Guitarist Barry Hyde plays a Gordon-Smith Gypsy with a double cutaway.

▼
Released in 2008, *This Is Not The World* was The Futureheads' third album.

| | |
|---|---|
| **Body style:** | Semi-hollow single cutaway (with solid-body and double cutaway options) |
| **Materials:** | Mahogany body with set mahogany neck; optional birch on the body and maple on the neck |
| **Finish:** | Assorted colors and finishes |
| **Fretboard:** | Rosewood |
| **Frets:** | 22 |
| **Inlays:** | Abalone dot |
| **Scale:** | 24 3/4" |
| **Width at nut:** | 1 5/8" |
| **Bridge:** | Vibrato |
| **Pickups:** | Gordon Smith humbuckers with coil-tap; 3-way selector switch |
| **Electrics:** | Dedicated volume and tone controls (push-pull initiates coil tap) |
| **Tuners:** | Schaller |

# GRETSCH : THE STORY

In 1883, German immigrant Friedrich Gretsch set up the Fred Gretsch Manufacturing Company in Brooklyn, producing his own range of musical instruments. His son, Fred Gretsch, quickly expanded the company, in particular carving a reputation for its drums and percussion. By the start of the 1930s, with the guitar growing in popularity, Gretsch produced its first range of acoustic instruments. In 1939, the first electric Gretsch appeared, the Electromatic Spanish. 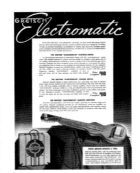 Bundled with a small amplifier, it retailed at $110 but made little impression on the market.

In 1942, Fred Gretsch retired, handing the business over to his son, Fred Jr., under whose leadership the name would achieve international recognition by concentrating on the marketing of high-end drums and guitars and procuring endorsements from the top musicians in their fields.

Important in the early days of Gretsch guitars was freelance worker Jimmie Webster, who conceived many of the classic designs and generally acted as an evangelist for the brand. By the early 1950s, he had developed the "Electromatic" archtop series capable of rivaling the popular Gibson models for quality. When Gibson launched the Les Paul model, Gretsch countered in 1953 with the sparkling Duo Jet. Retailing at $235, it was five dollars more expensive than the Gibson. But the most significant figure in the popularization of Gretsch guitars was ace country picker Chet Atkins, who had earlier been offered his own range of instruments.  The Chet Atkins Hollow Body 6120 appeared at the start of 1955—just as Atkins' Nashville fame was beginning to spread nationally. The Chet Atkins models, as Gretsch vice president Phil Grant was happy to admit, "put us on the map."

During the same period, Jimmie Webster conceived the most iconic Gretsch of them all—the White Falcon.  A mighty 17-inch single cutaway archtop hollow body finished in gleaming white gloss with gold "sparkle" decorations (from a Gretsch drum kit), the White Falcon retailed at $600 (around $5,000 today), becoming the ultimate fantasy guitar.

In 1967, Fred Gretsch Jr. sold out to the Baldwin Piano & Organ Company. The brand was run down when, in 1989, Fred Gretsch III (nephew of Fred Jr.) returned it to the family fold. The luxuriant, retro looks of the classic 1950s Gretsch guitars are now more popular than ever, and most of the company's designs are once again in production.

The 1939 Gretsch brochure featured the company's first Electromatic Spanish guitar and amplifier bundle.

Chet Atkins (*right*) cradles his Gretsch solid-body guitar as he poses with singer Porter Waggoner.

Jimmie Webster displays his specially made Gretsch Project-O-Sonic White Falcon.

1883 Friedrich Gretsch makes banjos and drums in New York City

1955 Gretsch introduces the hollow-body White Falcon

1955 Chet Atkins endorses a range of Gretsch guitars

1967 Gretsch is bought by Baldwin Piano & Organ Company

1981 After a decade of decline Gretsch production is terminated

1989 Fred Gretsch III buys the Gretsch company back from Baldwin

2002 Gretsch markets and produces its guitars through Fender

# GRETSCH

## FAMILY TREE

# GRETSCH WHITE FALCON 1954

The spectacular Gretsch White Falcon is one of the most visually distinctive production-line guitars ever made. Conceived by Gretsch marketing executive Jimmie Webster, it was intended to be a "dream guitar" capable of outperforming anything else on the market.

Already more than seventy years old, Gretsch had begun—unlike most other noteworthy guitar manufacturers—as a general producer of musical instruments, and some of the eye-catching visual features of the White Falcon betray this varied heritage. The thick sparkly gold plastic used in the binding, for example, derives from the flamboyant livery of the company's range of drum kits.

With its unusually large body (17 inches wide by 2 ¾ inches deep), the White Falcon was presented as "the Cadillac of guitars." Created initially as a one-off showpiece for the 1954 NAMM trade show, it created such a stir that the following year it went into production. Advertised as "The finest guitar we know how to make," the White Falcon had a price to match—at $600 (over $4,000 at today's prices), only Gibson's top-of-the-range Super 400 guitar cost more.

▲
The Cult's Billy Duffy, one of a long line of notable White Falcon users. Others include Stephen Stills, Brian Setzer of the Stray Cats, and Dave Stewart of Eurythmics.

▼
Duffy's White Falcon appears throughout The Cult's 1985 *Love* album, which also features the band's breakout single "She Sells Sanctuary."

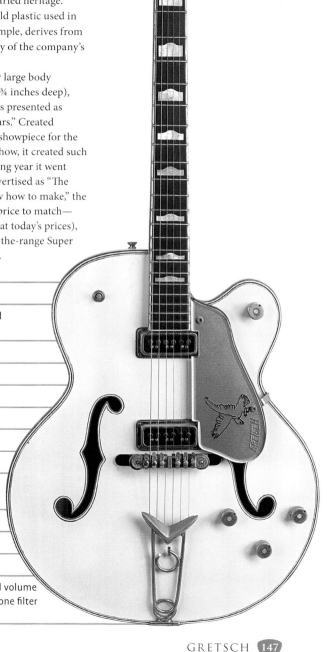

| | |
|---|---|
| **Body style:** | Single cutaway hollow body |
| **Materials:** | Mahogany body with laminated rock maple top; mahogany set neck |
| **Finish:** | Gloss white nitrocellulose lacquer |
| **Fretboard:** | Ebony |
| **Inlays:** | Mother-of-pearl |
| **Frets:** | 22 (.070" wide) |
| **Scale:** | 25 ½" |
| **Width at nut:** | 1 ¹¹⁄₁₆" |
| **Bridge:** | Melita Synchro-Sonic (Space Control from 1958) |
| **Tailpiece:** | Gretsch G Cadillac |
| **Pickups:** | DynaSonic (FilterTron from 1958) |
| **Machine heads:** | Grover Imperial |
| **Electrics:** | Master tone, master volume, and volume for each pickup (tone control replaced by tone filter switches after 1958) |

# GRETSCH CHET ATKINS 1955

not been impressed. Atkins tells the story: "He kept after me . . . He really wanted me to play one of their guitars. So finally he said, 'Well, why don't you design one that you would like?'"

Atkins himself played a limited role in the design of the Chet Atkins. Gretsch had wanted to aim the guitar at country players, using the same Western motifs found on the Round Up; Atkins didn't care for "all that junk," nor did he like the f-holes. But he insisted on a Bigsby vibrato arm. Despite reservations he gave in: "I wanted to be known all over the world as a great guitarist . . . and this would help that happen."

As Chet Atkins's fame spread, so did the Gretsch brand. As Atkins puts it: "If Jimmie Webster were alive today he would tell you the most important thing he ever did was to sign me, because they started selling the hell out of guitars!"

Just as Gibson had named its first solid-body electric after Les Paul, Gretsch lured emerging country star Chet Atkins with the offer of his own signature model. Atkins had been approached by Jimmie Webster to endorse an existing design, but had

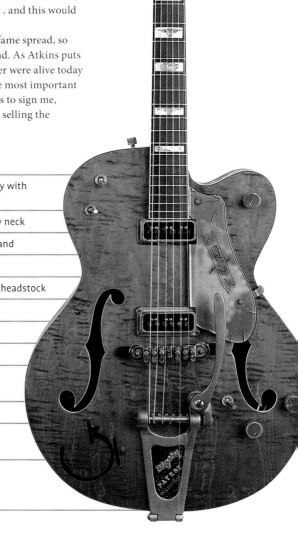

▲
Chet Atkins gave his name to a range of instruments for the Fred Gretsch company, among them the Country Gentleman, the Tennessee Rose, and the first of the series (*above*) named after him.

▼
*Neck And Neck* (1990) brings together Chet Atkins and Mark Knopfler: master pickers from two different generations.

| | |
|---|---|
| **Body style:** | 16" single cutaway hollow body with two bound f-holes |
| **Materials:** | Maple body with set mahogany neck |
| **Finish:** | Amber red/orange with G cattle brand |
| **Fretboard:** | Rosewood (ebony from 1958) |
| **Inlays:** | Western motifs; longhorn steer on headstock |
| **Frets:** | 22 |
| **Scale:** | 24½" |
| **Width at nut:** | 1¹¹⁄₁₆" |
| **Bridge:** | Compensating aluminum Bigsby bridge |
| **Tailpiece:** | Bigsby vibrato |
| **Pickups:** | 2 DeArmond single-coil pickups (Filter'Trons from 1958); 3-position switch |
| **Electrics:** | Dedicated volume controls for each pickup; master volume control; 2 tone filter switches |

# GRETSCH COUNTRY GENTLEMAN 1957

Chet Atkins proved to be the perfect endorsee, rarely seen without a Gretsch in his hands. Over time, the cactus-and-cattle decoration he'd so disliked was toned down, and the f-holes later became merely decorative. However, his biggest gripe was about the tone of the

DeArmond pickups, which he felt were insensitive to his picking style. Atkins turned to an inventor he'd met selling amplifiers in Nashville. Ray Butts came up with a twin-coil humbucking pickup around the same time that Seth Lover designed the P.A.F. at Gibson—both would argue that their own design came first. Butts agreed to a royalty deal with Gretsch, and in 1957 the Filter'Tron pickup appeared— a year later becoming standard on most of the Gretsch range.

That same year, new models were added to the Chet Atkins range, among them the Country Gentleman, a guitar that has since proved to be even more popular outside of the country music world. Indeed, in 1964, with Beatlemania running riot across the United States, Gretsch's magazine adverts could boast: "Among the top artists who play it is a member of that world-famous Liverpool rock 'n' roll group!"

▲
**More than *merely* the greatest country guitarist of all time,** Atkins had his finger in many business pies, including studio production, label management, and guitar endorsement.

▼
**The cover of *Chet Atkins' Workshop* (1960) shows the "Country Gentleman"** himself playing a Gretsch 6122.

| | |
|---|---|
| **Body style:** | Single cutaway hollow body |
| **Materials:** | Mahogany body with binding; set mahogany neck |
| **Finish:** | Natural mahogany |
| **Fretboard:** | Bound ebony |
| **Frets:** | 22 (not including zero fret, added in 1959) |
| **Inlays:** | Thumbnail |
| **Scale:** | 24 ¼" |
| **Width at nut:** | 1 11/16" |
| **Bridge:** | Bigsby vibrato and "metal bar bridge" |
| **Pickups:** | 2 humbucking Filter'Trons (no selector switching) |
| **Electrics:** | Dedicated volume controls for each pickup; overall volume control on cutaway bout; 2 tone filter switches on opposite bout |

# GRETSCH ANNIVERSARY 1958

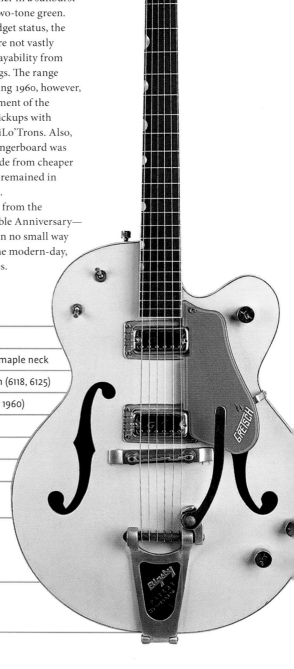

Gretsch guitars, by virtue of their price tags alone, had deliberately targeted the well-heeled or professional musician. In 1958, to mark the seventy-fifth birthday of the Fred Gretsch Music Company, a cheaper series of models was launched—named, appropriately enough, the Anniversary. Taking the basic Chet Atkins shape, the Anniversary models were available with two pickups (often called a "Double Anniversary") or one neck pickup ("Single Anniversary"). Each model was offered either in a sunburst finish or a beautiful two-tone green.

In spite of their budget status, the early Anniversaries are not vastly different in tone or playability from their expensive siblings. The range was downgraded during 1960, however, including the replacement of the original Filter'Tron pickups with cheaper single-coil HiLo'Trons. Also, the unbound ebony fingerboard was replaced with one made from cheaper rosewood. The guitar remained in production until 1975.

All Gretsch guitars from the 1950s—even the humble Anniversary—are collectible, aided in no small way by the high price of the modern-day, Japanese-built reissues.

▲
**Early 1970s British blues band Vinegar Joe launched the careers of vocalists Robert Palmer and Elkie Brooks. Palmer (*above*) also provided rhythm guitar duties.**

▼
**Palmer's rhythm playing with Vinegar Joe can be heard on 1972's *Rock 'n' Roll Gypsies*, an album that captures the raw energy of their shows.**

**Body style:** Single cutaway hollow body

**Materials:** Laminated maple body with set maple neck

**Finish:** Sunburst (6117, 6124); Two-tone green (6118, 6125)

**Fretboard:** Unbound ebony (rosewood after 1960)

**Frets:** 22

**Scale:** 24 ³/₅"

**Width at nut:** 1 ¹¹/₁₆"

**Bridge:** Roller bridge with G tailpiece or Bigsby vibrato

**Pickups:** 1 Filter'Tron pickup (6124, 6125); 2 Filter'Tron pickups (6117, 6118); HiLo'Trons used after 1960; 3-position selector switch

**Electrics:** Volume controls for each pickup; master volume control on cutaway bout; 2 tone filter switches on opposite bout

# GRETSCH DUO JET 1953

Fender's solid-body guitars. Indeed, it was only when Gibson entered the field that he sanctioned his own rival, and in 1953 the model Duo Jet first saw the light of day.

In truth, the Duo Jet is not a *true* solid-body guitar. While Leo Fender used a slab of solid ash for the bodies of his guitars, the Duo Jet's body was built using a number of pieces of mahogany with widely routed channels through which cables could be laid and electronic components fitted. A thin "lid" was then glued over the top of the arched body: on the earliest models this was covered in a shiny black plastic layer used on Gretsch drum shells.

The Duo Jet initially featured a pair of single-coil DeArmond pickups with a selector switch on the upper bout. The control layout is unorthodox in that there are three knobs (two volume and one tone) positioned directly beneath the bridge, but, curiously, an *overall* volume control on the cutaway bout.

Although the Gretsch company had existed since the 1880s, it wasn't until after the end of World War II that the brand established itself as a maker of high-quality instruments. Fred Gretsch had been skeptical about the lack of craftsmanship behind Leo

▲
George Harrison played Gretsch guitars on most of the early Beatles recordings— a Duo Jet (*above*) or a Country Gentleman. A controller styled on Harrison's Duo Jet is used with *The Beatles: Rock Band* game.

▼
One of the biggest-selling singles ever, "I Want To Hold Your Hand" (1963) features Harrison playing his Duo Jet.

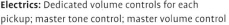

| | |
|---|---|
| **Body style:** | Single cutaway chambered solid body |
| **Materials:** | Mahogany with arched laminated maple top; set mahogany neck |
| **Finish:** | Black plastic finish (a few early examples exist in green) |
| **Fretboard:** | Ebony |
| **Frets:** | 22 |
| **Inlays:** | Block (Gretsch thumbnail on models from 1958) |
| **Scale:** | 24 3/5" |
| **Width at nut:** | 1 11/16" |
| **Bridge:** | Melita Synchro-Sonic |
| **Pickups:** | Two DeArmond (Filter'Trons used from 1958); three-way selector switch (two from 1958) |
| **Electrics:** | Dedicated volume controls for each pickup; master tone control; master volume control |

# GRETSCH SILVER JET 1955

the Silver Jet is an almost identical instrument except that it features a shimmering silver finish, again achieved with materials used on the shell coverings from Gretsch's drum range. This sort of finish, disliked by some players, was largely restricted to manufacturers that produced drums or accordions as well as guitars.

Like the Duo Jet, the Silver Jet featured Gretsch's revolutionary Melita Synchro-Sonic bridge. Designed by Sebastiano "Johnny" Melita, the bridge was the first to enable independent intonation adjustment for each string—a small screw on each of the six saddles could be turned to lengthen or reduce the scale length of the string.

Gretsch also added a third model derived from the Duo Jet. The 6130 Roundup aimed to cash in on the growing popularity of country music, and was adorned with western motifs, such as steer heads, cactuses, and a big G branded on the orange body.

Most Gretsch guitars show the name of the instrument on the headstock or pickguard. Each model also has a four-digit identity code. These can reflect cosmetic variations or differences in construction or components used. Issued shortly after the Duo Jet,

▲
**Billy Zoom emerged in the late 1970s with Los Angeles punk band X. He has played a Gretsch Silver Jet for most of his career. In 2009 Gretsch honored him with a signature model, the G6129BZ.**

▼
**Billy Zoom's Silver Jet is heard on *Los Angeles*, X's 1980 debut album.**

| | |
|---|---|
| **Body style:** | Single cutaway chambered "solid" body |
| **Materials:** | Mahogany with arched laminated maple top; set mahogany neck |
| **Finish:** | Silver "sparkle" plastic covering |
| **Fretboard:** | Ebony |
| **Frets:** | 22 |
| **Inlays:** | Block (Gretsch thumbnail on models from 1958) |
| **Scale:** | 24 3/5" |
| **Width at nut:** | 1 11/16" |
| **Bridge:** | Melita Synchro-Sonic |
| **Pickups:** | 2 DeArmond (Filter'Trons used from 1958); 3-way selector switch (2-way from 1958) |
| **Electrics:** | Dedicated volume controls for each pickup; master tone control; master volume control |

# GRETSCH WHITE PENGUIN 1955

T he "holy grail" of Gretsch instruments, the 1955 White Penguin is effectively the solid-body partner to the famous White Falcon (*see page 147*). It was so named, claimed long-term Gretsch employee Charles "Duke" Kramer, "because a penguin has a white front." It even

featured a cartoon penguin waddling its way across the gold pickguard.

The guitar's legendary status is largely down to the fact that nobody knows *precisely* how many originals were ever made: some experts have estimated that barely two dozen left the production line. This has created an unusual level of demand for such a modest guitar, with auction prices approaching $100,000—high for a guitar never owned by a noted deceased musician.

The White Penguin was issued to compete with the Gibson Les Paul, but was based broadly on the existing Duo Jet. It appeared in a snow-white finish with a metal armrest, gold-sparkle trim, gold-plated hardware, and red rhinestones set into the controls. The original White Penguin featured a Melita bridge and DeArmond pickups, which were replaced in 1958 with Filter'Tron double-coils. From 1961, the body design was changed from a single to a double cutaway.

▲
Jack White of both The White Stripes and The Raconteurs is one of an elite group that owns an original White Penguin. His very rare 1957 model can be seen in the video for the track "Icky Thump."

▼
Released in 2007, *Icky Thump* was The White Stripes' Grammy-winning sixth album. White's Gretsch 6134 features prominently.

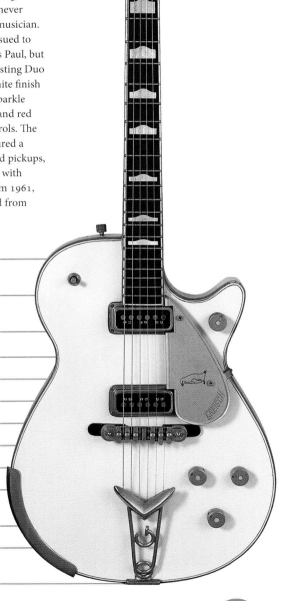

| | |
|---|---|
| **Body style:** | Single cutaway solid body (double cutaway from 1961) |
| **Materials:** | Mahogany body with laminated maple top; mahogany set neck |
| **Finish:** | Gloss white polyurethane lacquer |
| **Fretboard:** | Ebony |
| **Frets:** | 22 |
| **Inlays:** | Mother-of-pearl |
| **Scale:** | 24 ⅗" |
| **Width at nut:** | 1 ¹¹⁄₁₆" |
| **Bridge:** | Melita Synchro-Sonic |
| **Pickups:** | 2 DeArmond single-coil pickups (Gretsch Filter'Trons from 1958) |
| **Machine heads:** | Grover Imperial |
| **Electrics:** | Volume control for each pickup; master tone control; master volume control |

# GUILD F SERIES 1954

The Guild Guitar Company was founded in 1952 by music-store owner Avram "Al" Dronge and George Mann, a former executive with the rapidly declining Epiphone brand. Located in Manhattan, New York, the Guild workshop initially focused on archtop jazz guitars, both electric and acoustic. The Guild brand swiftly established itself as a maker of high-quality instruments, and the company was quickly forced to relocate to a larger factory in Hoboken, New Jersey.

At the beginning of the 1960s, sensing at close quarters the rapid international expansion of the New York folk scene, Guild shifted focus to acoustic guitars, producing two important ranges. The Dreadnought D series competed successfully with Martin's well-established D-18 model, Richie Havens famously opening 1969's Woodstock Festival with his Guild D-40. Meanwhile, the Jumbo F series became hugely popular with acoustic blues players, and was prized both for its volume and deep, rich, clear tone.

Even though Guild no longer exists as an independent company, both the brand and the F and D series are still in production, representing some of the best acoustic instruments available.

▲
**Mississippi John Hurt was one of a number of acoustic blues players to turn to the Guild F series in the 1960s.**

▼
**First recording in the 1920s, Hurt was rediscovered four decades later working as a sharecropper. His appearance at the 1964 Newport Folk Festival relaunched his career.**

| | |
|---|---|
| **Body style:** Jumbo acoustic | |
| **Materials:** Maple back and sides, Sitka spruce top; 3-piece mahogany/walnut/mahogany neck | |
| **Finish:** Gloss nitrocellulose lacquer | |
| **Bracing:** Scalloped red spruce | |
| **Fretboard:** Rosewood | |
| **Nut:** Bone | |
| **Inlays:** Mother-of-pearl and abalone block | |
| **Frets:** 20 | |
| **Scale:** 25 ⅝" | |
| **Width at nut:** 1 ¹¹⁄₁₆" | |
| **Bridge:** Ebony with bone saddle pins | |
| **Machine heads:** Gotoh | |
| **Electrics:** Optional D-TAR pickup on contemporary models | |

# GUILD DE-500 1960

Anyone asked at the beginning of 1960 to name the world's most famous guitarist probably would have come up with Duane Eddy. From the late 1950s Eddy enjoyed a string of hits—simple melodic instrumentals played on a twangy, reverberated guitar. Who

better, then, to be honored by a young, ambitious guitar company like Guild as the first rock 'n' roll musician to be given a signature model?

In 1960, Guild produced two Duane Eddy guitars, the DE-400 and the upscale DE-500. These were luxury instruments crafted from the finest woods and kitted out with gold-plated hardware and high-output DeArmond humbuckers, designed to produce Eddy's hallmark clean tone.

Guild thrived in the early 1960s, but struggled as the acoustic blues/folk vogue passed. In 1966 electronics giant Avnet Inc. took over and operations moved to a larger factory at Westerly, Rhode Island, until, in 1995, the Guild brand—like so many other classic guitar names—was brought under the wing of the mighty Fender corporation.

Guild guitars are now built in the former Ovation factory (also owned by Fender), at New Hartford, Connecticut.

▲
**Duane Eddy playing one of his Guild DE-500 signature models. Eddy was also associated with the Gretsch Chet Atkins range.**

▼
**The Duane Eddy sound can best be experienced on one of the many available *Greatest Hits* packages.**

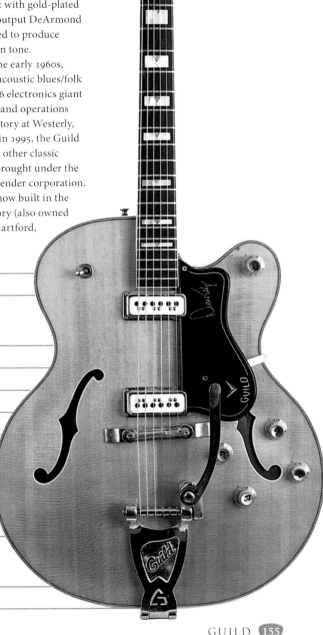

| | |
|---|---|
| **Body style:** | Single cutaway hollow body |
| **Materials:** | Curly maple back and sides, laminated spruce top; 3-piece mahogany /walnut/mahogany neck |
| **Finish:** | Natural or sunburst |
| **Fretboard:** | Bound ebony |
| **Inlays:** | Mother-of-pearl and abalone block |
| **Frets:** | 21 |
| **Scale:** | 24½" |
| **Width at nut:** | 1 11/16" |
| **Bridge:** | Guild Bigsby vibrato |
| **Pickups:** | 2 DeArmond humbuckers with 3-way selector switch |
| **Electrics:** | Dedicated volume and tone controls for each pickup; master volume on the cutaway bout |
| **Machine heads:** | Grover Rotomatic |

# GUYATONE LG-350 SHARP 5 1965

Founded in 1933 by Mitsuo Matsuki and Atsuo Kaneko, the company that became Guyatone was one of Japan's first guitar manufacturers and exporters to the United States. In Europe, the late 1950s LG range (including the LG-50) often arrived under other brand names (most famously Antoria). It was a first electric guitar for many teenagers, among them Hank Marvin and Rory Gallagher.

The success of U.S. surf band The Ventures with their Mosrite guitars had a huge impact on Guyatone models of the period, as it did on guitars from other Japanese makers active in the early 1960s. The body shape of the LG-350 is almost a mirror image of the famous Mosrite Ventures model—the beveled edging even has something approaching a German carve.

Guyatone generally produced guitars for the lower end of the market. Indeed, most that were exported to the U.S. were cheap, low-quality copies of well-known American models. However, the LG-350 is something

of an exception. Unusually, what we have here is a signature instrument built for a Japanese band, in this case a guitar instrumental five-piece called The Sharp 5—one of the country's most popular "eleki" acts of the mid-1960s. The band featured lead guitarist Nobuhiro Mine, who was an important influence on young Japanese players.

Armed with two single-coil pickups and an extremely sensitive vibrato mechanism, the LG-350 was ideally suited to The Sharp 5's guitar instrumentals, with a clinical tone that could cut clearly through an audio mix.

One of the best Japanese electric guitars of the mid-1960s, the LG-350 stood out among the plethora of poor imitations. Unfortunately, by the end of the decade the Japanese guitar industry had foundered, with the 1970s being mainly devoted to making cheap plywood copies of Fenders and Gibsons. But the LG-350 is evidence that Japan produced some fascinating and worthwhile curiosities during the 1960s.

▼
**The Sharp 5 were one of the most popular of Japan's "eleki" bands during the mid-1960s. Nobuhiro Mine was one of Japan's most famous guitarists of the period. He remains active today.**

| | |
|---|---|
| **Body style:** | Double cutaway solid body |
| **Materials:** | Maple with solid maple set neck |
| **Finish:** | Wide variety of color and "sparkle" finishes |
| **Fretboard:** | Rosewood |
| **Inlays:** | Acrylic dot |
| **Frets:** | 22 (not including zero fret) |
| **Scale:** | 25 ½" |
| **Width at nut:** | 1 ¹¹⁄₁₆" |
| **Bridge:** | Fixed vibrato |
| **Pickups:** | 2 or 3 high-powered single-coil Guyatone pickups; 3-way selector switch |
| **Electrics:** | Master volume and tone controls |

# HAGSTROM P46 DELUXE 1958

Based in Älvdalen, Sweden, Albin Hagström began building accordions in 1932, quickly establishing a reputation across Europe.

In 1958, Hagstrom became one of the first large-scale producers of electric guitars outside of the United States. The company's manufacturing roots are very apparent on the early Deluxe models, which feature a distinctive sparkle and pearloid celluloid finish previously used to decorate accordions.

Top of the early Hagstrom line was the P46 Deluxe. While the guitar itself appeared a relatively unremarkable take on a Les Paul, the pickup assembly was certainly unorthodox. Arguably the first production-line instrument sporting four pickups, the P46 provided an unusual degree of sonic versatility. The pickups were grouped as pairs in the standard neck and bridge positions, separated by a gold grill. Master volume and tone was controlled by roller wheels on either edge of the unit above the pickups. Pickup selection was achieved through six push-button switches covering numerous combinations of the four single-coil pickups.

Also unusual is the translucent lucite fingerboard—an effect reminiscent of Hagstrom's accordion range.

▲
**Nick McCarthy of Scottish band Franz Ferdinand has frequently performed with a Hagstrom P46 Deluxe.**

▼
**The P46 Deluxe can be heard on Franz Ferdinand's 2004 debut album.**

| | |
|---|---|
| **Body style:** | Single cutaway solid body |
| **Materials:** | Birch covered with pearloid celluloid finish; bolt-on birch neck with H-bar truss rod |
| **Finish:** | Assorted pearloid finishes |
| **Fretboard:** | Lucite |
| **Inlays:** | Acrylic block |
| **Frets:** | 22 |
| **Scale:** | 25 ½" |
| **Width at nut:** | 1 11/16" |
| **Bridge:** | Vibrato |
| **Pickups:** | 4 single-coil pickups in two pairs; 6 switches: LH (bridge and neck together); L (bridge); H (neck); O (off); Solo (or lead, a volume boost); Acc (rhythm, allows volume cut) |
| **Electrics:** | Roller-wheel master volume and tone controls |

# HAUSER 1935

The Hauser name represents the most prominent dynasty in the world of classical guitar. The workshop, founded by Josef Hauser in Munich, Germany, in the 1870s, primarily produced zithers. It was Josef's son, Hermann, who would establish Hauser as the most significant luthier since Torres, filing patents on aspects of construction, such as the body-neck joint.

Leading classical players of the early twentieth century, such as Segovia and Llobet, all used instruments crafted by Hermann Hauser I. (The numeral is used to differentiate him from the son and grandson who succeeded him, both named Hermann.)

In 1930 Hauser's son Hermann II joined his father's business, taking over in 1952. His own son, Hermann III, began building guitars independently in the same workshop, and is now widely viewed as one of the world's leading luthiers.

Crafting each Herman III guitar takes up to 240 hours, and so the workshop, based in Reisbach since the heavy bombing of Munich in World War II, can rarely produce more than seventeen guitars a year. Potential buyers can expect to join a waiting list of well over five years.

The model shown here was built in 1935 by Hermann Hauser I.

▲
**Between 1959 and 1963, British classical maestro Julian Bream exclusively used a guitar built for him by Hermann Hauser II.**

▼
**Segovia used a Hauser as his concert guitar from 1932 to 1937. Bream's own Hauser can be heard on *The Art Of Julian Bream* (1960).**

| | |
|---|---|
| **Body style:** | Classical |
| **Materials:** | Indian rosewood back and sides; German spruce soundboard; Honduran mahogany neck |
| **Fretboard:** | Ebony |
| **Finish:** | French polished |
| **Fan struts:** | 3 center fans left square underneath the bridge area |
| **Bridge plate:** | Spruce bridge plate with fan struts notched over plate |
| **Frets:** | 19 (including partial fret) |
| **Scale:** | 25 3/5" |
| **Width at nut:** | 2 1/20" |
| **Bridge:** | Top constructed flat, the bridge bellied and top forced into bridge |

# HERNÁNDEZ 1925

Flamenco evolved from the folk music of the southern regions of Spain. Initially unaccompanied singing, songs were later accompanied by guitar, hand-clapping, foot-stamping, and dance. Flamenco guitar evolved into a popular art form in its own right, with outstanding musicians such as Sabicas and Ramón

Montoya widely admired throughout the world. The flamenco guitar differs from its classical counterpart. Reflecting the poverty of flamenco players, cheaper woods such as cypress were used for the body. Lighter than traditional rosewood, this helps give the instrument its charactertistically earthy percussive tone.

Santos Hernández has been described as "the Stradivarius of flamenco." Born in 1873 in Madrid, Hernández learned his craft under master luthier Manuel Ramirez, by whom he was employed for twenty-three years. When Ramirez died in 1916 he set up on his own, his workshop becoming a popular meeting place for flamenco players of the day.

Hernández guitars were built in the tradition of Antonio Torres. They were designed for a strong attack and power. But Santos added an innovative downward-sloping harmonic bar beneath the soundboard, giving the treble a firmer sound.

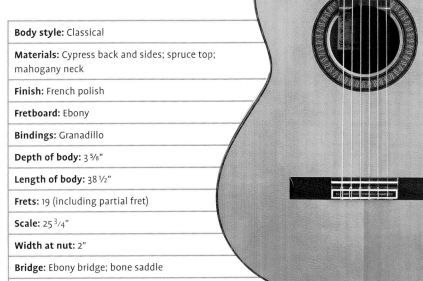

▲

Sabicas is one of the most celebrated flamenco guitarists. He played Hernández guitars throughout his career.

▼

Sabicas appears on the album *Flamencan Guitar Solos*. Chet Atkins thought Sabicas the world's most technically gifted guitarist.

| | |
|---|---|
| **Body style:** | Classical |
| **Materials:** | Cypress back and sides; spruce top; mahogany neck |
| **Finish:** | French polish |
| **Fretboard:** | Ebony |
| **Bindings:** | Granadillo |
| **Depth of body:** | 3 ⅝" |
| **Length of body:** | 38 ½" |
| **Frets:** | 19 (including partial fret) |
| **Scale:** | 25 ¾" |
| **Width at nut:** | 2" |
| **Bridge:** | Ebony bridge; bone saddle |
| **Bracing:** | 7-strut fan bracing |

# HOFNER GALAXIE 1960

O ver the past two decades, as the well of vintage American guitars has gradually dried, and prices have spiraled ever higher, there has been a growing interest among collectors in instruments built in Europe and Japan. During the 1960s Hofner was one of the largest manufacturers of electric guitars outside of America, and, while few would claim they produced instruments to rival Gibson, Fender, or Gretsch, they are now viewed as increasingly desirable to collect.

Violin maker Karl Höfner founded the company in Schönbach, Germany, in 1887. Establishing a reputation for craftsmanship and innovation, Höfner—later joined by his two sons, Josef and Walter—quickly became the largest manufacturer of stringed and fretted instruments in Germany.

In the prewar years, Hofner's small guitar production concentrated on low-cost student instruments, but from the 1950s attempts were made at producing upmarket archtop acoustics and solid-body electric guitars and basses.

Most early Hofners were variations on standard Fender designs. Launched in 1960, the Galaxie featured three humbucking pickups with an unusual array of controls, notably dedicated on/off switches and a rotary tone wheel for each pickup.

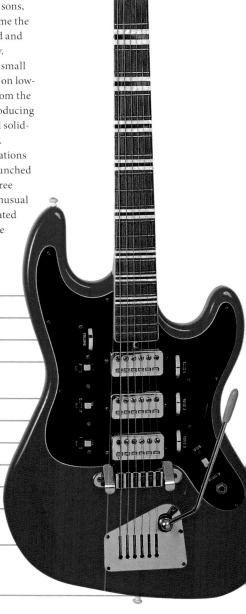

▲
Hofner guitars were marketed widely outside Germany. In the U.K. at the end of the 1950s, when a trade embargo made desirable Fender and Gibson models almost impossible to find, many young guitar players saw owning a Hofner as a decent alternative. The Hofner brand fared less well in the U.S. where transit costs and import duty rendered them absurdly expensive—even rivaling Gibsons and Gretsches.

| | |
|---|---|
| **Body style:** | Double cutaway, offset waist solid body |
| **Materials:** | Obeche body; maple set neck |
| **Fretboard:** | Rosewood |
| **Finish:** | Assorted finishes possible, but most were red cellulose or red vinyl |
| **Inlays:** | Celluloid |
| **Frets:** | 22 |
| **Scale:** | 25 ½" |
| **Width at nut:** | 1 ¹¹⁄₁₆" |
| **Bridge:** | Hofner vibrato assembly |
| **Pickups:** | 3 humbucking pickups; individual on/off switches for each pickup |
| **Electrics:** | Master volume and tone control; rotary wheel tone controls for each pickup (some models fitted with rhythm/solo switch) |

# HOFNER 500/1 1956

By the end of World War II, Walter Höfner, a creative businessman as well as innovative guitar and violin maker, was running the company. In 1955 he used his expertise in these two disciplines to create the extraordinary model 500/1, a semi-hollow bass guitar with a violin-shaped body.

In 1961, while The Beatles were serving a grueling apprenticeship in the nightclubs of Hamburg's Reeperbahn, bass guitarist Stu Sutcliffe was ejected from the band. Paul McCartney agreed a switch from guitar and hastily began checking out Hamburg's music stores for a bass of his own. The problem for the left-handed McCartney was that all of the right-handed bass guitars he tried felt awkward when turned upside down . . . until he found the symmetrical 500/1, which could easily be played either way.

McCartney would use a Hofner bass throughout his Beatles career, providing Hofner with the kind of publicity that no money could ever buy.

The Hofner story cannot, of course, be told without mention of the most famous pop group of them all—The Beatles. Just as the patronage of John Lennon and George Harrison had turned Rickenbacker into a household name, Hofner would enjoy the Paul McCartney effect.

▲
Paul McCartney owned two 500/1s: his original 1961 model, and a modified 1962 model (*above*) given to him by the Hofner company.

▼
McCartney exclusively played his "violin bass" until 1965, after which he also used a Rickenbacker 4001. The 500/1 can be heard on 1965's *Rubber Soul*.

| | |
|---|---|
| **Body style:** | Violin-shaped hollow body |
| **Materials:** | Spruce top, laminated maple back and sides; 2-piece set maple neck |
| **Finish:** | Sunburst; nitrocellulose lacquer |
| **Fretboard:** | Rosewood |
| **Inlays:** | Pearloid |
| **Frets:** | 22 |
| **Scale:** | 30" |
| **Width at nut:** | 1 9/16" |
| **Bridge:** | Hofner ebony |
| **Pickups:** | 2 Hofner Nova-Sonic humbuckers; selector switch for each pickup |
| **Electrics:** | Volume control for each pickup; bass/treble switch |

# IBANEZ : THE STORY

The Ibanez product catalog of 1975.

1985 Ibanez Axstar.

Steve Vai plays the Ibanez Jem.

T he Japanese Ibanez brand is now one of the largest guitar manufacturers in the world. However, the Ibanez name has a curiously convoluted history dating back to 1870, when luthier Salvador Ibáñez opened his first workshop in Valencia, Spain. Ibáñez made highly regarded classical guitars that were sold throughout Europe and imported to Japan by the Hoshino Gakki company of Nagoya. The Spanish Civil War (1936–39) saw periods of heavy fighting in Valencia—and, in one bloody battle, the Ibáñez workshop was destroyed, with many of the workforce losing their lives. The two Ibáñez sons who had taken over the company after Salvador's death in 1920 also perished in the Civil War.

No longer able to supply Ibáñez guitars, Hoshino Gakki bought the rights to the name from the surviving members of the family in Spain, and began successfully building Salvador Ibáñez guitars exclusively for the Japanese market. In an unfortunate repetition of the fate of the Salvador Ibáñez workshop in Valencia, the Hoshino factory was destroyed in 1945 during a bombing raid and was not able to resume business for another five years.

In 1957, guitars produced by Hoshino were being branded simply "Ibanez," and in 1962 the company first entered the electric guitar market. Early catalogs show a mixture of curious Japanese designs and copies of well-established American and European models, notably— and perhaps surprisingly—models by Hagstrom and Burns. But at the end of the 1960s, demand for low-end electric guitars started to wane, and many manufacturers failed to weather the storm.

By the end of the 1970s, guitars such as the Yamaha SG-2000 had proved that instruments of the highest quality could be made in Japan, and Ibanez set a new course by concentrating primarily on making original instruments. ❶ The next decade saw the appearance of such fine ranges as the Iceman, Maxxas, Blazer, Roadstar, and Axstar. ❷

Also important to Ibanez has been its artist collaborations. They began in the late 1970s with the George Benson and Paul Stanley (of KISS) models, continuing from the late 1980s with the Jem and 7-string Universe ranges developed with guitar pyrotechnician Steve Vai. ❸

Ibanez now carries one of the world's largest ranges of production guitars, catering to the pocket of any level of musician.

**1870**
Salvador Ibáñez starts to build guitars in Valencia, Spain

**1929**
Matsujiro Hoshino imports Salvador Ibáñez acoustic guitars

**1935**
Hoshino Gakki builds its own Salvador Ibáñez acoustic guitars

**1945**
Hoshino factory is destroyed during a wartime bombing raid

**1975**
Ibanez produces the Iceman model as part of the Artist series

**1977**
Ibanez produces the George Benson signature model

**1987**
Ibanez produces the critically lauded Jem with Steve Vai

# IBANEZ : THE FAMILY TREE (1964-PRESENT)

The sheer volume of different models produced since the late 1950s makes an exhaustive Ibanez family tree an impossibility. Shown here are a number of strands that indicate the way in which Ibanez—above all other Japanese guitar makers—evolved from supplying cheap imitations of Fender, Gibson, Rickenbacker, and Burns guitars; then creating copies that sometimes outperformed the originals; and finally producing originals that leading players have often chosen over the classic U.S. brands.

**2375N (1975–78)**

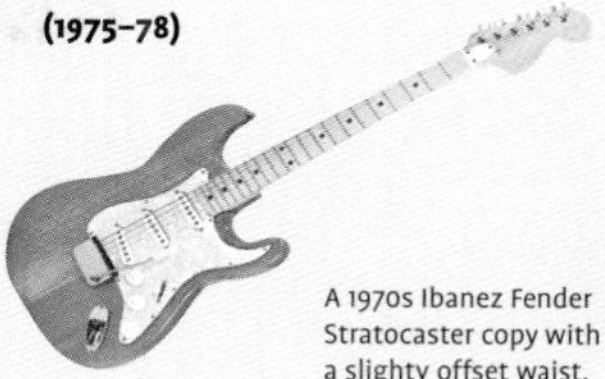

A 1970s Ibanez Fender Stratocaster copy with a slighty offset waist.

**FIREBRAND (1974–77)**

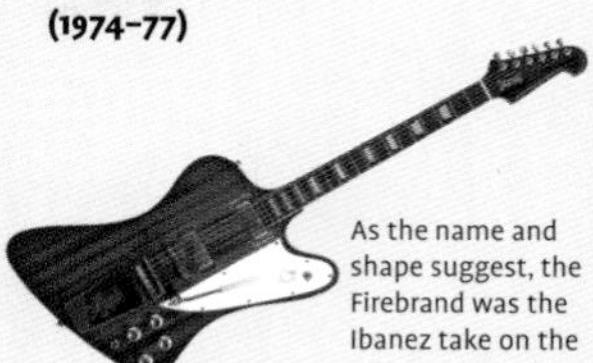

As the name and shape suggest, the Firebrand was the Ibanez take on the Gibson Firebird.

**3 (64)**

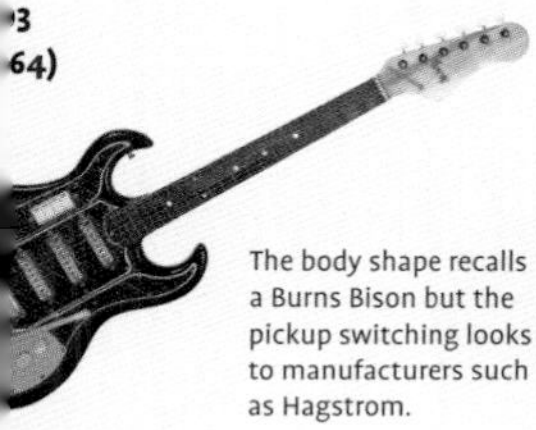

The body shape recalls a Burns Bison but the pickup switching looks to manufacturers such as Hagstrom.

**2350 CUSTOM (1975–78)**

A high-quality Les Paul copy. One of the "lawsuit guitars" that prompted legal action by Gibson.

**ROADSTAR (1979–PRESENT)**

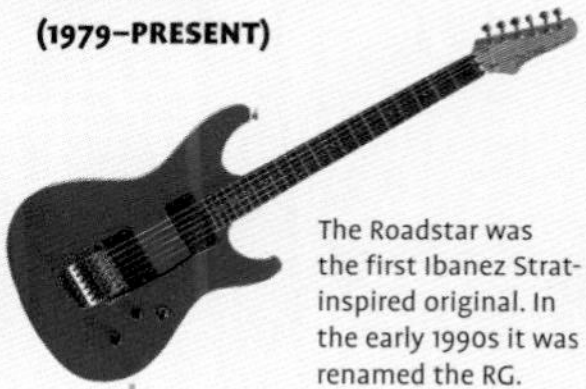

The Roadstar was the first Ibanez Strat-inspired original. In the early 1990s it was renamed the RG.

**ICEMAN (1975–PRESENT)**

An Ibanez classic, the Iceman is the Firebird shape given a uniquely oriental twist.

**STAR 85–86**

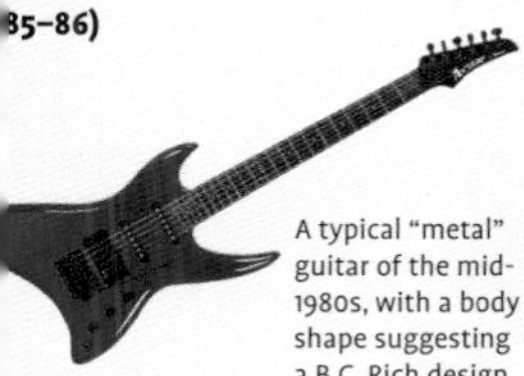

A typical "metal" guitar of the mid-1980s, with a body shape suggesting a B.C. Rich design.

**SABER (1987–PRESENT)**

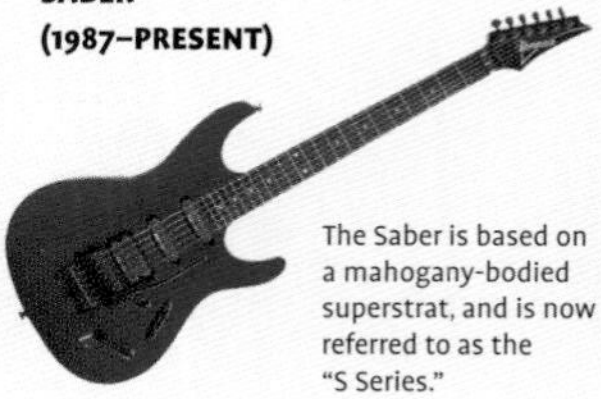

The Saber is based on a mahogany-bodied superstrat, and is now referred to as the "S Series."

**PRO LINE (1985–86)**

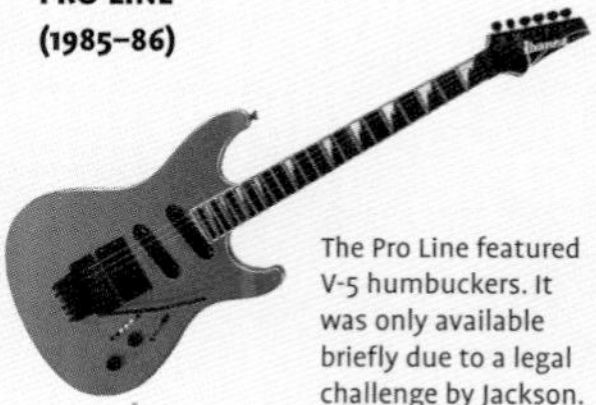

The Pro Line featured V-5 humbuckers. It was only available briefly due to a legal challenge by Jackson.

**DESTROYER (1975–PRESENT)**

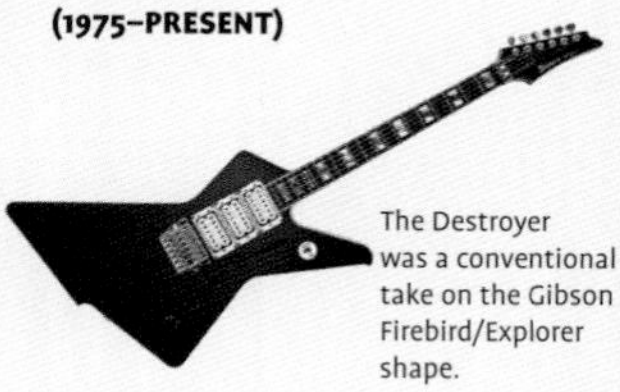

The Destroyer was a conventional take on the Gibson Firebird/Explorer shape.

**500 85–87**

Uncommon Ibanez from the "hair rock" era.

**UNIVERSE (1990–PRESENT)**

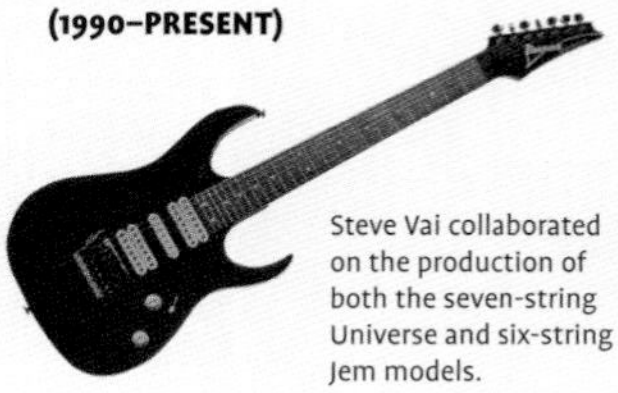

Steve Vai collaborated on the production of both the seven-string Universe and six-string Jem models.

**JEM (1987–PRESENT)**

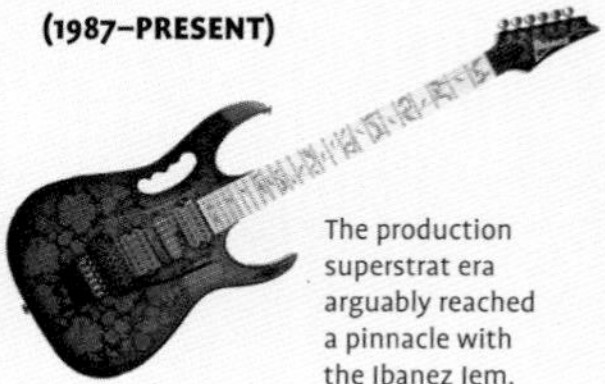

The production superstrat era arguably reached a pinnacle with the Ibanez Jem.

## IBANEZ "LAWSUIT" GUITARS

Guitars initially made by Ibanez, like most of the instruments produced by the major Japanese companies in the 1960s, were copies of famous models from the West. During the 1970s, high-quality Ibanez Gibson copies began to infiltrate the U.S., resulting in a lawsuit in 1977. Strangely enough, the case was brought by Gibson for copying headstock designs rather than body shapes. Ibanez agreed an out-of-court settlement, and Ibanez thereafter concentrated on producing "original" guitars, including some of the best production superstrats.

**XXAS 7–90**

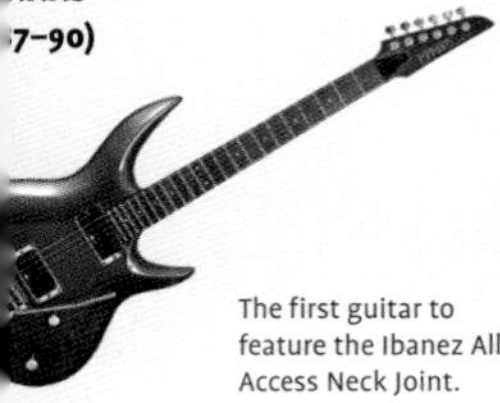

The first guitar to feature the Ibanez All Access Neck Joint.

**SHRG1Z (2007–8)**

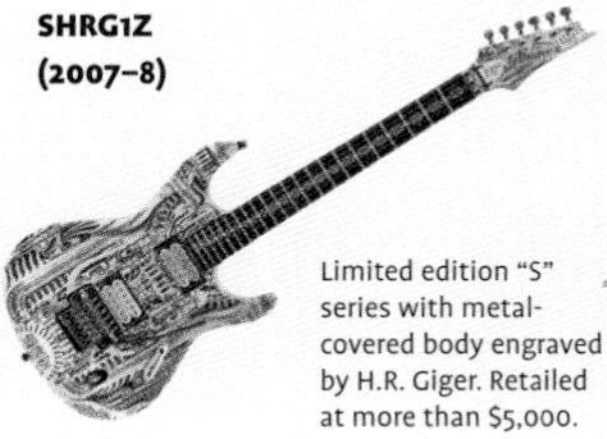

Limited edition "S" series with metal-covered body engraved by H.R. Giger. Retailed at more than $5,000.

**JEM 10TH ANNIVERSARY (1996–97)**

Limited edition model with chrome hardware and certificate of authenticity signed by Steve Vai.

# IBANEZ 1803 "BISON" 1964

Like other Japanese guitar manufacturers of the 1960s, Ibanez responded to the "eleki" craze—which saw Japanese youth *en masse* forming electric guitar-based beat groups, often to play instrumental music—by building cheap copies of guitars from the West.

The earliest Ibanez solid-body electric guitars appeared in the late 1950s and were built by Guyatone. The instruments appeared under the brand names of either Ibanez or Star. However, in 1962, Hoshino Gakki, the company owning the Ibanez brand name, built its own factory and began producing its own guitars.

In the early 1960s, rather than attempting to emulate the famous American guitars produced by Gibson, Fender, Mosrite, and others, Ibanez launched a number of instruments reflecting European designs, from such makers as Sweden's Hagstrom, Italy's Eko, and Britain's Burns.

The Ibanez 1803 guitar featured here (*see right*) is clearly modeled on the Burns Bison (*see below*). Not only

are the unique double cutaway horns of the Burns closely reproduced, but also the original's unusual narrow six-in-line headstock. In one departure from the Burns, the design of the 1803 gives a passing nod to Fender; its asymmetric lower bout design is highly reminiscent of the Jazzmaster.

There is even a distinctly European influence on the electrical components. Like many German and Italian guitars of the period, this Ibanez features a series of chunky on/off rocker switches for each pickup, rather than the three-way toggle selector switching more typically found on American guitars of the period. The advantage of the European arrangement is that it provides the player with every possible configuration of pickup combinations—something a conventional American three- or five-way switch cannot match.

The Hoshino factory was closed in 1966, a casualty of a downturn in the Japanese guitar market, and guitar production switched to the Teisco plant in Tokyo.

▼
**The horns of the British-built Burns Bison are somewhat sharper than those of the Ibanez copy.**

| | |
|---|---|
| **Body style:** | Heavily curved double cutaway solid body |
| **Materials:** | Mahogany body with maple neck |
| **Finish:** | Sunburst |
| **Fretboard:** | Rosewood |
| **Inlays:** | Acrylic dot |
| **Frets:** | 21 |
| **Scale:** | 25" |
| **Width at nut:** | 1 11/16" |
| **Bridge:** | Vibrato |
| **Pickups:** | 3 single-coil pickups; individual rocker switches for each pickup |
| **Electrics:** | Master volume, bass, and treble controls |

# IBANEZ ICEMAN 1975

and the Greco guitar company produced a peculiarly oriental take on the Gibson Explorer body shape. Greco retained the exclusive rights to sell the guitar in Japan, calling it the Mirage; Hoshino held the export rights, and, when first issued in 1975, it was a part of the Ibanez Artist range—three years later this was changed to the Iceman.

The Iceman/Mirage came in a number of different forms, with pickup configurations, woods, and construction methods varying with price. Production continued into 1983 when the Iceman II was issued, the principal visual difference being the introduction of six in-line tuners.

Paul Stanley of US glam-rockers Kiss was the first major rock celebrity to use an Ibanez, favoring an Iceman until he began endorsing his own Washburn signature models. Daron Malakian of System Of A Down has his own signature guitar, the Ibanez DMM1, based on the Iceman shape.

**D**uring the 1970s Hoshino Gakki, the company that owned the Ibanez brand name, took a decision to step away from making cheap Gibson and Fender replicas, instead producing a guitar with a uniquely Japanese flavor. A design collaboration between Hoshino

▲
Daron Malakian of high-speed metal band System Of A Down plays his modern-day signature version of the Iceman.

▼
Malakian used his DMM1 Iceman on System Of A Down's *Mezmerize* album from 2005.

| | |
|---|---|
| **Body style:** | Offset waist single cutaway with extended upper treble bout |
| **Materials:** | Mahogany body with maple neck |
| **Finish:** | Available in a wide variety of colors and designs |
| **Fretboard:** | Rosewood |
| **Inlays:** | Acrylic block |
| **Frets:** | 22 |
| **Scale:** | $24\,^3/_4$" |
| **Width at nut:** | $1\,^{11}/_{16}$" |
| **Bridge:** | Gibraltar bridge with Quickchange tailpiece |
| **Pickups:** | Depending on model, 1 or 2 Super 70 anti-hum (*shown right*), Super 2000, Triple Coil, and V2; 3-way selector switch on 2-pickup models |
| **Machine heads:** | Velve-Tune |
| **Electrics:** | Master volume and tone controls (dedicated on 2-pickup models) |

# IBANEZ JEM 77 BFP 1987

since the 1980s with Steve Vai, one of rock's most technically gifted guitarists.

Vai had previously used a custom-built instrument by Tom Anderson, but in 1986 took up an offer to design his own production guitar for Ibanez. The result, the Jem, is perhaps the ultimate superstrat, designed for high-speed playing with an unusual configuration of DiMarzio pickups providing every sound a rock guitarist could require.

First appearing in 1987, the Jem series polarized players over its garish looks—bright clashing colors, floral patterns, and pyramid imagery—and the unique "monkey grip" handle. But every aspect of the guitar had been carefully considered for the metal player, from the dive-bomb Floyd Rose vibrato to the scalloped frets at the top of the scale. On the five-way pickup selector, positions two and four combine the center single-coil with *one* of the coils from the humbuckers.

B y the end of the twentieth century, Ibanez was one of the world's leading guitar manufacturers, with arguably the largest range of instruments in production. Underlining the firm's ambitions has been their involvement

▲
**Steve Vai received a perfect grounding as a young player, subjected to the rigorous discipline of the Frank Zappa band. In 2004 he published his *30-Hour Path To Virtuoso Enlightenment*—a practice regimen to be worked through in three ten-hour sessions!**

▼
**Vai's pyrotechnical Jem playing can be heard on his 1996 *Fire Garden* album.**

| | |
|---|---|
| **Body style:** | Double cutaway solid body with "monkey grip" |
| **Materials:** | American basswood body with bolt-on maple neck (scalloped on top 4 frets) |
| **Finish:** | Wide assortment of plain and decorative finishes |
| **Fretboard:** | Maple |
| **Inlays:** | Dependent on model |
| **Frets:** | 24 |
| **Scale:** | 25½" |
| **Width at nut:** | 1 $^{11}$⁄₁₆" |
| **Bridge:** | Ibanez Edge tremolo (licensed from Floyd Rose) with stud lock and block lock |
| **Pickups:** | 2 DiMarzio X2 PAF Pro humbuckers, 1 DiMarzio X1 single-coil pickup; 5-position switch (1, bridge humbucker; 2, center + one coil of bridge humbucker; 3, center; 4, center + one coil of neck humbucker; 5, neck humbucker) |
| **Electrics:** | Master volume and tone controls |

# IBANEZ UNIVERSE 1990

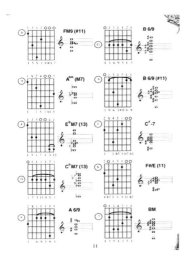

W hen the Ibanez Jem was launched in 1987, the company made a further declaration of innovation by producing the Universe—the first ever large-scale production seven-string guitar. Such instruments were by no means a new concept: in Russia, the seven-string acoustic guitar was the norm until well into the twentieth century, and similar instruments are used in Brazilian music. In 1938, Epiphone created interest by building a seven-string archtop guitar for American jazz musician George Van Eps, but the idea of adding an extra string interested only a tiny number of players.

Driven by Steve Vai's interest in evolving the electric guitar, Ibanez produced a seven-string version of the Jem. Vai took the most common approach and added a bass string tuned to B—the same interval as the bottom four strings on a standard guitar: thus, a twenty-four-fret instrument like the Universe has an extraordinary note range: four octaves and five half-steps.

The Universe may not have exactly changed the electric guitar landscape, but it has found a niche among forward-thinking metal players.

▲
All Ibanez Universe models were accompanied by Steve Vai's own introductory book containing chord and scale exercises designed for seven-string playing.

▼
Vai showcased the Universe on 1990's *Passion And Warfare*, viewed by many as the greatest guitar instrumental album of all time.

| | |
|---|---|
| **Body style:** Double cutaway solid body | |
| **Materials:** American basswood with bolt-on maple or wenge neck | |
| **Finish:** Assorted plain and decorative finishes | |
| **Fretboard:** Rosewood (occasionally maple) | |
| **Inlays:** Dependent on design | |
| **Frets:** 24 | |
| **Scale:** 25 ½" | |
| **Width at nut:** 1 ⁹/₁₀" | |
| **Bridge:** Ibanez Edge tremolo (licensed from Floyd Rose) with stud lock and block lock | |
| **Pickups:** 2 DiMarzio X2 PAF Pro humbuckers, 1 DiMarzio X1 single-coil pickup; 5-position switch (1, bridge humbucker; 2, center + one coil of bridge humbucker; 3, center; 4, center + one coil of neck humbucker; 5, neck humbucker) | |
| **Electrics:** Master volume and tone controls for each pickup | |

# JACKSON GUITARS : THE STORY

**Eddie Van Halen with his custom-built Charvel superstrat.**

**Corey Beaulieu of U.S. metal band Trivium plays a Jackson Randy Rhoads model.**

**First produced in 1990, the Warrior was one of Jackson's high-spec rock guitars.**

It would be difficult to tell the story of Jackson Guitars without detailing the company's close relationship to the Charvel brand . . . and, indeed, the man who founded the company, Wayne Charvel.

Wayne Charvel had opened Charvel's Guitar Repair in Azusa, California, in the early 1970s. Beginning with set-ups, light repair, and refinishing, the business gradually evolved to building custom guitars. Charvel ran into problems when a failed sales and marketing deal ended in litigation. During this time, jobbing guitarist Grover Jackson—then contemplating an alternative career—met Charvel while looking for guitar parts at his shop. Jackson, convinced he could turn around Charvel's business, agreed to work for him in exchange for 10 percent of the business. Slowly, the Charvel brand began to gain recognition among rock guitar players on the West Coast. A year later, in 1979, Charvel's personal financial worries became more acute, and to prevent Charvel declaring the company bankrupt Jackson offered to buy him out for around $40,000.

With the more dynamic Jackson in control of the business, the profile of the Charvel brand was already on the rise when a young guitar player named Eddie Van Halen began to use a Charvel superstrat. In 1978, Van Halen appeared on the cover of his band's debut album—viewed widely as one of *the* great rock classics—sporting his Charvel, complete with what would become his hallmark personally customized striped decor. ① Demand for Charvels exploded as the album gained recognition.

That same year, Jackson was approached by Ozzy Osbourne's guitarist, Randy Rhoads, to produce a high-spec Flying V. ② The resulting instrument, which would eventually be named after the guitarist following his untimely death in 1982, was deemed too extreme to fit in with the Charvel range, and so was launched under the Jackson brand, which would quickly gain a reputation for producing high-end rock guitars. ③

The Jackson and Charvel lines flourished alongside each other. In the mid-1980s, wanting to expand his business, Jackson merged with the International Music Corporation. Finding himself unsuited to corporate life, Jackson sold the rest of his share to IMC in 1990. In 2002, the Jackson and Charvel brands were bought by the mighty Fender Corporation, already owner of such distinguished marques as Gretsch and Guild.

**1979**
Grover Jackson buys Charvel company from Wayne Charvel

**1980**
Debut album by Van Halen features a Charvel on the cover

**1982**
Launch of the Jackson Randy Rhoads model

**1984**
Jackson Soloist superstrat goes into production

**1985**
Charvel guitar production switches to Japan

**1990**
Grover Jackson sells his shares in the company to IMC

**2002**
Fender buys Jackson and Charvel brands. All new models are built in Corona, California

# JACKSON : THE FAMILY TREE (1981-PRESENT)

Grover Jackson is often described as the "Father of the superstrat." His background working with Wayne Charvel was in modifying existing production instruments, or producing "souped-up" alternatives from scratch.

If we look at the complete catalog of Jackson and Charvel guitars, it is clear that almost all are based on classic American designs from the 1950s. Most, of course, are modeled on the Fender Stratocaster, but also significant in the Jackson evolutionary path are the late 1950s Gibson

"modernist" guitars—the Flying V and Explorer. The drooping headstock of the latter would become a feature of many "metal" guitars produced from the 1980s, starting with Jackson's own Soloist. The two vintage Gibsons also merged to produce Jackson's first, and arguably most enduring design, the Randy Rhoads.

The vogue for superstrats began to fade during the 1990s, and, somewhat ironically, in 2002 Jackson found itself the subject of a takeover . . . by Fender.

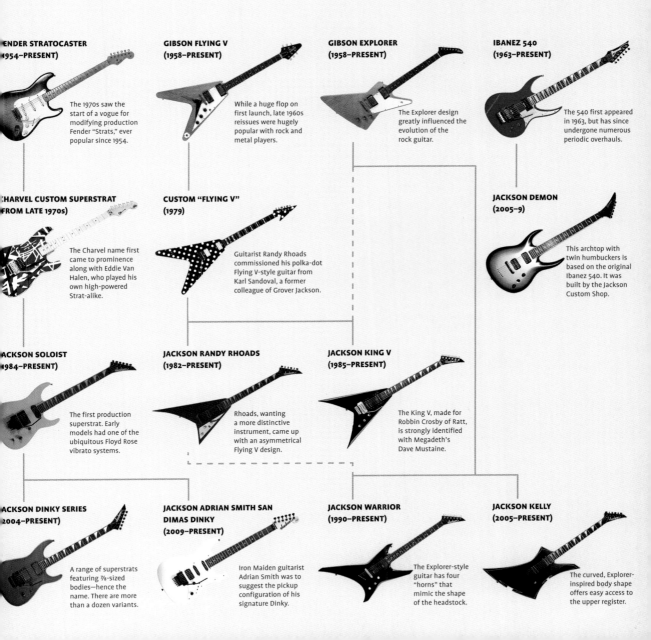

**FENDER STRATOCASTER (1954–PRESENT)**

The 1970s saw the start of a vogue for modifying production Fender "Strats," ever popular since 1954.

**GIBSON FLYING V (1958–PRESENT)**

While a huge flop on first launch, late 1960s reissues were hugely popular with rock and metal players.

**GIBSON EXPLORER (1958–PRESENT)**

The Explorer design greatly influenced the evolution of the rock guitar.

**IBANEZ 540 (1963–PRESENT)**

The 540 first appeared in 1963, but has since undergone numerous periodic overhauls.

**CHARVEL CUSTOM SUPERSTRAT (FROM LATE 1970s)**

The Charvel name first came to prominence along with Eddie Van Halen, who played his own high-powered Strat-alike.

**CUSTOM "FLYING V" (1979)**

Guitarist Randy Rhoads commissioned his polka-dot Flying V-style guitar from Karl Sandoval, a former colleague of Grover Jackson.

**JACKSON DEMON (2005–9)**

This archtop with twin humbuckers is based on the original Ibanez 540. It was built by the Jackson Custom Shop.

**JACKSON SOLOIST (1984–PRESENT)**

The first production superstrat. Early models had one of the ubiquitous Floyd Rose vibrato systems.

**JACKSON RANDY RHOADS (1982–PRESENT)**

Rhoads, wanting a more distinctive instrument, came up with an asymmetrical Flying V design.

**JACKSON KING V (1985–PRESENT)**

The King V, made for Robbin Crosby of Ratt, is strongly identified with Megadeth's Dave Mustaine.

**JACKSON DINKY SERIES (2004–PRESENT)**

A range of superstrats featuring ¾-sized bodies—hence the name. There are more than a dozen variants.

**JACKSON ADRIAN SMITH SAN DIMAS DINKY (2009–PRESENT)**

Iron Maiden guitarist Adrian Smith was to suggest the pickup configuration of his signature Dinky.

**JACKSON WARRIOR (1990–PRESENT)**

The Explorer-style guitar has four "horns" that mimic the shape of the headstock.

**JACKSON KELLY (2005–PRESENT)**

The curved, Explorer-inspired body shape offers easy access to the upper register.

# JACKSON RANDY RHOADS 1981

The Jackson story begins in 1981 when Randy Rhoads, the highly rated guitarist with Ozzy Osbourne's Blizzard Of Ozz approached Charvel Guitars to build him his own take on the Flying V. Soon after, he commissioned a second instrument, this time with the upper half of the body extended to resemble a shark's fin. Charvel owner Grover Jackson decided to put the design into production but, considering its outrageous shape, decided to brand it a Jackson guitar. Christened the Concorde, it quickly became Rhoads' main guitar. Two further production prototypes were built for Rhoads' approval, but they were never tested: tragically, on March 19, 1982, Rhoads was killed in an air crash. The guitar would go into production that same year but was renamed in honor of the late guitarist.

The Jackson Randy Rhoads features Seymour Duncan humbucking pickups, a Floyd Rose locking tremolo system, and flattened frets to aid high-speed lead work. Unsurprisingly, the guitar has been embraced principally by the hard rock fraternity, in particular metal soloists.

Randy Rhoads is now acknowledged as an influential player, and frequently appears near the top of "all-time-great" playing polls.

▲
**Randy Rhoads was playing guitar with the band Quiet Riot when he came to the attention of former Black Sabbath frontman Ozzy Osbourne.**

▼
*Diary Of A Madman* **was Rhoads's final album. He played his Jackson Concorde throughout.**

| | |
|---|---|
| **Body style:** | Extended "Flying V" solid body |
| **Materials:** | Maple body and maple through-neck (later versions have featured an alder body and a bolt-on maple neck) |
| **Finish:** | Black (original); many different colors and custom graphics available on later models |
| **Fretboard:** | Ebony |
| **Inlays:** | Acrylic diagonally sliced block |
| **Frets:** | 22 (24 on later models) |
| **Scale:** | 25 ½" |
| **Width at nut:** | 1 ¹¹⁄₁₆" |
| **Bridge:** | Locking tremolo system (originally Floyd Rose) |
| **Pickups:** | 1 or 2 Seymour Duncan humbuckers; 3-way selector switch |
| **Electrics:** | Master volume and tone controls (dedicated volume controls on early models) |

# JACKSON SOLOIST 1984

Best known as a Stratocaster man, Jeff Beck also used a Jackson Soloist during the mid-1980s.

Whether or not Grover Jackson was indeed the "Father of the superstrat," he was certainly instrumental in the popularization of the genre. During the 1970s, the reputations of Fender and Gibson were at their lowest levels, and rock guitarists began to seek out other avenues. One popular approach was to take a basic Stratocaster and add the latest technological innovations, such as high-powered active pickups and the Floyd Rose locking tremolo that enabled "divebomb" pitch bends to be made without putting the guitar out of tune.

The first great production superstrat was the Jackson Soloist. Although only launched on the market in 1984, prototypes combining Stratocaster-type bodies with Gibson Explorer-inspired headstocks had existed within Jackson's Charvel workshop since the late 1970s.

At this time, Jackson was essentially a custom guitar maker, and so the Soloist was made available with the widest possible array of user options: Floyd Rose or Kahler vibrato, or a string-through-body fixed bridge; Seymour Duncan pickups were standard, although any type required by the customer was possible; and finishes were simply unlimited.

On his 1989 album *Jeff Beck's Guitar Shop*, Beck used a Jackson Soloist, as he says, "to get some high tones."

| | |
|---|---|
| **Body style:** | Double cutaway solid body |
| **Materials:** | Alder body with maple top and maple straight-through neck (many other combinations of materials and construction have been used) |
| **Finish:** | Standard colors were black, Ferrari red, ivory, and platinum pink, but any customer-specified finish was possible |
| **Fretboard:** | Ebony (other woods used on later models) |
| **Frets:** | 24 (jumbo) |
| **Scale:** | 25 1/2" |
| **Width at nut:** | 1 11/16" |
| **Bridge:** | Floyd Rose or Kahler vibrato; fixed options |
| **Pickups:** | Seymour Duncan humbuckers standard, but any alternatives requested by the customer were possible |
| **Electrics:** | Master volume and tone controls |

# KRAMER 650G 1976

The Kramer company was founded in 1976 by Gary Kramer and Dennis Berardi. Kramer set up his factory in Neptune, New Jersey to manufacture aluminum-necked guitars, the bold concept that he and his former partner Travis Bean had pioneered two years earlier.

The Travis Bean guitars were built to an extremely high specification, and had created a great deal of interest in the industry. They were constructed using a straight-through aluminum neck to which the pickups were also attached—wooden wings were then added. The theory behind the revolutionary idea of an aluminum neck was that it would aid sustain. There was general agreement about the sound quality of Travis Beans, but the aluminum adapted poorly to temperature change, making the guitars difficult to keep in tune, and made them extraordinarily heavy. After Bean left the company, Kramer conceived an alternative approach to using aluminum, reducing weight with epoxy-secured inserts of walnut or maple—making the guitars also, conveniently, distinct enough to avoid an infringement of Bean's patent.

The most distinctive visual feature of the early Kramers is the "tuning fork" headstock, each prong housing three tuners (or two on basses)—a design for which conventional neck woods would not be sturdy enough. The fingerboards were also unorthodox, being molded from Ebonol, a man-made material similar to that used for bowling balls. The guitar bodies were often carved from exotic tonewoods such as koa, afromosia, bubinga, walnut, and shedua, as well as conventional maple.

Kramer introduced basses using the same principles. It was these instruments that benefited most from the Bean/Kramer philosophy, and they have left much the greater impression on guitar history.

▼
**Travis Bean TB1000, the upscale precursor to Kramer's aluminum-necked guitars. The T-hole in the headstock makes them instantly recognizable.**

| | |
|---|---|
| **Body style:** | Double cutaway solid body |
| **Materials:** | Black burl walnut and bird's eye maple; aluminum straight-through neck with walnut/maple inserts |
| **Finish:** | Natural |
| **Fretboard:** | Ebonol |
| **Inlays:** | Aluminum dot (mother-of-pearl on later models) |
| **Frets:** | 22 (not including zero fret) |
| **Scale:** | 25" |
| **Width at nut:** | 1 $\frac{11}{16}$" |
| **Pickups:** | 2 humbuckers; 3-way switch |
| **Electrics:** | Dedicated volume and tone controls for each pickup |
| **Machine heads:** | Schaller M-6 |

# KRAMER FLOYD ROSE SUSTAINER 1989

By 1981, Gary Kramer was gone, and the aluminum with him. Kramer guitars now favored Stratocaster-inspired designs aimed at the heavy metal market.

The Kramer name, however, would still be linked to innovation. Recognizing the growing importance to rock players of a reliable wide-pitch vibrato system, Kramer exclusively licensed the powerful, if bulky, Rockinger tremolo system. This attracted Rock God *du jour*, Eddie Van Halen, who for the next decade played an assortment of personally modified Kramer guitars, each given his trademark white-stripe custom finish. Kramer was also the first major company to see the potential of the Floyd Rose locking tremolo system, and by the mid-1980s was the only one fitting original rather than licensed versions on all its guitars.

The 1989 Sustainer is notable for its Floyd Rose-designed neck pickup, which, at the flick of a switch, emits an electromagnetic field able to sustain the vibrating strings indefinitely. This innovation never had the chance to succeed as Kramer went out of business shortly afterwards. The brand, bought in 1998 by Gibson, is now used on budget rock guitars.

▲ **Eddie Van Halen with one of his customized Kramer guitars. He was impressed with the Floyd Rose Sustainer's potential: "Incredible! With the Sustainer you can perform techniques that usually take years to master!"**

▼ **Van Halen's Kramers can be heard on 5150, (1986) the band's first chart-topping album.**

| | |
|---|---|
| **Body style:** | Double cutaway solid body |
| **Materials:** | Alder body with bolt-on maple neck |
| **Finish:** | Black, blue stain, candy blue, candy red, champagne, creme, flip flop blue, flip flop red, flip flop white, fluorescent pink, red stain, seafoam green, violet, white, and assorted "holoflash" finishes |
| **Fretboard:** | Rosewood or maple |
| **Inlays:** | Dot or shark-tooth; Kramer name on 12th fret |
| **Frets:** | 22 |
| **Scale:** | 25½" |
| **Width at nut:** | 1 ¹¹⁄₁₆" |
| **Bridge:** | Original Floyd Rose vibrato |
| **Pickups:** | 1 humbucker (bridge); 1 single-coil Floyd Rose Sustainer pickup (bridge); 3-way selector switch; Sustainer on/off switch |
| **Electrics:** | Master volume and tone controls; Sustainer intensity control; Sustainer mode switch |

# MARTIN : THE STORY

For well over a century, the Martin brand has been recognized as producing among the finest flat-top acoustic guitars—indeed, it was the Martin company that largely established this uniquely American strand of guitar production in 1833 at its home in Nazareth, Pennsylvania. And yet, like most other nineteenthth-century American business successes, the roots of the Martin story begin over 4,000 miles to the east, on the other side of the Atlantic Ocean.

The Martin family business can be traced back as far as 1807 in the Saxony town of Markneukirchen (in modern-day Germany), where Johann Georg Martin was a successful cabinetmaker. At this time, the guitar was still far from established as a respected musical instrument. While makers of violins enjoyed the prestige of having a guild, the trade of luthier was not recognized as worthy of its own guild, so guitars were generally made by cabinetmakers who built guitars as a sideline, including Martin. As these earliest Martin guitars have been lost to history we are unable to assess their quality—although it would be fair to say that Johann Georg Martin's name was not noted by connoisseurs at this time.

In keeping with the tradition of his day, Johann's son, Christian Friedrich (who was born in 1796 and was later to anglicize his name to Christian Frederick Martin)  entered the same trade as his father. Showing early promise, at the age of fifteen he was sent to Vienna as an apprentice to Johann Stauffer, one the leading luthiers of the Austrian/German school of guitar making, whose guitars featured innovations, hitherto unseen, such as tuning pegs arrayed in a single row on the headstock.

When Christian Friedrich Martin returned to Markneukirchen he became embroiled in a trade dispute. Observing the growing popularity of the guitar, the guild of violin makers saw itself in danger of missing the opportunity of a potentially valuable new market, and so they argued that they should be given the exclusive right to make other musical instruments. For Martin the dispute sowed seeds of discontent. In 1931, a close friend and fellow luthier, Heinrich Schatz, had emigrated to the United States and, two years later, Martin agreed to become his business partner.

In 1833, Christian Frederick Martin (as he was now calling himself) and his young family left Saxony for what was then termed the New World. The

One of the few known photographs of C.F. Martin, founder of the world's oldest guitar company.

A guitar built by noted luthier Johann Stauffer in Vienna in around 1830. C.F. Martin worked for Stauffer for fourteen years.

Martin began his business career in America working as a partner of friend Heinrich Schatz.

MARTIN & SCHATZ,
from VIENNA. Pupils of the celebrated STAUFFER.
Guitar & Violin Manufacturers
Importers of
MUSICAL INSTRUMENTS
196
Hudson Street.
NEW YORK.

1796
Christian Friedrich Martin born in Markneukirchen, Saxony

1811
Martin becomes apprentice to Johann Stauffer in Vienna

1833
Martin emigrates with family to New York City

1838
Unhappy in New York, Martin moves to rural Pennsylvania

1850
Martin introduces the use of X-brace design in his guitars

1852
C.F. Martin introduces the first Style 28 guitars

1867
C.F. Martin II takes over from ailing father, who dies in 1873

first business address registered by Martin was 196 Hudson Street, New York City. ③ At these premises, Martin sold his own guitars as well as a wide array of other musical instruments, most of which he and his partner imported in some form from many contacts they maintained in Europe.

Although the business flourished, the Martin family found it hard to settle in the alien environment of New York City; indeed, at one stage they came close to returning to Saxony. Once again, it was Martin's friend Heinrich Schatz, now known as Henry, who provided the solution. Schatz had moved his home to Pennsylvania, and after inviting them to visit he convinced them to stay. Pennsylvania had a long-established German population and the architecture reminded the family of Markneukirchen. In 1838, Martin sold his entire retail stock to a New York competitor, and by the end of the year he had bought an eight-acre plot of rural land near Nazareth, Pennsylvania. His plan was now to concentrate wholly on building guitars.

During the 1830s, the guitars Martin built were, unsurprisingly, crafted in the German/Austrian school of luthiery. ④ Indeed, if we were to look at a Stauffer guitar built in the 1820s, we would see very few differences from an early Martin model. The most notable feature is Stauffer's curled headstock, with its ornately engraved brass backplate and unusual array of "six-in-a-line" tuning pegs. ⑤ Described by Martin in the company ledgers as "Vienna Screws," they were imported by him at great expense from Vienna—an indication, perhaps, of the importance he placed on them. Martin also used Stauffer's idea of an adjustable neck, the angle of which was controlled by a key inserted into the heel. ⑥

Martin's business offered a wide variety of guitars at this time, from instruments that were among the most ornate to be seen outside of Europe, to no-frills models that retailed at a quarter of the price. The suggestion by some music historians that Martin's top-of-the-range models at this time were, in fact, imported from Vienna can be laid to rest simply by looking at Martin's highly detailed ledgers. They reveal that delivery time on these instruments was somewhere in the region of two months—an interval of time that would have been quite impossible to achieve by shipping orders to Europe, having the guitars built in Vienna, and then shipping the finished instruments back to America.

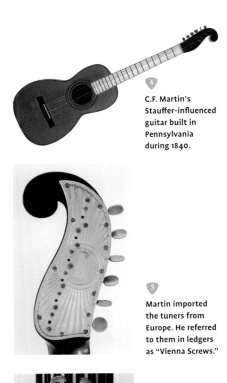

④
C.F. Martin's Stauffer-influenced guitar built in Pennsylvania during 1840.

⑤
Martin imported the tuners from Europe. He referred to them in ledgers as "Vienna Screws."

⑥
Martin used the Stauffer key for neck adjustment on his early guitars.

**1888**
Frank Henry Martin, grandson of C.F. Martin takes over

**c.1890**
Martin takes over distribution from Zoebisch & Sons

**1916**
Dreadnought style developed for Oliver Ditson Company

**1929**
First "OM" Orchestral Models are built

**1931**
Martin introduces necks that join the body at the fourteenth fret

**1931**
"C.F. Martin & Co." gold headstock logos introduced

**1931**
Launch of the D-1 and D-2—the first Martin Dreadnoughts

Martin 1-40 from 1874—standard size "1", and style 40.

By the 1850s, the Stauffer influence had diminished, and Martin was well established as the premium name in American-built guitars. At this time, Martin adopted X-bracing for its instruments, rather than the fan bracing more commonly used in Europe. The company also attempted to standardize the sizing of its guitars: "1" was the standard model; "2" was a smaller parlor size; "0" was a larger concert style; "00" (introduced in 1877) was the largest, a grand concert model. There were also many styles, each denoted by a two-digit number—the low-numbered styles were generally simpler and cheaper; the high numbers more costly and ornate.

In 1867, with C.F. Martin now elderly and in poor health, his son Christian Frederick Martin Jr. took over, and, in 1888, his own son Frank Henry Martin took charge of the company. It was later in his reign, in the early decades of the twentieth century, that the Martin brand would see its greatest period of growth and innovation. The style of the day was for larger, louder instruments, so a "000" orchestral model was made available. Later, more dramatically, the "Dreadnought" style was launched. Named after a British battleship, this guitar had a larger body than any previous model, was louder, and exhibited a rich bass tone. Ideal for accompanying a vocalist, the Dreadnought is now accepted as a standard design, and has long been a basic ingredient of pop, rock, and country music, attracting the attention of stars as varied as Neil Young and Hank Williams. Other later styles included the Jumbo (J) and the Orchestral Model (OM).

In 1928, all of the Martin standard designs were altered to take account of two factors. One was the transition from gut to steel strings, which required greater strength from the bracing and neck joints; the other was a lengthening of the neck. Previous fingerboards had tended to join the neck at the twelfth fret; if they joined at the fourteenth, the player had access to higher notes. This, again would become standard throughout the industry.

C.F. Martin & Company is now the oldest guitar manufacturer in the world. Surprisingly, however, it nonetheless remains a family business, of which current CEO Chris Martin represents the sixth generation. The company's reputation for the quality of its instruments remains as strong as ever, even if the vast majority of its popular range is based on designs likely to have been created well over a century earlier.

Frank Henry Martin presided over the company's most innovative period.

Country legend Hank Williams plays his famous Martin D-28 to Hank Jr.—himself destined to be a major name in country music.

The Martin factory, still in Nazareth, Pennsylvania.

**1931** First Martin D-28 models introduced

**1933** Martin's most famous guitar, the D-45, built for "Singing Cowboy" Gene Autry

**1948** Christian Frederick Martin III takes over the running of the company

**1958** Martin introduces its first electric guitar

**1979** Martin launches E-18 solid-body electric guitar and accompanying EB-18 electric bass

**1995** The first Martin signature model launched—the Eric Clapton 000-42ECM

# MARTIN & CO
## FAMILY TREE

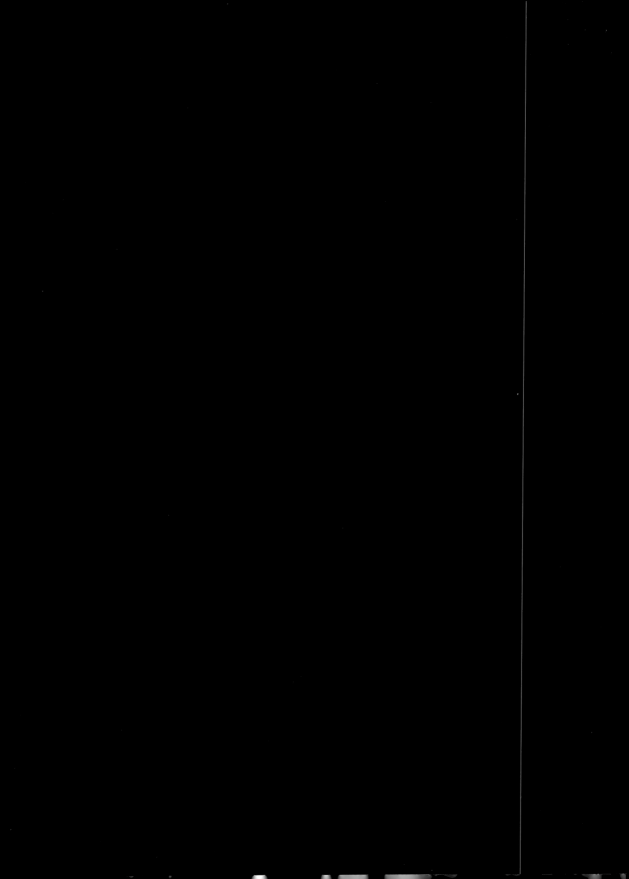

# MARTIN STAUFFER 1820

Johann Georg Stauffer (1778–1853) was the leading guitar maker of the Vienna School. His most famous instrument design resulted from his collaboration with Italian concert guitarist Luigi Legnani.

Legnani had trained as a string player but later devoted himself to performing as a guitarist and vocalist. A noted composer, Legnani is best remembered for his thirty-six caprices for the guitar—some of the most demanding pieces in the classical repertoire. Legnani worked with a number of luthiers, eventually creating instruments in his own right.

Stauffer first built these guitars from about 1815 and they would become very influential among luthiers of Northern Europe. Stauffer's work is interesting, not only for his own instruments, but because one of the apprentices working for him during this time was a young man named Christian Friedrich Martin.

Although Martin's early history is patchy, it seems likely that he joined Stauffer in around 1813. Evidently a diligent and skillful worker, he became one of Stauffer's foremen in the workshop shortly after the end of his training. He would later return to his hometown, Markneukirchen in Germany. He emigrated to the United States in 1833 after a trade dispute arose between the guilds of the violin and cabinet makers over who should be allowed to build guitars.

There is no certain evidence to suggest that Martin himself worked on the guitar shown (*see right*), but the instruments designed by Stauffer at this time would be a critical influence on Martin's own guitars.

The headstock with its six-in-a-line tuners is notable. When Martin started making guitars in the U.S. from 1833, he used a similar headstock design, which was rarely seen again until the first Fenders in 1940.

| | |
|---|---|
| **Body style:** | Hollow-body, figure-eight |
| **Materials:** | Maple back and sides; spruce top; rosewood binding veneered neck (adjustable with a key) |
| **Body dimensions:** | Body length—15 $^{17}/_{36}$"; lower bout: 11 $^{16}/_{35}$"; upper bout: 8 $^{41}/_{42}$" |
| **Finish:** | French polish |
| **Fretboard:** | Ebony |
| **Frets:** | 17 |
| **Scale:** | 22 $^1/_{21}$" |
| **Width at nut:** | 1 $^{13}/_{16}$" |
| **Bridge:** | Ebony "mustache" design with bone saddle and mother-of-pearl inlays |
| **Tuners:** | 6-in-a-line, mechanism hidden beneath brass plate |

# MARTIN & SCHATZ 1840

In the late 1820s, Christian Friedrich Martin found himself embroiled in a dispute between Germany's cabinetmakers (a trade that incorporated the relatively new discipline of luthiery) and violin makers for the exclusive right to produce musical instruments. Deterred by the restrictions of the guild system, he decided to follow the path taken by his friend and fellow luthier, Heinrich Schatz. Martin and his young family emigrated to the United States in 1833 and set up business in New York City. As well as making his own guitars, Martin also ran a retail establishment, selling other kinds of instruments, many of which he imported using his contacts back in Germany and Austria.

By 1840, it was becoming clear that the Martin family were struggling to adjust to the pace of their new country. Once again at the suggestion of Schatz, Martin moved his family out to rural Nazareth, Pennsylvania, where many

other central European émigrés had also settled. Here Martin was able to concentrate his efforts wholly on building guitars, both on his own and in collaboration with others.

Christian Frederick Martin and Henry Schatz (both by this time had anglicized their names) ran their own separate workshops, even though their business activities intersected frequently. There is no evidence that any formal arrangement existed to cover the jointly-built models, but that may simply have been because, as long-standing friends, they may have deemed it unnecessary.

Built in 1840, this guitar has a characteristically Northern European-style body, and still features Stauffer's unique six-in-a-line arrangement of tuners—which Martin now referred to as Viennese Screws. It shows quite clearly that Martin was yet to move beyond the design and construction style of his former employer.

| | |
|---|---|
| **Body style:** | Hollow-body, figure-eight |
| **Materials:** | Figured mahogany back and sides; spruce top; Spanish cedar neck (adjustable with a key) |
| **Finish:** | French polish |
| **Fretboard:** | Ivory |
| **Rosette:** | Delicate ivory marquetry |
| **Frets:** | 18 |
| **Scale:** | 22 1/21" |
| **Width at nut:** | 1 13/16" |
| **Bridge:** | Ivory bridge with ornate inlays; ivory pins with inlays; bone saddle |
| **Tuners:** | 6-in-a-line, mechanism hidden beneath brass plate |

# MARTIN 2-27 1874

When C.F. Martin and Co.'s first price list appeared in 1874, the model 2-27 was shown retailing at $58.50. This would equate to around $1,000 at today's prices, suggesting that it was aimed squarely at the serious and/or wealthy player. Fascinatingly, at the bottom of the sheet is the comment: "No. 2 ½ and No. 2—Ladies' Sizes." Until the middle of the nineteenth century there had been a wide perception that the guitar was a woman's instrument, especially small-bodied "parlor" guitars such as the Martin size 2. This would indeed have contributed to the guitar's struggle to be taken seriously, along with the view that it was an uncouth folk instrument. Certainly, if we look at earlier works of art depicting the instrument, the player is invariably a young woman—the most notable example perhaps being Johannes Vermeer's *De Gittaarspeelster*, which he painted around 1670.

As far as Martin's designs were concerned, there were even smaller-bodied guitars produced, such as the size 5. This type of instrument was known as a "terz" guitar; it was named after the German word for "third," and so called because the standard tuning was raised by three half steps—which is a note interval of a minor third.

The model 2-27 is described as being "inlaid with pearl" and "ivory bound," making it—unusually—somewhat fancier than the higher-numbered style 28; the 28, however, was only available in the larger 0 size. The most expensive models listed by Martin's are *all* ornate "ladies'" parlor guitars, right up to the 2-42 which is "richly inlaid"—at $90, the 2-42 was considerably more expensive than the 2-27.

Although it was one of the most popular instruments in the entire Martin range during the nineteenth century, the 2-27 model no longer appeared in advertisements after 1898.

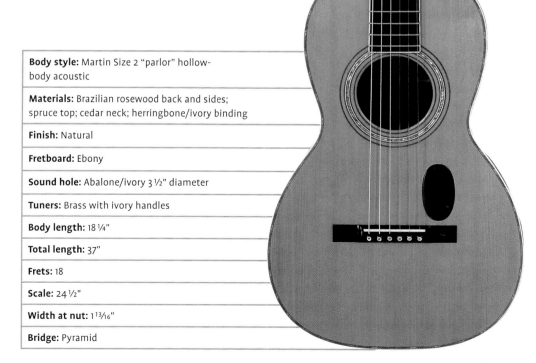

| | |
|---|---|
| **Body style:** | Martin Size 2 "parlor" hollow-body acoustic |
| **Materials:** | Brazilian rosewood back and sides; spruce top; cedar neck; herringbone/ivory binding |
| **Finish:** | Natural |
| **Fretboard:** | Ebony |
| **Sound hole:** | Abalone/ivory 3 ½" diameter |
| **Tuners:** | Brass with ivory handles |
| **Body length:** | 18 ¼" |
| **Total length:** | 37" |
| **Frets:** | 18 |
| **Scale:** | 24 ½" |
| **Width at nut:** | 1 ¹³⁄₁₆" |
| **Bridge:** | Pyramid |

# MARTIN OM-28 1929

The Orchestral Model (OM) body shape was first introduced in 1929 and marks a significant moment in the history of Martin guitars. Earlier Martins, like all standard acoustic guitars of the time, were built with the neck joint close to the twelfth fret, giving a usable playing range of one octave per string. The OM models extended the length of the neck so that it met the body at the fourteenth fret, giving far easier access to notes in the upper register.

At the same time as the OM models were introduced, Martin also offered a range of archtop guitars, once again with fourteen-fret access. Both models proved popular, following the gradual shift from gut to steel strings. Martin recognized that steel-string players wanted bigger, louder guitars with longer, narrower necks. As a result, by 1934 all the standard Martin body shapes had been redesigned to accommodate the "fourteen-fret neck."

The OM-28 was the first of the Orchestral Models to appear, featuring Martin's Pyramid Bridge. It only stayed in production until 1934 when its designation was changed to the 000-28. The coveted guitar reappeared on the Martin pricelist in 1995, available only as a special order.

John Mayer was given his first signature Martin in 2003. The OMJM was intended to have the characteristics of his OM-28 but at a more affordable price.

▼
John Mayer's third album, *Continuum* (2006), marked a change in direction toward a new, more blues-oriented sound.

| | |
|---|---|
| **Body style:** | Hollow-body Martin "OM" size |
| **Materials:** | Rosewood back and sides; spruce top; cedar neck fixed with dovetail joint |
| **Body dimensions:** | Length 19 ³/₈"; upper width 11 ¼"; lower width 15"; maximum depth 4 ⅛" |
| **Binding:** | Ivory with herringbone top trim |
| **Finish:** | French polish |
| **Fretboard:** | Ebony |
| **Inlays:** | Mother-of-pearl dot |
| **Frets:** | 20 |
| **Scale:** | 25 ²/₅" |
| **Width at nut:** | 1 ¾" |
| **Bridge:** | Martin "Pyramid"; ebony with bone saddle |

# MARTIN D-28 1931

T he name of any standard Martin guitar is a combination of codes for the size and style of the body. All Dreadnought-sized Martins take the prefix of D; other prefixes include J (Jumbo), and OM (Orchestral Model). The numbers that follow indicate the style—a higher number usually indicates a more elaborate finish. The D-28 is one of the most famous Dreadnought guitars.

The Style 28, with its rosewood back and sides, spruce top, and cedar neck, first appears in Martin's ledgers in 1852. At this time it was a Size 0 instrument and would become Martin's most popular guitar during the nineteenth century. Well into the twentieth century, Martin was recommending the 0-28 as "the finest model for the solo guitarist using gut strings." Shortly afterward, Martin guitars were redesigned for use with steel strings, and new bracing systems were introduced to enable the body to withstand the additional tension.

In 1928, this style was made available in a Dreadnought body for the first time. At this time Style 28 featured a luxurious herringbone trim around the top of the soundboard; this changed to black and white checker in 1947.

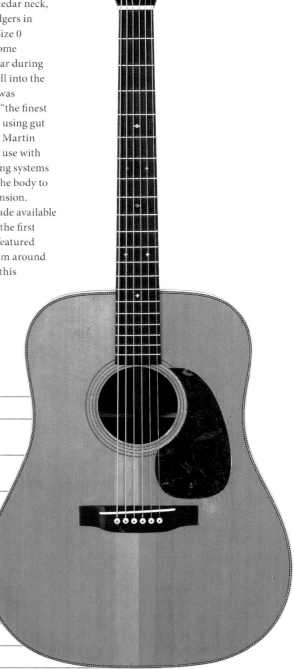

▲
**Neil Young owns and plays one of the most famous D-28s—a 1941 model that once belonged to country star WIlliams.**

▼
**Young continues to use the Hank Williams D-28 on stage and in the studio. Among the albums on which it can be heard is 1974's *On The Beach*.**

| | |
|---|---|
| **Body style:** Dreadnought | |
| **Materials:** Rosewood back and sides; spruce top; cedar neck fixed with dovetail joint | |
| **Body dimensions:** Length 20"; upper width 11 ½"; lower width 15 ⅝"; maximum depth 4 ⅞" | |
| **Binding:** Ivory with herringbone top trim | |
| **Finish:** French polish | |
| **Fretboard:** Ebony | |
| **Inlays:** Mother-of-pearl dot | |
| **Frets:** 20 | |
| **Scale:** 25 ⅖" | |
| **Width at nut:** 1 ¹¹⁄₁₆" | |
| **Bridge:** Ebony with bone saddle | |

# MARTIN D-45 1933

T he prewar Martin D-45 has a special attraction for the wealthiest collectors of flat-top acoustic guitars.

Style 45 was the fanciest design offered by Martin, with abalone pearl inlay on practically every border of the body, not to mention the ornate fingerboard and headstock inlays. It first appeared as a Dreadnought in 1933 when a custom one-off was built for Gene Autry, the singing cowboy star of numerous Western movies (and also a hugely important figure in the popularization of the guitar). Opulent in looks and cost, the D-45 was into production between 1938 and 1942 (when wartime austerity put a halt on manufacture of all Style 45s). During that period only ninety D-45s were built. These are among the most collectible production acoustic guitars—particularly those built in 1938 with the "snowflake" fingerboard inlay—the remaining original D-45s would feature hexagonal inlays.

In 1968 Martin reissued the Style 45 in Dreadnought size only. It has remained in production, with a number of D-45 variants added along the way. In 2000 an Orchestra Model OM-45 was made available for the first time in almost sixty years.

▲
Gene Autry, the Singing Cowboy, was one of the biggest Western stars of the 1940s. A war hero and astute businessman, he was long in the "Forbes 400" list of wealthiest Americans.

▼
The 2003 compilation album *Tumbling Tumbleweeds* contains Autry's signature song "Back In The Saddle Again."

| | |
|---|---|
| **Body style:** | Dreadnought |
| **Materials:** | Rosewood back and sides; spruce top; cedar neck fixed with dovetail joint |
| **Body dimensions:** | Length 20"; upper width 11½"; lower width 15⅝"; maximum depth 4⅞" |
| **Binding:** | Ivory |
| **Finish:** | French polish |
| **Fretboard:** | Ebony pyramid bridge |
| **Inlays:** | Mother-of-pearl snowflake (1938), hexagonal blocks (1939–43); "C.F. Martin" inlaid vertically in headstock |
| **Frets:** | 20 |
| **Scale:** | 25 ⅖" |
| **Width at nut:** | 1 ¹¹⁄₁₆" |
| **Bridge:** | Ebony with bone saddle |

# MARTIN 000-42ECM 1995

In 1992, British guitar legend Eric Clapton took part in MTV's *Unplugged*—a series of small-venue concert television broadcasts where electric artists were given the opportunity to play their songs on acoustic instruments. Such was the critical success of Clapton's show that the recordings were released on an album that would sell over ten million copies, and earn him six Grammy Awards.

Both the TV show and recordings were widely believed to have sparked a surge of interest in acoustic guitars. During the performance, Clapton used his two favorite Martin guitars: a 1939 000-42 and a 1966 000-28, which had been customized by Martin employee Mike Longworth to a "45" level of decorative finish. Martin received many enquiries about Clapton's instruments and so decided to produce a signature guitar bearing the initials ECM (Eric Clapton Model).

Martin's "000" body size is prized both for its tonal balance and its clarity in the treble register. Consequently, it is more likely to find favor among fingerpickers than strummers. This can be heard to great effect in the playing of both Clapton and fellow guitarist Andy Fairweather-Low on the acoustic reworking of rock classic "Layla."

▲
**Eric Clapton has featured acoustic segments in his live performances since the mid-1980s.**

▼
***Unplugged*** **was voted by Q magazine as being among the 100 best British albums of all time.**

| | |
|---|---|
| **Body style:** Hollow-body, flat-top Martin "000" size | |
| **Materials:** Solid Carpathian spruce top; solid Madagascar rosewood; "select hardwood" modified V-profile neck | |
| **Finish:** Natural; nitrocellulose gloss finish | |
| **Fretboard:** Ebony | |
| **Frets:** 20 | |
| **Scale:** 24 9/10" | |
| **Width at nut:** 1 3/4" | |
| **Bridge:** Ebony | |
| **Electrics:** Optional | |
| **Tuners:** Waverly nickel with "Ivaroid" butterbean knobs | |

# MICRO-FRETS GOLDEN MELODY 1967

Micro-Frets is one of the more individualistic names in the pantheon of American-built electric guitars in the 1960s.

Ralph S. Jones was an engineer with some strong ideas on how the electric guitar could be improved. Bankrolled by a millionaire real-estate man named Marion Huggins, Jones set up a workshop in Frederick, Maryland.

At first, Jones concentrated on marketing his inventions, notably the Micro-nut, which was akin to an early Buzz Feiten-style "tempered" approach to dealing with the intonation issues affecting most guitars. Jones also invented the Calibrato vibrato arm, which allowed for individual string adjustment: unlike standard vibratos, this made it possible to bend complete chords that would remain in tune as the pitch altered.

The first Micro-Frets guitars appeared in 1967 and, true to the time, were quite colorful, sporting such exotic names as Venus Sunset and Martian Sunrise, or the green sunburst effect (see right). Models such as the Huntington and Golden Melody featured body shapes that were quite unlike those of the main American manufacturers of the time, although they did bear a passing resemblance to Rickenbackers of the period. The Golden Melody was capable of creating a distinctive biting sound, generated by the two single-coil Bill Lawrence-designed Hi-Fi pickups.

As the company grew, Ralph Jones's experiments became more daring. One example was the Orbiter, a guitar with an in-built FM transmitter that could relay stereo sound to any radio or hi-fi that was tuned to 102.3 MHz.

The Micro-Frets story came to an abrupt halt in the early 1970s with the unexpected death of Ralph Jones. During the company's brief life it is estimated to have produced around 3,000 guitars in total.

▼
Multi-tracking guitar artist Buddy Merrill used at least eight different guitars in many combinations on his album *Guitars Express* (1998); they included the Micro-Frets Huntington.

| | |
|---|---|
| **Body style:** | Semi-solid double cutaway with single Rickenbacker-inspired sound hole |
| **Materials:** | Maple body with bolt-on maple neck |
| **Finish:** | Martian sunburst, standard sunburst, black (other colors available as custom orders); white celluloid binding on front and back of body |
| **Fretboard:** | Rosewood or maple |
| **Inlays:** | Acrylic dot |
| **Frets:** | 22 |
| **Scale:** | 24" |
| **Bridge:** | Tune-o-matic style with patented Calibrato vibrato arm |
| **Nut:** | Patented Micro-nut |
| **Pickups:** | 2 single-coil Hi-Fi pickups designed by Bill Lawrence; 3-way selector switch |
| **Electrics:** | Master volume and tone controls under pickguard |

# MODULUS GRAPHITE QUANTUM 1984

Technological innovation in the musical instrument world can emerge from the most unexpected of sources: in the case of Modulus instruments, that came from bass-playing aerospace scientist Geoff Gould.

Employed in the mid-1970s by Ford Aerospace, Gould was a member of the team that designed the carbon fiber dish antenna for the *Voyager I* space probe. As he learned about carbon fiber he saw that it could solve problems he had faced with his bass guitars, such as dead spots and warping.

Joining up with the innovative Alembic company in 1976, he experimented with carbon fiber bass guitar necks. His ideas captured the imagination of Phil Lesh of the Grateful Dead, one of rock's most forward-thinking bass players, who would later become Gould's most important endorsee.

The Modulus brand was born in 1979, with a small workforce based in San Francisco. The company's reputation was quickly established with the Quantum bass, constructed from a hand-laid carbon fiber neck and featuring beautifully crafted bodywork using exotic woods.

Gould sold his company in 1995, but the brand has continued down its founder's innovative path—with the 1996 Genesis neck design, for example, which marries a carbon fiber skeleton with lightweight tonewoods.

▲
**Grateful Dead bassist Phil Lesh switched to one of the first carbon fiber-necked basses in the 1990s after visiting Modulus.**

▼
**Phil Lesh and his Modulus Quantum bass can be heard on the 2002 album *There And Back Again*.**

| | |
|---|---|
| **Body style:** | Solid body with double cutaway |
| **Materials:** | Alder body with maple top (flamed maple, bubinga, chechen, and walnut also available); carbon fiber neck |
| **Finish:** | Assorted color finishes |
| **Fretboard:** | Ebony or chechen |
| **Frets:** | 24 |
| **Scale:** | 35" |
| **Width at nut:** | 1 ⅗" |
| **Bridge:** | Adjustable |
| **Pickups:** | Active—EMG or Bartolini |
| **Electrics:** | Dependent on pickup option |

# MOSRITE VENTURES MARK 1 1963

and Roger Rossmeisl, a German immigrant who had brought traditional luthier techniques to the electric guitar manufacturing process, and would later create the classic Thinline series for Fender.

Mosrite began as a boutique brand, creating custom instruments, but recognition came in 1963 when Moseley built a guitar for Nokie Edwards of The Ventures, America's most popular instrumental surf band.

The Mosrite Ventures Mark 1 set the visual tone for the models that would follow, with its characteristic reverse Stratocaster body and the German Carve beveled edge, a technique Moseley had learned from Rossmeisl.

The Mark 1 also incorporated Moseley's own hardware, hand-wound pickups, and a vibrato arm, the Vibramute—a design that used wheeled saddles to reduce string wear and, as its name suggests, also included a foam rubber pad that could be deployed to deaden the strings.

Mosrite was formed in 1956 in California by a young ex-Rickenbacker employee, Semie Moseley. He had a fine pedigree, having apprenticed under both Paul Bigsby, a strong claimant for having built the first solid-body electric guitar (not to mention the inventor of the ever-popular Bigsby vibrato unit),

▲
**Johnny Ramone of seminal punk band The Ramones is seen here playing a Mosrite Ventures at a 1977 concert in New York.**

▼
**Ramone's Mosrite Ventures is heard on *Ramones* (1976), the debut album widely credited for kick-starting punk rock.**

| | |
|---|---|
| **Body style:** | Double cutaway with over-extending treble bout and German Carve beveled edging |
| **Materials:** | Alder body with bolt-on maple neck |
| **Finish:** | Assorted colors (metallic finishes an optional extra); cellulose lacquer |
| **Fretboard:** | Rosewood |
| **Inlays:** | Acrylic dot |
| **Frets:** | 22 (not including the zero fret) |
| **Scale:** | 24 ¾" |
| **Width at zero fret:** | 1 ¹¹/₁₆" |
| **Bridge:** | Vibramute combined bridge, tailpiece and vibrato unit |
| **Pickups:** | 2 single coil; 3-position switch |
| **Electrics:** | Master volume and tone controls for each pickup |

# MOSRITE STRAWBERRY ALARM CLOCK 1967

bands such as the Strawberry Alarm Clock, whose neatly crafted multi-harmonied bubblegum psychedelia took them to the top of the charts in 1967.

Moseley had achieved recognition with his Ventures models, but they were costly to build, and retailed at considerably more than a Fender. In 1967, Moseley hoped to reach a wider market by hooking up with America's most popular psychedelic band, producing for them a set of guitars and a bass. The resulting instruments shared the same hardware and construction as other Mosrites, but featured a bizarre outer skeleton.

After completion, the guitars were shipped out to Californian artist Von Dutch (Kenny Howard), a figure well known for producing custom surfboards, automobile pinstriping, and other painted body designs. He proceeded to give each instrument its own paint job, creating what now appear as fascinating period pieces.

The "psychedelic era" was a curious time for popular culture. There were those who lived on the edge, experimented with mind-expanding substances and took music to hitherto unexplored regions. But most musicians settled for raiding their girlfriends' wardrobes and singing songs about peace and love—

▲
The Strawberry Alarm Clock may not have been at the cutting-edge of psychedelia but their music and image evoke the period beautifully.

▼
"Incense and Peppermints" was the band's first hit single and also the title of its 1967 debut album.

| | |
|---|---|
| **Body style:** | Double cutaway with external skeleton frame fixed at the headstock |
| **Materials:** | Alder body with bolt-on maple neck |
| **Finish:** | Green (6-string); red (12-string and bass); psychedelic hand-painted artwork by Von Dutch |
| **Fretboard:** | Rosewood |
| **Inlays:** | Acrylic dot |
| **Frets:** | 22 (not including the zero fret) |
| **Scale:** | 24 ¾" |
| **Width at zero fret:** | 1 ¹¹⁄₁₆" |
| **Bridge:** | Vibramute combined bridge, tailpiece, and vibrato unit |
| **Pickups:** | 2 single-coil pickups; 3-position switch |
| **Electrics:** | Master volume and tone controls |

# MOSRITE V88 1988

Having begun as a business by making guitars to order, Mosrite was, by the mid-1960s, established as a credible manufacturer of high-quality instruments. At the peak of production in 1968, Mosrite employed a staff of more than a hundred and were producing over a thousand guitars a month—acoustics, electrics, double- and triple-necks, basses, and even resonators (Moseley had bought Dobro in 1966). They also began to move into unchartered territory, producing amplifiers and effects. Unfortunately, although Moseley may have been an inspired luthier, he could be equally naive in business matters. After a number of unsuccessful distribution deals, by 1968 the company was declared bankrupt.

Two years later, Moseley was able to acquire the right to use the Mosrite name again, and even though the 1970s were a difficult time for the company, slowly he began to rebuild his business, concentrating on exporting guitars to Japan where The Ventures, although no longer affiliated with the brand, were still very popular.

With few exceptions, Mosrite guitars from this period were all but reissues of the basic Ventures design, with a few variations, such as humbucking pickups, which were used on some models in the early 1970s.

The V88 was based on the 1963 Ventures design, but without the German Carve on the edging. The bridge unit is also unusual for Mosrite in that there is no vibrato arm. Models produced at this time were signed by Moseley himself.

In 1992, Semie Moseley died. His family and employees continued to run the company for two more years before finally closing down.

The famous Mosrite body shape is still being manufactured in Japan, even using the Mosrite brand name. These guitars are, however, unconnected to the original company.

▼
**The 1988 Mosrite catalog presents Semie Moseley on the cover holding a V88 under the banner "History Comes Alive." Mosrite reproductions and adaptations of classic designs from earlier decades are of increasing interest to collectors.**

| | |
|---|---|
| **Body style:** | Double cutaway with over-extending treble bout |
| **Materials:** | Alder body with bolt-on maple neck |
| **Finish:** | Assorted colors (metallic finishes an optional extra); cellulose lacquer |
| **Fretboard:** | Rosewood |
| **Frets:** | 22 (not including zero fret) |
| **Scale:** | 24 3/4" |
| **Width at nut:** | 1 11/16" |
| **Bridge:** | Combined bridge and tailpiece |
| **Pickups:** | 2 single-coil pickups; 3-position switch |
| **Electrics:** | Master volume and tone controls |

# MOSRITE VENTURES BASS 1967

roles with the more technically adept Nokie Edwards.

Perhaps the most interesting aspect of the Ventures/Mosrite story is how the band's success would go on to affect the evolution of the electric guitar. By 1964, The Ventures were on the wane commercially in their homeland, a new generation of beat groups rendering their twang a little outdated. At the same time, as if passing through some strange cultural twilight zone, The Ventures became increasingly successful in Japan—more so even than The Beatles.

Suddenly every young Japanese male wanted an electric guitar—and preferably a Mosrite. Since these were expensive and not available in large numbers, a new industry began to emerge in Japan, creating cheap, home-produced electric guitars, at first with a strong Mosrite influence. This explosion would see the emergence of many of the great names in Japanese guitar manufacture.

Moseley produced a range of Ventures models, not only guitars but also a bass version. The first celebrated player of the Mosrite bass was, unsurprisingly, The Ventures' own Bob Bogle—who had originally played lead guitar in the band, notably on their signature hit "Walk, Don't Run", before swapping

**Big in Japan! The Ventures were one of the first bands from the U.S. to make a big impression in the Far East.**

**In 1964, the band shifted from using Fender to Mosrite instruments. They can be heard on the classic album of the same year, *The Ventures In Space*.**

| | |
|---|---|
| **Body style:** | Double cutaway with over-extending treble bout and German Carve beveled edging |
| **Materials:** | Alder body with bolt-on maple neck |
| **Finish:** | Assorted colors (metallic finishes an optional extra); cellulose lacquer |
| **Fretboard:** | Rosewood |
| **Inlays:** | Acrylic dot |
| **Frets:** | 20 (not including the zero fret) |
| **Scale:** | 30" |
| **Width at zero fret:** | 1 7/16" |
| **Bridge:** | Fixed with foam mute |
| **Pickups:** | 1 or 2 pickups; 3-position switch |
| **Electrics:** | Master volume and tone controls |

# MUSICMAN SILHOUETTE 1986

By the end of the 1960s, life at Fender had become difficult for some long-standing employees. Unhappy with the way Fender was being managed under CBS, in 1971 Forrest White and Tom Walker left to start their own venture. The plan was to involve their former boss Leo Fender who, having signed a "no compete" clause when he sold out to CBS, would participate as a silent partner.

The first product to emerge was a hybrid valve/solid-state amplifier designed by Walker and Fender. When his contractual clause with CBS ran out in 1975, Fender was made president of the company, and a year later his consulting business CLF Research began producing instruments bearing the MusicMan name.

Under its new management, the MusicMan brand enjoyed a spectacular renaissance producing guitars and basses. The new company's first significant success was the Silhouette. Launched in 1986, this superstrat featured a twenty-four-fret fingerboard and a combination of single-coil and humbucking pickups. It was a performance guitar geared to the rock player who sought a wide array of sounds. It also featured a graphite-coated truss road, adjusted by an easily accessible wheel, without the need for special tools.

▲
**Toronto-based guitarist Elmer Ferrer mixes classic blues/rock with music from his native Cuba.**

▼
**Ferrer's Music Man Silhouette is prominent on his 2009 album *No Guitars Allowed*.**

| | |
|---|---|
| **Body style:** | Double cutaway solid body |
| **Materials:** | Poplar, alder, or ash; bird's-eye maple, 6-hole bolt-on neck |
| **Finish:** | Black, white, fire engine red, translucent red, blueburst, sunburst ash, and periodic "specials" |
| **Fretboard:** | Maple or rosewood |
| **Frets:** | 24 |
| **Scale:** | 25 ½" |
| **Width at nut:** | 1 ⅝" (1 ¹¹⁄₁₆" optional) |
| **Bridge:** | Floating vibrato unit |
| **Pickups:** | Combinations of DiMarzio single-coil and custom-wound humbuckers; 5-way switching |
| **Electrics:** | Master volume and tone control |
| **Tuners:** | Schaller (in a 4+2 formation) |

# MusicMan StingRay 1976

MusicMan's unusual business arrangement was problematic. CLF Research and MusicMan were effectively separate companies: Leo Fender headed CLF, which built the guitars and basses; Tom Walker headed MusicMan, which built the amplifiers and sold the guitars. A rift between the two companies arose over payments, and Fender began a new company, G&L, with another of his old colleagues, George Fullerton. MusicMan went to a young luthier named Grover Jackson in an attempt to continue production, and the company soldiered on until 1984 when it was bought out by string manufacturer Ernie Ball.

MusicMan instruments combined Fender-style bodies with the brand's asymmetric tuner arrangements. The StingRay bass appeared in 1976. Similar visually to a Fender Precision, it featured a "soapbar" humbucking pickup and the first active pre-amp to appear in a production guitar. The 3+1 headstock arrangement—with the G-string tuner fitted to the underside— was also unorthodox and gained the instrument notice, along with its distinctive oval-shaped pickguard.

The StingRay bass is well known for its punch, making it a good choice for funk applications and music requiring slapping techniques.

▲
Bernard Edwards, cofounder of seminal R&B group Chic, used a MusicMan StingRay for most of his career.

▼
Chic produced a string of dance classics in the 1970s before Edwards and cofounder Nile Rodgers departed. *Risqué* (1979) was their third studio album and included the hit "Good Times."

| | |
|---|---|
| **Body style:** | Double cutaway solid body |
| **Materials:** | Ash (or sometimes alder) body with maple bolt-on neck |
| **Finish:** | Wide assortment of natural and color finishes |
| **Fretboard:** | Maple, rosewood, or pau ferro |
| **Inlays:** | Acrylic dot |
| **Frets:** | 22 |
| **Scale:** | 34" |
| **Width at nut:** | 1 5/8" |
| **Bridge:** | Fixed (4- or 5-string) |
| **Pickups:** | 1 or 2 high-output "soapbar" humbucking pickups, with optional piezo pickup located in the bridge |
| **Electrics:** | Volume control and pre-amplifier with active 2- or 3-band tone controls (powered by a 9-volt battery) |

# NATIONAL TRICONE 1927

Before the invention of the magnetic pickup, the guitar had been a low-profile instrument. The problem was simply one of volume: it couldn't be heard among naturally louder acoustic instruments.

During the 1920s there were a number of ingenious attempts to make the guitar louder, one of which was to use mechanical amplification. Also in the 1920s, instrument maker John Dopyera produced the first "resonating" guitar—an instrument with a thin aluminum cone, rather like a loudspeaker, fitted inside the body. When the guitar strings were struck the cone would pick up the vibrations and amplify the sound.

In 1927 Dopyera and guitarist George Beauchamp (who had first requested such an instrument) founded the National String Instrument Corporation. The first instrument they produced was a metal-bodied guitar fitted with three conical aluminum resonators connected at the center by a T-shaped aluminum bridge, on top of which is a maple bridge saddle. This system was called the Tricone.

There were four different Tricones available, each with differently etched body designs: Style 1 was plain, Style 2 featured a wild rose, Style 3 had a lily of the valley, and Style 4 showed a chrysanthemum.

▲
**1930s duo Jim Holstein and Bob Pauole billed themselves as The Genial Hawaiians. Holstein played his National Tricone in both conventional guitar style and horizontal lap style.**

▼
**The pair can be heard on *Hula Blues* (2000), a compilation of lap-steel music from the 1930s.**

| | |
|---|---|
| **Body style:** | Tricone resonating, slatted sound hole |
| **Materials:** | "German silver" body (nickel alloy with nickel plating) with mahogany neck |
| **Finish:** | Engraving |
| **Fretboard:** | Ebony |
| **Inlays:** | Ivoroid diamond |
| **Frets:** | 19 |
| **Scale:** | 24 ¾" |
| **Width at nut:** | 1 27/32" |
| **Bridge:** | T-bar |
| **Tailpiece:** | Trapezoid |
| **Resonators:** | 3 x 6" units (2 on bass side; 1 on treble side) |
| **Tuners:** | Nickel with ivaroid buttons |

# NATIONAL STYLE O 1930

F riction existed between National's two founders from the start, and both would later claim to have played the greater part in the invention of the resonator. We do know, however, that guitarist George Beauchamp had initially wanted, for reasons of economy, to produce a single-cone instrument, just as instrument maker John Dopyera was convinced that this would be a poor-sounding compromise. In 1929, Beauchamp would file for a patent for the single-cone resonator and Dopyera would leave National to form his own rival company, Dobro.

So it was that in 1930 Beauchamp produced his first single-cone instrument, the now-famous National Style O. The amplification principle was the same as with the Tricone models, only that the bridge was now connected to a single 9 ½-inch cone in the center of the body.

The difference between the two approaches was in tone and volume. The Style O was much louder than the Tricone, with a sharper attack, but was lacking in warmth. Although resonators had not been created with blues musicians in mind, the Style O quickly gained popularity among popular artists of the period, such as Son House and Reverend Gary Davis.

In 1931, Beauchamp was fired by the shareholders of National. In 1934 Dopyera and his brothers merged the businesses to form the National-Dobro Corporation.

▲
**Mark Knopfler of Dire Straits is known for his Strat playing, but he is also a frequent user of National resonator guitars.**

▼
**Knopfler's National Style O featured on the front and back cover art of *Brothers In Arms* (1985).**

| | |
|---|---|
| **Body style:** | Single resonating, f-holes in upper bout; diamond shapes cut into resonator cover |
| **Materials:** | Nickel-plated steel (brass from 1932); bolt-on mahogany neck |
| **Finish:** | Assorted sand-blasted Hawaiian-style designs on front and sides |
| **Fretboard:** | Bound ebony |
| **Frets:** | 19 |
| **Scale:** | 24 ¾" |
| **Width at nut:** | 1 ²⁷⁄₃₂" |
| **Inlays:** | Dot |
| **Resonator:** | Single 9 ½" |

# NATIONAL STUDIO 66 1962

The National name is so closely associated with the resonator that it is easy to forget that the company also made electric instruments. And yet the last of the original National resonators came off the production line as early as 1942. The following year, three of the partners in the National Dobro Company, Victor Smith, Al Frost, and Louis Dopyera, reorganized themselves under the Valco brand (the company name was derived from the initials of their forenames).

Valco produced a large variety of fretted instruments under different marques, among them Supro, Airline, and Oahu, and, as their premium brand, National. At the same time, the company also produced amplification under contract for other well-known guitar makers, such as Danelectro, Gretsch, Harmony, and Kay.

The first guitars to bear the new National brand were archtop acoustics and hollow-body electrics. During the early 1960s, however, Valco briefly produced a range of National solid-body guitars. These were unusually shaped instruments with an appearance that could be described as Art Deco in character, with a sideways visual reference perhaps to the D'Angelico guitars built in New York several decades earlier.

The most unusual aspect of this National electric range was the body material, which was a proprietary man-made fiber. Valco called it "Res-O-Glas," gloriously describing it in a 1962 advert: "Polyester resins embedded with threads of pure gleaming glass provide a new climatically immune miracle material of the super space age . . . super durable . . . classically beautiful . . . functionally perfect."

Valco eventually ran into financial difficulties and merged with Kay in 1967. A year later the joint company went out of business.

▼
The jacket of the 1961 National sales catalog is as much a piece of period design as the instruments displayed inside. By this period, the National brand, once famed for its revolutionary acoustic resonators, was exclusively devoted to electric guitars—many of which were built using newly developed man-made materials.

| | |
|---|---|
| **Body style:** | 15" by 19" single cutaway solid body |
| **Materials:** | Res-O-Glas fiberglass body incorporating "bat wing" molded pickguard |
| **Finish:** | Sand buff |
| **Fretboard:** | Rosewood |
| **Inlays:** | Pearl dot |
| **Frets:** | 20 (not including zero fret) |
| **Scale:** | 24 ¾" |
| **Width at nut:** | 1 ¹¹⁄₁₆" |
| **Bridge:** | Rosewood, adjustable with thumb wheels |
| **Tailpiece:** | Trapezoid |
| **Pickups:** | Single bridge pickup |
| **Machine heads:** | Kluson |
| **Electrics:** | Single volume and tone controls |

# NATIONAL WESTWOOD 77 1962

All of the guitars produced during this time were characterized by their unique body shape, most famously the "map" models, such as the Glenwood and Newport ranges, with body designs that seemed to have been inspired by the outline of a map of the United States. The National Westwood range shared a similar styling but without the Res-O-Glas body.

The semi-solid Westwood was made available in three different models. At the top of the range, the cherry red 77 boasted a pair of Vista Power pickups (described as "treble" and "bass") and the Silver Sound bridge unit which featured a built-in pickup for "perfect acoustic string tone reproduction." The Westwood also boasted the impressive-sounding Val-Trol electrics—which were, in fact, no more than tone and volume controls for each pickup.

Due to their unorthodox shapes, National solid-body guitars of the period are now highly collectible.

Valco produced National solid-body electric guitars between 1962 and 1966. Even if some of these models featured plastic bodies, they were by no means cheap instruments. Indeed, they were comparable in price with some models produced by Fender and Gibson.

▲
**Bob Dylan uses a National Glenwood—the Westwood's Res-O-Glas sibling—as a slide guitar on the *Rolling Thunder Revue* tour.**

▼
**One of the most "bootlegged" of artists, Dylan documents his *Rolling Thunder Revue* on the widely available *Live 1975* album.**

| | |
|---|---|
| **Body style:** | Semi-hollow single cutaway "map of America" design |
| **Materials:** | Unspecified "hard wood" body, with bolt-on True-Pro neck |
| **Finish:** | Cherry red (Westwood 77), blonde ivory (Westwood 72), red sunburst (Westwood 75) |
| **Fretboard:** | Rosewood |
| **Frets:** | 20 (not including zero fret) |
| **Scale:** | 24 ¾" |
| **Width at nut:** | 1 ¹¹⁄₁₆" |
| **Bridge:** | "Compensated" adjustable Silver Sound unit |
| **Pickups:** | 2 Vista Power single-coil pickups; Silver Sound bridge pickup with 3-way switching |
| **Electrics:** | Master volume, and dedicated Val-Trol electrics consisting of volume and tone controls for each pickup |

# OVATION : THE STORY

For a man whose activities in the field of luthiery were little more than a footnote to a hugely impressive aeronautical business career, Charles Huron Kaman managed to make a permanent impact by bringing new technology to the conservative world of the acoustic guitar.

Born in Washington, D.C. in 1919, Kaman worked for helicopter pioneer Igor Sikorsky after graduating with a degree in aeronautics. Hugely ambitious, he had founded his own company by 1945, building groundbreaking helicopters such as the Kaman K-125  and K-225 models, using his own revolutionary design for intermeshing rotor blades. Fabulously successful, the Kaman Corporation diversified to include manufacture of airforce armaments and aviation components.

From his teen years, Kaman had also been an enthusiastic guitarist, and in the 1960s he further diversified, making use of his advanced technological knowledge to produce a new type of guitar. It had long been held by classical luthiers that the most significant key to a guitar's tone was in the design and materials of the soundboard. Kaman turn his attention to the back and sides—traditionally made from a "lesser" tonewood. He reasoned that by changing the back of the body to a rounded bowl, the flow of sound through the guitar would be improved, much as it is in the smaller body of a lute. He then looked into producing a body that integrated a traditional tonewood soundboard with a composite "bowl." For this he used a proprietary fiberglass developed at Kaman's aerospace laboratories with the name of Lyrachord.  The advantage of using a composite was that it combined minimal weight with great strength, it did not require internal bracing, which blocked soundwaves traveling inside the guitar's body, and it was economical to mass-produce. The Ovation Balladeer,  launched in 1966, was the first guitar built to Kaman's design and was an immediate success.

Ovation quickly became well known as a brand pushing the envelope of technology. For example, the piezo pickup fitted beneath the bridge was able to produce an excellent acoustic tone when plugged into an amplifier—bypassing the problem of microphone feedback. Consequently, by the 1980s a significant proportion of large-venue stage performers were seen playing Ovation electroacoustic guitars.

**Helicopters remained Charles Kaman's great passion. The 1947 Kaman K-125 was his first model.**

**The deep Lyrachord bowl of an Ovation electroacoustic guitar.**

**The Custom Balladeer, a 1990s version of the original Ovation "roundback."**

1919 · Charles Huron Kaman born in Washington, D.C.

1945 · Kaman Aircraft begins to produce helicopters

1966 · Ovation Balladeer launched with Lyrachord back and sides

1971 · Piezo pickups and preamplifiers fitted to Ovation acoustic guitars

1971 · Launch of the Breadwinner, the first Ovation solid-body

1977 · Ovation Adamas uses graphite top and multiple offset sound holes

2011 · Charles Huron Kaman dies

# OVATION : THE FAMILY TREE (1966-PRESENT)

The Ovation name has a unique position in the history of the acoustic guitar. Founder Charles Kaman was an aerospace engineer and guitar enthusiast. He was struck by the revolutionary idea of creating a bowl-backed instrument, rather like a traditional lute, but made from a proprietary form of glass fiber. This made the guitar stronger and louder but did not affect the tone, which is mostly determined by the tonewood used in the soundboard.

Kaman's contributions to guitar making did not stop there. In a second important development, he used piezo pickups built into the bridge, which enabled the acoustic player to plug the guitar into an amplifier yet still produce a convincing "acoustic" sound. During the 1980s, Ovation dominated the market for electroacoustic guitars.

In the early 1970s, Ovation also briefly entered the solid-body electric market, starting with two visually unorthodox instruments—the Breadwinner and Deacon. At that time, a guitar, especially an electric guitar, was referred to in popular slang as an "ax," and the body shapes of both of these models were something of a visual pun on that idea.

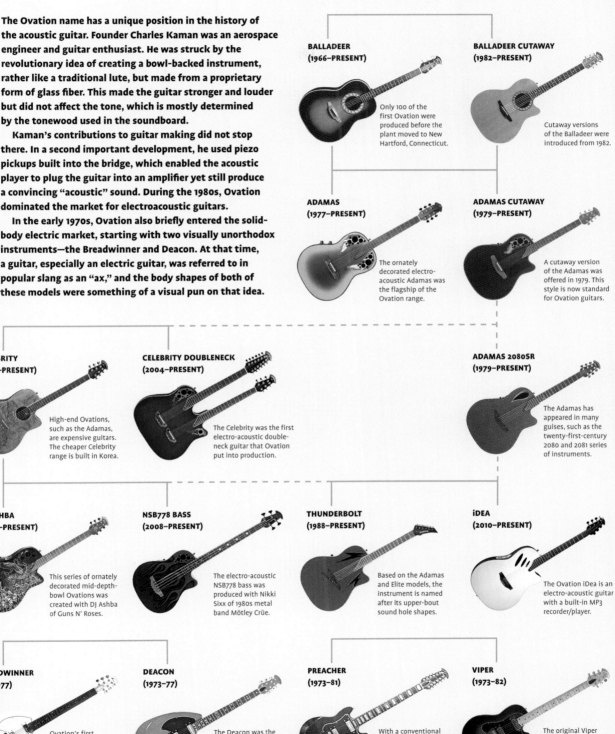

**BALLADEER (1966–PRESENT)**

Only 100 of the first Ovation were produced before the plant moved to New Hartford, Connecticut.

**BALLADEER CUTAWAY (1982–PRESENT)**

Cutaway versions of the Balladeer were introduced from 1982.

**ADAMAS (1977–PRESENT)**

The ornately decorated electro-acoustic Adamas was the flagship of the Ovation range.

**ADAMAS CUTAWAY (1979–PRESENT)**

A cutaway version of the Adamas was offered in 1979. This style is now standard for Ovation guitars.

**[CE]LEBRITY ([1]982–PRESENT)**

High-end Ovations, such as the Adamas, are expensive guitars. The cheaper Celebrity range is built in Korea.

**CELEBRITY DOUBLENECK (2004–PRESENT)**

The Celebrity was the first electro-acoustic double-neck guitar that Ovation put into production.

**ADAMAS 2080SR (1979–PRESENT)**

The Adamas has appeared in many guises, such as the twenty-first-century 2080 and 2081 series of instruments.

**[A]SHBA ([2]010–PRESENT)**

This series of ornately decorated mid-depth-bowl Ovations was created with DJ Ashba of Guns N' Roses.

**NSB778 BASS (2008–PRESENT)**

The electro-acoustic NSB778 bass was produced with Nikki Sixx of 1980s metal band Mötley Crüe.

**THUNDERBOLT (1988–PRESENT)**

Based on the Adamas and Elite models, the instrument is named after its upper-bout sound hole shapes.

**iDEA (2010–PRESENT)**

The Ovation iDea is an electro-acoustic guitar with a built-in MP3 recorder/player.

**[B]READWINNER ([1]971–77)**

Ovation's first solid-body electric guitar featured a solid mahogany body coated in Lyrachord.

**DEACON (1973–77)**

The Deacon was the deluxe version of the Breadwinner. A third model, the LTD, had a top cutaway.

**PREACHER (1973–81)**

With a conventional body shape, the Preacher featured twin humbuckers and a stereo output.

**VIPER (1973–82)**

The original Viper featured a pair of high-output single-coil pickups, claimed to be "6db hotter!"

# OVATION BALLADEER 1966

The invention in the twentieth century of man-made fibers permeated and transformed every area of life. Some industries, however, would prove stubbornly resistent to change, and while there have been numerous attempts to produce guitars from materials other than wood, few have succeeded beyond the initial novelty stage. One very significant exception has been the Ovation Guitar Company of New Hartford, Connecticut.

The Ovation story begins with aeronautical engineer and amateur guitarist Charles Kaman, wealthy owner of the Kaman Corporation, a company formed in 1945 with interests including helicopters and the testing of chemical and nuclear weapons.

In the early 1960s Kaman conducted research into the viability of producing an acoustic guitar with a fiberglass rounded-bowl back and sides and a new bracing system for the wooden top. Kaman developed a man-made fiber he called Lyrachord to make the acoustic bowl. The bowl shape proved to be a great success, enabling greater volume and projection to be achieved without any loss of tone. The first Ovation guitar to appear, the Balladeer, was launched in 1966.

▲
Joan Armatrading is one of the best-known singer/songwriters in the U.K. Here she can be seen playing an Ovation Balladeer in concert in 1977.

▼
Armatrading's delicate acoustic guitar work can be heard on her 1976 eponymous third album, which features her signature hit "Love And Affection."

**Body style:** Symmetrical figure-eight hollow body (single cutaway option available on later models)

**Materials:** Sitka spruce top with Lyrachord bowled back and sides; maple neck

**Finish:** Natural

**Fretboard:** Rosewood

**Inlays:** Acrylic trapezoid

**Frets:** 24

**Scale:** 25 ¼"

**Width at nut:** 1 ¹¹⁄₁₆"

**Bridge:** Walnut

**Pickups:** None (piezo bridge transducer on later models, *see right*)

**Electrics:** None (different Ovation preamps have since appeared on models equipped with piezo transducer)

# OVATION ADAMAS 1977

considerable R&D resources were tasked with developing a revolutionary pickup to overcome the inherent problems of amplifying an acoustic guitar in a live scenario, that Ovation began to achieve widespread interest.

The technology that resulted featured a "musically balanced" piezo pickup housed in an intonated bridge saddle, mounted on the underside of the soundboard. This connected to an internal pre-amp, which could then be plugged into an external guitar amplifier or PA system.

And thus a new category was born—the electroacoustic guitar. Ovation have dominated this field, their guitars finding a home in every style of music. Introduced in 1979, the Adamas remains one of the company's most important electroacoustics. They proudly boast that the labor going into each Adamas guitar "exceeds the number of man hours it takes General Motors to assemble a Cadillac Seville."

The Ovation Lyrachord-backed acoustic guitars quickly found a niche. Not only were they excellent lightweight instruments, but the molded back was so strong that it required no bracing at all—indeed, Ovation described their guitars as "virtually indestructible." However, it was not until the 1970s, when Kaman's

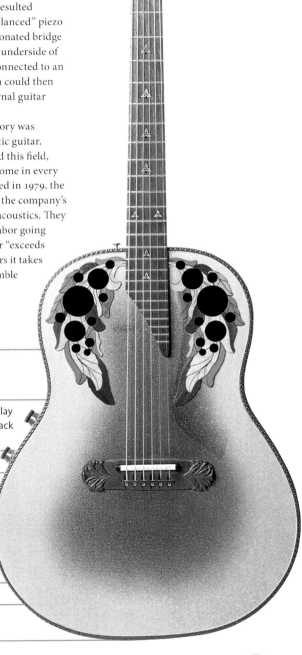

▲
**Kaki King heads a new generation of primarily acoustic instrumental musicians. She is seen here playing an Ovation Adamas with a cutaway.**

▼
**Kaki King's 2003 debut was *Everybody Loves You*, her only fully acoustic album to date. She has since been honored with a signature Ovation.**

**Body style:** Symmetrical figure-eight hollow body (single-cutaway option also available on later models)

**Materials:** Carbon and birch top, decorative inlay around sound holes, with Lyrachord bowled back and sides; maple neck

**Finish:** Assorted finishes

**Fretboard:** Rosewood

**Frets:** 24 (including 6 partial frets)

**Scale:** 25 ¼"

**Width at nut:** 1 ¹¹⁄₁₆"

**Bridge:** Walnut

**Pickups:** Piezo bridge transducer

**Electrics:** FET preamplifier with master volume and tone controls

# OVATION BREADWINNER 1971

O vation's reputation at the end of the 1960s was based on the development of its revolutionary fiberglass-backed acoustic guitars. As a new decade turned, Ovation was quick to make a mark on the electric guitar world. Applying transducer-equipped bridges to its existing instruments changed the way that acoustic musicians performed on stage—a field Ovation would lead for the next three decades. The company fared less well, however, in the world of the solid-body guitar.

Launched in 1971, the Breadwinner was Ovation's first non-acoustic instrument. A visually bold statement, the unusual mahogany body shape of the Breadwinner was, Ovation claimed, designed for its balance; the designer, however, claimed that as an artist he knew nothing of such matters and came up with a shape that resembled an ax head—because "ax" was popular slang for a guitar. The Breadwinner was coated in Lyrachord—the material used to make Ovation acoustics—meaning that most models still appear "ding-free."

Ovation also issued the upmarket Deacon, which took the Breadwinner shape and added a rather functionless additional cutaway in the upper body.

▲
**Wire, headed by Colin Newman, emerged dramatically in 1977 with the art-punk album *Pink Flag*. Always fascinating, Wire has continued to function into the twenty-first century.**

▼
**Chairs Missing (1978) was the second of Wire's many inspirational albums.**

| | |
|---|---|
| **Body style:** | Single cutaway solid body |
| **Materials:** | Mahogany body with 2-piece maple bolt-on neck |
| **Finish:** | Black, white, tan, blue; Lyrachord covering |
| **Fretboard:** | Ebony |
| **Inlays:** | Acrylic dot |
| **Frets:** | 24 |
| **Scale:** | 24 ¾" |
| **Width at nut:** | 1 11/16" |
| **Bridge:** | Fixed adjustable with tripoint mount |
| **Pickups:** | 2 toroidal single-coil pickups (later versions featured humbuckers); 3-position switch |
| **Electrics:** | Master volume and tone control; FET active pre-amplifier; phase switch on humbucking models |

# OVATION VIPER 1973

T he Ovation Breadwinner was not a major success. Most agreed that from a sonic perspective it was a fine guitar, but some found it visually off-putting. Hardly surprising, then, that in 1973 two new solid-body electrics—the Viper and Preacher—were introduced with the line: "For years, performers

have been asking Ovation to make a conventional-shaped guitar." So conventional, in fact, were the new models that their bodies were based simply on a scaled-down Ovation acoustic shape with cutaways: single for the Viper; double for the Preacher.

The Viper featured a pair of single-coil pickups, which, claimed Ovation, had 30 percent more windings, generating an output 6dB higher than other similar pickups—because, in the words of a 1970s advertisement, "the hotter the better." Its powerful, cutting sound was intended to appeal to Fender users. Ovation also increased the scale length; the company had used the Gibson-standard 24 ¾-inch for the Breadwinner but the Viper had the 25½-inch scale used on Fender guitars.

The Viper appeared in a number of different variants and was produced until late 1982. Ovation continues to produce acoustic and electro-acoustic instruments but no longer participates in the solid-body market.

▲
The Arctic Monkeys, led by singer, guitarist, and songwriter Alex Turner (here playing a Viper), was one of the most significant bands to emerge at the start of the twenty-first century.

▼
Released in 2009, *Humbug* is the third album from the Arctic Monkeys.

| | |
|---|---|
| **Body style:** | Solid single cutaway |
| **Materials:** | Alder body; 1-piece maple bolt-on neck |
| **Finish:** | Sunburst, red, natural, white, nutmeg |
| **Fretboard:** | Maple |
| **Frets:** | 24 |
| **Scale:** | 25 ½" |
| **Width at nut:** | 1 ¹¹⁄₁₆" |
| **Bridge:** | Fixed adjustable with tripoint mount |
| **Pickups:** | 2 "overwound" single-coil pickups; 3-way switching |
| **Electrics:** | Master volume and tone controls |

# PANORMO 1836

The label on a small-bodied English guitar built in 1836 reads: "Louis Panormo. The only Maker of Guitars in the Spanish Style. 46 High Street, Bloomsbury, London. Guitars of every description from 2 to 15 Guineas." Panormo was one of an elite group of luthiers active during the first half of the nineteenth century whose instruments were used by concert performers.

Panormo had trained under his father, a noted violin maker. While performing in London, Fernando Sor, the greatest virtuoso player-composer of the period, spent time with Panormo, showing him Spanish instruments built by Pagés and Martinez. Under Sor's instruction Panormo began building guitars in the Spanish style, notably using fan bracing, unknown at the time outside of Spain.

In 1854, Panormo left London with his sons to resettle in New Zealand. Eight years later he died. During his lifetime Panormo produced a large quantity of instruments of variable quality, many of which still survive. The best of these guitars are thought to rival anything else being produced at the time; other models suffer from a tone that is harsh and thin.

▲
One of the few portraits of nineteenth century virtuoso Fernando Sor, shown here playing a Panormo guitar.

▼
Music by Fernando Sor, on a guitar built by Louis Panormo, can be heard on the 2003 album *Plucked Instruments In The Edinburgh University Collection*, performed by Rob MacKillop.

| | |
|---|---|
| **Body style:** | Early 19th-century Spanish style |
| **Materials:** | 1-piece spruce soundboard edged in rosewood, with alternate thin strips of maple and rosewood; rosewood back and sides; band of rosewood at the bottom, edged on either side by strips of maple and rosewood. The back is 1-piece, veneered on to a spruce backing |
| **Finish:** | French polish |
| **Fretboard:** | Rosewood |
| **Purfling:** | Alternate strips of rosewood and maple |
| **Inlays:** | Mother-of-pearl on bridge ends |
| **Frets:** | 18 |
| **Scale:** | $1^{35}/_{38}$" |
| **Bridge:** | Ebony; ebony bridge pins with mother-of-pearl eyes |

# PARKER FLY ARTIST 1993

Arguably the most radical production guitar developed over the past twenty years, the Parker Fly, has managed to buck this trend.

The Fly was developed in 1993 by Ken Parker, who set out to build an instrument that was lower in mass than a regular guitar but that was just as solid in strength. It consists of a wooden frame with an exoskeleton made from a powerful carbon fiber/epoxy composite; the neck also features a similar composite fingerboard.

Also revolutionary, the Fly's electrics feature not only a pair of switchable humbuckers but also an internal battery-powered Fishman piezo pickup, which makes for a highly effective amplified acoustic sound.

In 2003 Parker Guitars was sold to U.S. Music Corporation and the Fly underwent a number of "refinements" aimed at reducing the high production costs. Other Fly variants include MIDI and bass versions.

The very fact that the first solid-body electric guitars produced at the beginning of the 1950s remain the most popular perhaps speaks volumes about the innate conservatism of the guitarist. Subsequent developments have been rare and generally not widely accepted.

▲
Best known for his work with King Crimson, Adrian Belew is an extraordinarily versatile guitarist. He has been an avid Fly user since becoming a Parker endorsee in 2004.

▼
Belew's work with the Parker Fly can be heard on his 2005 album *Side One*.

| | |
|---|---|
| **Body style:** | Solid with double cutaway and thin extended horns |
| **Materials:** | Body frame and set neck made from assorted tonewoods with a carbon fiber exoskeleton |
| **Finish:** | Assorted color finishes |
| **Fretboard:** | Carbon fiber |
| **Frets:** | 24 |
| **Scale:** | 25½" |
| **Width at nut:** | 1 15/22" |
| **Bridge:** | Parker vibrato |
| **Pickups:** | 2 humbucking pickups; 6-element Fishman piezo system fitted beneath bridge; pickup selector switch |
| **Electrics:** | Master volume and tone controls; piezo volume and tone controls; magnetic/piezo selector switch; stereo/mono switch |

Ted Nugent—gun in one hand; PRS guitar in the other.

Peter Frampton was one of Paul Reed Smith's earliest clients.

Al Di Meola's *Elegant Gypsy* (1977) was one of the first albums to feature prominently a Paul Reed Smith guitar.

If one guitar manufacturer has threatened the traditional axes of power over the past two decades, it has been PRS—Paul Reed Smith guitars. A typical PRS instrument is built to an extremely high standard, looks exquisite, plays easily, and is very versatile—capable of a wide range of sounds. Unsurprisingly, this luxury comes at a rather high retail price, meaning that PRS players are likely to be either professionals, or amateurs who take their playing very seriously indeed.

Paul Reed Smith was born in 1956 in Bethesda, Maryland. He was a music-obsessed teenager and played in numerous short-lived high-school bands. Sensing that this was not to be his calling, at the age of sixteen he began building his own instruments, initially making new bodies from existing necks. Shortly after, a local guitar store was sufficiently impressed with the repair he had done on a friend's Les Paul Junior that he was offered a part-time job while he finished high school.

While briefly pursuing a degree in mathematics, Smith also started to build his own instruments from scratch, while hanging around backstage at the major rock venues in Washington, D.C. and Baltimore, hoping to make contacts. He first managed to arouse the interest of a rock celebrity in 1975 when he turned up at a Ted Nugent concert with a guitar he had built. Nugent commissioned him to build a solid-body version of a Gibson Byrdland, a hollow-body archtop electric favored by jazz musicians of the 1960s. An increasingly confident Smith made a deal with Nugent: "If you don't fall in love with the guitar, you get your money back." Nugent did, and apparently still owns the instrument.

Smith understood that the key to getting known as a luthier lay in having his instruments played by rock stars. Before handing over Nugent's guitar, he had the chance to show it to Peter Frampton, the English guitarist then enjoying worldwide success with his *Frampton Comes Alive!* album. Frampton also gave him a commission to build a guitar.

By this stage in his career, Smith was becoming increasingly successful at securing meetings with rock's rich and famous musicians: "I'd show the roadies the guitars. They'd spend half an hour with me checking them out . . . decide that I'm cool and I'm not going to kill their artist . . . then they'd give me backstage passes. That's how I always get in!"

**1956** Paul Reed Smith born in Bethesda, Maryland

**1972** Paul Reed Smith builds his first guitar

**1975** Smith sells a guitar to rock star Ted Nugent

**1976** Al Di Meola commissions a guitar from Paul Reed Smith

**1980** Smith's idol, Carlos Santana, commissions a guitar

**1985** PRS Guitars founded—factory opens in Annapolis, Maryland

**1985** PRS Custom production model released

In 1976, a concert at Washington's Capital Center gave Smith the opportunity to meet one of his prime targets on a bill that featured Carlos Santana and Chick Corea's band, Return To Forever. Although Santana liked the guitar, he didn't elect to buy one. However, Return To Forever's Al Di Meola had been deeply impressed, and a deal was done—Di Meola has been using PRS guitars ever since. ③

An indication of the clarity of Paul Reed Smith's vision may be gained by looking at the guitars the luthier was now making. It is quite striking how closely they resemble the models that a decade later would be rolling off the production line, with their post-1958 double-cutaway Les Paul-style bodies, gently arched tops, and ornate fingerboards with bird inlays.

By the summer of 1977, Smith had built only seventeen guitars but was beginning to amass an impressive client roster. Yet he still had an elusive goal: "I figured if I could make a guitar for Carlos Santana, I'd be made." Smith was given a second shot at the end of 1980, and this time he took away a commission from the Mexican rock star. ④

By 1985, Smith felt that he had taken custom guitar-building as far as he could, and raised enough capital to set up a small factory in Annapolis, Maryland. The first instruments to come off the production line were the PRS Custom models with a range of optional variations. The guitars retailed at around the $1,500 mark—twice the cost of a U.S.-built Fender Vintage Stratocaster of the time. Other models followed, such as the Standard, Signature, and Limited Edition models, and later the Artist, McCarty, and exotic Private Stock instruments. ⑤

In 1992, PRS began an irregular series of Dragon guitars. Inspired by a dream Smith had had as a sixteen-year-old, featuring a guitar with a dragon inlaid down its neck, the Dragon 1 appeared in a limited run of fifty, individually decorated with startling dragon mosaics constructed from abalone, turquoise, and mother-of-pearl. Despite carrying a retail price of around $8,000 each, they sold out almost immediately—the rare guitars now have an estimated value approaching $30,000. ⑥

The PRS brand is admirably uncompromising. Exotic tonewoods and quality American craftsmanship do not come cheaply, but these are the foundations on which the company's success has been built.

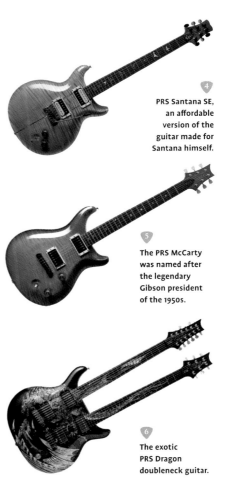

④ PRS Santana SE, an affordable version of the guitar made for Santana himself.

⑤ The PRS McCarty was named after the legendary Gibson president of the 1950s.

⑥ The exotic PRS Dragon doubleneck guitar.

**1986** PRS Signature model first produced with "ultimate quality wood"—each guitar personally signed by Paul Reed Smith

**1987** Bass-4 and Bass-5—the first PRS bass guitars

**1991** First version of the PRS Dragon in limited run of 50

**1995** PRS moves to larger factory premises on Kent Island, Maryland

**1995** PRS 10th Anniversary model

**1996** Private Stock range launched—each guitar is made to order and comes with a letter from Paul Reed Smith documenting its history

# PRS : THE FAMILY TREE (1975-PRESENT)

Paul Reed Smith built his first guitar in 1975 as a nineteen-year-old college student. His first guitars were modeled on the twin cutaway Gibson Les Paul Junior built in the 1950s. Indeed, this period of Gibson's evolution so consumed Smith that he would eventually collaborate with Ted McCarty, Gibson's president during that period—and after whom a line of PRS guitars would be named.

A comparison of the first custom model Smith built for Carlos Santana in 1980 (*below, top left*) with a large proportion of the PRS guitars manufactured since produces evidence of a singular vision; apart from the later Les Paul Junior-inspired single cutaways, there has been a surprising lack of cosmetic variation. After elongating the bass horn for the first factory PRS Customs in 1985, the body shape has remained largely constant.

Much the most significant manufacturer to have emerged toward the end of the twentieth century, PRS has produced guitars that are highly popular, in spite of their high cost, because of their combination of outstanding playability, versatile tonal range, and exquisite—often exotic—finishes.

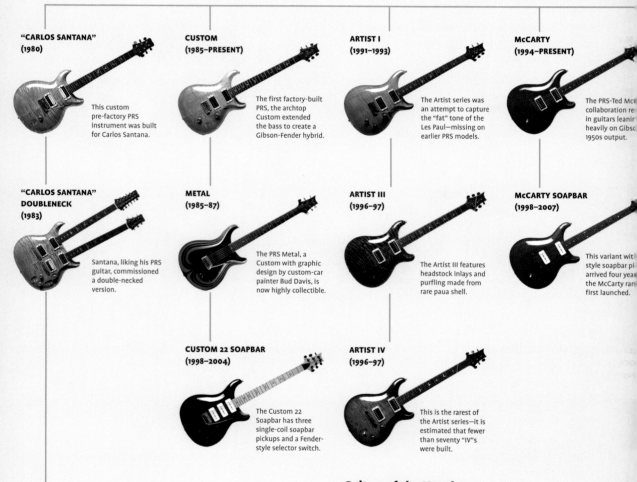

**"CARLOS SANTANA"**
**(1980)**

This custom pre-factory PRS instrument was built for Carlos Santana.

**CUSTOM**
**(1985–PRESENT)**

The first factory-built PRS, the archtop Custom extended the bass to create a Gibson-Fender hybrid.

**ARTIST I**
**(1991–1993)**

The Artist series was an attempt to capture the "fat" tone of the Les Paul—missing on earlier PRS models.

**McCARTY**
**(1994–PRESENT)**

The PRS-Ted McC[...] collaboration re[...] in guitars leanin[...] heavily on Gibso[...] 1950s output.

**"CARLOS SANTANA"**
**DOUBLENECK**
**(1983)**

Santana, liking his PRS guitar, commissioned a double-necked version.

**METAL**
**(1985–87)**

The PRS Metal, a Custom with graphic design by custom-car painter Bud Davis, is now highly collectible.

**ARTIST III**
**(1996–97)**

The Artist III features headstock inlays and purfling made from rare paua shell.

**McCARTY SOAPBAR**
**(1998–2007)**

This variant wit[...] style soapbar pi[...] arrived four yea[...] the McCarty ran[...] first launched.

**CUSTOM 22 SOAPBAR**
**(1998–2004)**

The Custom 22 Soapbar has three single-coil soapbar pickups and a Fender-style selector switch.

**ARTIST IV**
**(1996–97)**

This is the rarest of the Artist series—it is estimated that fewer than seventy "IV"s were built.

## Guitars of the Month

Between December 1994 and March 1996, PRS produced a dozen limited-edition experimental models, referred to as "guitars of the month." For Smith it was an opportunity to experiment with finishes and hardware detailing. Among the models produced were a scarlet twelve-string prototype, the first PRS hollow-body electric with f-holes, and another, with a hand-painted space scene on the body and sterling-silver fingerboard inlays suggesting assorted constellations. The "guitars of the month" principle led directly to the later Private Stock range.

**SANTANA SE II**
**(2002–7)**

This Korean-built budget model retailed at under $750—a very low price for a PRS.

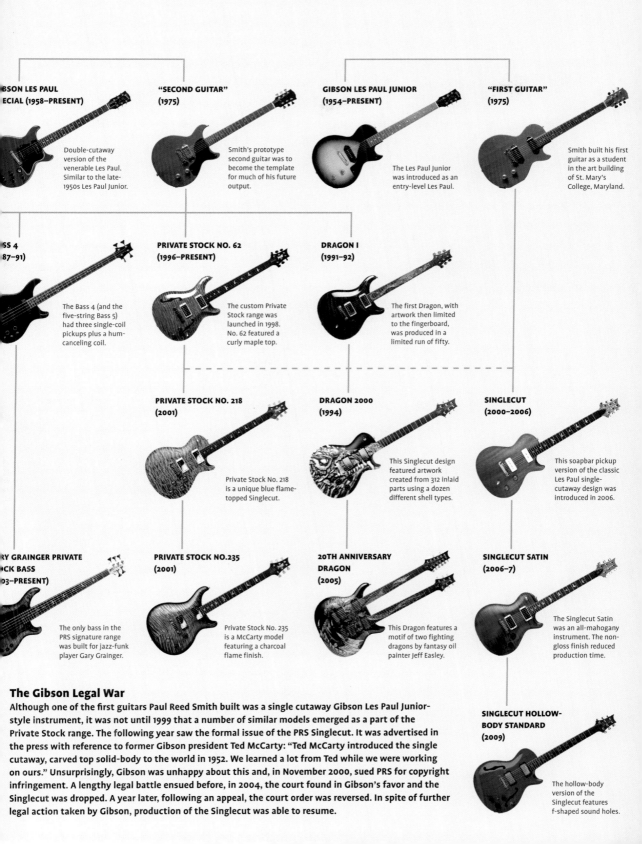

**BSON LES PAUL**
**ECIAL (1958–PRESENT)**

Double-cutaway version of the venerable Les Paul. Similar to the late-1950s Les Paul Junior.

**"SECOND GUITAR"**
**(1975)**

Smith's prototype second guitar was to become the template for much of his future output.

**GIBSON LES PAUL JUNIOR**
**(1954–PRESENT)**

The Les Paul Junior was introduced as an entry-level Les Paul.

**"FIRST GUITAR"**
**(1975)**

Smith built his first guitar as a student in the art building of St. Mary's College, Maryland.

**SS 4**
**87–91)**

The Bass 4 (and the five-string Bass 5) had three single-coil pickups plus a hum-canceling coil.

**PRIVATE STOCK NO. 62**
**(1996–PRESENT)**

The custom Private Stock range was launched in 1998. No. 62 featured a curly maple top.

**DRAGON I**
**(1991–92)**

The first Dragon, with artwork then limited to the fingerboard, was produced in a limited run of fifty.

**PRIVATE STOCK NO. 218**
**(2001)**

Private Stock No. 218 is a unique blue flame-topped Singlecut.

**DRAGON 2000**
**(1994)**

This Singlecut design featured artwork created from 312 inlaid parts using a dozen different shell types.

**SINGLECUT**
**(2000–2006)**

This soapbar pickup version of the classic Les Paul single-cutaway design was introduced in 2006.

**RY GRAINGER PRIVATE**
**CK BASS**
**03–PRESENT)**

The only bass in the PRS signature range was built for jazz-funk player Gary Grainger.

**PRIVATE STOCK NO.235**
**(2001)**

Private Stock No. 235 is a McCarty model featuring a charcoal flame finish.

**20TH ANNIVERSARY**
**DRAGON**
**(2005)**

This Dragon features a motif of two fighting dragons by fantasy oil painter Jeff Easley.

**SINGLECUT SATIN**
**(2006-7)**

The Singlecut Satin was an all-mahogany instrument. The non-gloss finish reduced production time.

## The Gibson Legal War

Although one of the first guitars Paul Reed Smith built was a single cutaway Gibson Les Paul Junior-style instrument, it was not until 1999 that a number of similar models emerged as a part of the Private Stock range. The following year saw the formal issue of the PRS Singlecut. It was advertised in the press with reference to former Gibson president Ted McCarty: "Ted McCarty introduced the single cutaway, carved top solid-body to the world in 1952. We learned a lot from Ted while we were working on ours." Unsurprisingly, Gibson was unhappy about this and, in November 2000, sued PRS for copyright infringement. A lengthy legal battle ensued before, in 2004, the court found in Gibson's favor and the Singlecut was dropped. A year later, following an appeal, the court order was reversed. In spite of further legal action taken by Gibson, production of the Singlecut was able to resume.

**SINGLECUT HOLLOW-**
**BODY STANDARD**
**(2009)**

The hollow-body version of the Singlecut features f-shaped sound holes.

# PRS Santana 1980

Like many 1970s American teenage musicians, Paul Reed Smith greatly admired Mexican latin/rock guitarist Carlos Santana. As a fledgling luthier, his dream was to build an instrument for his idol. In 1980, Smith met Santana before a concert and showed him his new dresser-draw maple model.

The guitarist was so impressed that he used the PRS for that evening's show. Santana loved the look and feel of the guitar but was not completely happy with the sound coming from the pickups. Nonetheless, the two discussed a specification for Santana's dream guitar and Reed went about trying to build it.

With the basic guitar unaltered, Smith added a specially designed vibrato arm (Santana had not wanted a Floyd Rose) and pair of humbuckers designed to order by Seymour Duncan. The guitar was a perfect fit for Santana's playing style, every note capable of feeding back consistently. More than impressed, the guitarist requested another two guitars be built.

The Santana model was not offered to the public until 1995, but Smith acknowledges the importance of Santana in establishing the PRS name: "We couldn't have done it without his support . . . He gave my instruments instant credibility."

Carlos Santana was one of the earliest guitar celebrities to make the switch to PRS; he has rarely played anything else since 1980.

Two decades after Santana's last commercial success, 1999's *Supernatural* was an international hit and a showcase for his PRS guitar sound.

| | |
|---|---|
| **Body style:** | Double cutaway solid body |
| **Materials:** | Mahogany body with figured maple top; set mahogany neck |
| **Finish:** | Natural figured maple |
| **Fretboard:** | Rosewood |
| **Inlays:** | "Eagle" inlays; "OM" symbol on truss-rod cover |
| **Frets:** | 24 |
| **Scale:** | 24 ½" |
| **Width at nut:** | 1 $^{21}/_{32}$" |
| **Bridge:** | PRS Tremolo unit |
| **Pickups:** | 2 humbuckers; 3-position switch |
| **Machine heads:** | PRS 14:1 ratio |
| **Electrics:** | Master volume and tone controls |

# PRS CUSTOM 1985

Paul Reed Smith launched his Custom series in 1985 at a time when guitar fashions were geared strongly to the metal end of the market, and where the vogue was leaning toward characteristically unorthodox sharp shapes and high-tech features—a stark contrast to the "old-school" lines of the PRS range. Of course, *anything* fashionable is doomed sooner or later to lose its luster. Sure enough, within a few years those metal monsters would appear absurdly dated while the PRS range positioned itself in the ranks of the timeless classics.

The Custom was constructed on the lines of the original Les Paul. It featured a one-piece mahogany neck set into a one-piece mahogany body "capped" with a distinctive maple top, bound at the edges. Like all PRS models, the Custom was something of a crossbreed, with Gibson-style humbucking pickups that could, when the five-way rotary selector switch was engaged in positions two and four, create Fender-style single-coil sounds.

In spite of its high price, the Custom was a major commercial success that would have a significant impact on the guitar world, not least in heralding a return to the traditional values that had briefly been abandoned.

▲
**Mikael Åkerfeldt,** guitarist, vocalist, and composer with influential Swedish progressive death metal band Opeth. Magazine polls have voted him among the ten greatest metal guitarists of all time.

▼
A variety of PRS Custom models can be heard throughout Opeth's 2008 album *Watershed*.

| | |
|---|---|
| **Body style:** | Solid double cutaway |
| **Materials:** | Mahogany with carved figured maple top, set mahogany neck |
| **Finish:** | Natural carved figured maple |
| **Fretboard:** | Rosewood |
| **Frets:** | 24 |
| **Inlays:** | Moons ("Shadow Birds" on anniversary models) |
| **Scale:** | 25" |
| **Width at nut:** | 1 21/32" |
| **Bridge:** | PRS Tremolo |
| **Machine heads:** | PRS 14:1 |
| **Pickups:** | 2 humbuckers with coil-taps for single-coil play controlled by a 5-way rotary selector switch |
| **Electrics:** | Master volume and tone controls |

# PRS DRAGON 1992

One of the hallmarks of the Paul Reed Smith brand has been the number of limited-edition models produced over the years, the most famous of which is the PRS Dragon.

When it was launched in 1992, the Dragon I had been a long time coming. As Smith himself related in that year's PRS catalog: "When I was sixteen I had a dream about a guitar with a dragon inlaid down the neck. Twenty years later the technology became available to inlay such a complicated design with precision."

A limited run of fifty Dragons was produced, each one with a beautiful dragon mosaic designed by Jude Van Dyke inlaid in the neck, comprising 201 pieces of abalone, turquoise, and mother-of-pearl. The Dragons were given a retail price of $8,000 and sold out almost immediately. These first Dragons are now estimated to have a value approaching $30,000.

Dragons II and III appeared in subsequent years, and once again sold out straightaway. However, PRS reserved the most dramatic design for the millennium Dragon 2000 (*see right*), on which the inlays were shifted from the fretboard to cover much of the guitar's lower bout. The guitar was advertised at the 1999 NAMM trade show in Anaheim, California, bearing the high tag of $20,000—advanced orders were placed for all fifty guitars before the show had closed.

With its intricate pattern spreading from the body into the fingerboard, the Dragon 2000 is unique in being the only single-cutaway Dragon made. Until 2000, all PRS models had been built around the same basic body shape: the Singlecut was controversial, its clear body resemblance to a Les Paul bringing about an injunction from Gibson in 2004. The lawsuit failed, however, and a year later production was allowed to resume.

▼
**The PRS Dragon is arguably the most collectible of modern-day production electric guitars. The PRS twentieth anniversary catalog, produced in 2005 for the lucrative Japanese market, prominently displays a Dragon on its cover.**

| | |
|---|---|
| **Body style:** | Solid single cutaway |
| **Materials:** | Mahogany with flame maple top, and set Brazilian rosewood neck |
| **Finish:** | Mosaic constructed from abalone, turquoise, and mother-of-pearl |
| **Fretboard:** | Brazilian rosewood |
| **Frets:** | 22 |
| **Inlays:** | No standard markers; mosaic from 15th fret |
| **Scale:** | 25" |
| **Width at nut:** | 1 21/32" |
| **Bridge:** | PRS Stoptail |
| **Machine heads:** | PRS 14:1 |
| **Pickups:** | 2 humbuckers; 3-way selector switch |
| **Electrics:** | Dedicated volume and tone controls for each pickup |

# PRS McCarty 1994

I n the early 1990s, Paul Reed Smith had begun looking at some of the design approaches taken during Gibson's golden era—the 1950s. The impetus to produce a new instrument came in 1992 when American session guitarist David Grissom approached Smith with a brief to produce a guitar that sounded like the old Les Paul used by Duane Allman on the 1971 album *The Allman Brothers Band at Fillmore East*. The guitar that emerged was named as a tribute to Theodore "Ted" McCarty, Gibson's president from 1950 to 1966, a man who had one way or another been responsible for most of the company's key electric guitars. During the 1980s Smith and McCarty had become close acquaintances.

The McCarty model took Smith's Dragon design and made the body thicker, the neck thinner, and the tuners lighter. It added an unusual tailstop bridge and covered humbucking pickups, based on the P.A.F. produced by Seth Lover at Gibson while McCarty was president.

Although the instrument was named in his honor, McCarty was not directly involved in the design—by then he was in his eighties and with failing eyesight. But Smith acknowledges his importance, and that "everything Ted was teaching me is incorporated."

▲
Jazz-rock virtuoso Al Di Meola came to prominence in the 1970s playing in Chick Corea's band, Return To Forever. He used a PRS McCarty for more than twenty years.

▼
Much of Di Meola's recent music has been acoustic, but *Consequence of Chaos* (2006) shows off his fine electric playing on the PRS McCarty.

| | |
|---|---|
| **Body style:** | Solid double cutaway |
| **Materials:** | Mahogany with East Coast maple top, set mahogany neck |
| **Finish:** | Natural East Coast maple |
| **Fretboard:** | Rosewood |
| **Frets:** | 22 |
| **Inlays:** | Moon; "McCarty" on truss rod cover |
| **Scale:** | 25" |
| **Width at nut:** | 1 21/32" |
| **Bridge:** | PRS Stoptail |
| **Machine heads:** | PRS Vintage |
| **Pickups:** | 2 brass-covered humbuckers; 3-way selector switch |
| **Electrics:** | Master volume and tone |

# PEAVEY RAZER 1983

Having designed and built his first amplifier at the age of sixteen, Hartley Peavey set up his own electronics company in his basement after graduating from Mississippi State University in 1965. From such modest beginnings, the Peavey brand expanded rapidly throughout the 1970s and is now one of the world's most significant names in audio electronics, with manufacturing bases in the U.S., U.K., and East Asia. Peavey holds more than 130 patents and has an unusually large product range of over 2,000 designs.

Although the Peavey brand has always been most strongly associated with guitar amplification, in 1978 the company introduced its first range of guitars. The T-60 guitar and accompanying T-40 bass were reputed to be the first production guitars built using computer-controlled carving machines; both instruments were highly regarded mid-market models.

Having established a reputation through their successive ranges of largely conventional-looking guitars, in 1983 Peavey entered the exotic metal market with a pair of highly unorthodox body shapes. First came the Mystic, which was broadly based on a standard spiky B.C. Rich design. Its counterpart, the Razer (*see right*), seemed to have no such precedent.

The most startling visual feature of the Razer is the unwaisted hard edge on the body's bass side—a straight line that passes from the tip of the horn to the lower bout. Construction, too, was unusual; the guitar featured Peavey's patented bilaminated maple neck—with laminates running in opposite directions to increase stability.

Finally, there were the Razer's unusual electrics—tone circuitry that incorporated a built-in coil tap; if the control is turned in one direction, the humbucker switches to a single coil.

▼
**The two "metal" Peaveys are premiered in the company's 1983 catalog. The Razer remained in production until 1986.**

| | |
|---|---|
| **Body style:** | Single-waisted double cutaway solid body |
| **Materials:** | Alder body with bolt-on bilaminated maple neck |
| **Finish:** | Assorted (*see color chart below left*) |
| **Fretboard:** | Maple |
| **Inlays:** | Acrylic dot |
| **Frets:** | 23 |
| **Scale:** | 24 ¾" |
| **Width at nut:** | 1 ¹¹/₁₆" |
| **Bridge:** | Die-cast chrome with adjustable saddles and vibrato mechanism |
| **Pickups:** | Fully shielded, high-output, full-range humbuckers with blade pole pieces for dual/single coil operation; 3-way selector switch |
| **Electrics:** | Master volume; tone control for each pickup—these also switch between single-pole and humbucker operation |

# PEDULLA PENTABUZZ 1990

Tim Landers (Al Di Meola), two of the leading lights of late 1970s jazz fusion. Pedulla was able to use their experience in the designs for his MVP model, and to tap into the Pastorius-inspired vogue for fretless bass with the Buzz.

Pedulla's reputation grew throughout the following decade, the business expanding accordingly, making it one of America's leading boutique bass brands. As the 1990s drew to a close, Pedulla became frustrated: "I was no longer doing what I loved to do . . . I did less in the shop, and more in the business end . . . I lost enthusiasm." Downsizing his operation, he now works on every instrument from the woodshop through finish and set-up.

The MVP and Buzz models are visually exotic, distinguished by beautiful finishes and the delicate line of two narrow teardrop horns. But in terms of sound and playability, many Pedulla owners would claim their instruments were matchless.

**M**ichael V. Pedulla set up his first workshop in 1975 in Rockland, Massachusetts. Although he began with acoustic and electric guitars, it was his first bass instruments that attracted interest and resulted in his taking on repairs for Mark Egan (Pat Metheny Group) and

▲
Mark Egan first became known on the New York jazz scene in the late 1970s as a member of the Pat Metheny Group. He has used Pedulla basses since 1980.

▼
Egan's jazz bass can be heard on a cover of Jimi Hendrix's "Little Wing" on Sting's 1987 double album *Nothing Like The Sun*.

Sting

| | |
|---|---|
| **Body style:** | Solid-body double cutaway |
| **Materials:** | 3-piece maple laminate straight-though neck with flame maple wings |
| **Finish:** | Natural and assorted finishes coated with gloss polyester |
| **Fretboard:** | Fretless ebony |
| **Inlays:** | 24 white inlaid fret lines; mother-of-pearl dots |
| **Scale:** | 34" |
| **Width at nut:** | 1½" |
| **Bridge:** | ABM 3-way adjustable machined brass with roller saddles |
| **Pickups:** | Bartolini PJ, JJ, or SB (specially built for Pedulla) with active electronics |
| **Electrics:** | Volume control; pan control between pickups; bass boost/cut switch; treble boost/cut switch; mid boost/cut switch |

# RAMÍREZ (JOSÉ III) 1956

The Ramírez dynasty is perhaps the most significant in the history of the classical Spanish guitar, instruments now having been built by four generations of the family.

The company was founded in 1882, when José Ramírez opened his first workshop in Madrid, Spain. After his death in 1923, his son José Ramírez II, a professional guitarist and luthier who had been living and working in South America, returned to Madrid to take over the company.

Plagued by material shortages in the aftermath of the Spanish Civil War, José II's son and apprentice, José III, began experimenting with unorthodox construction techniques, such as the use of North American cedar in the soundboard. When José III took control in 1957 he was able to oversee such important innovations as longer scale lengths and asymmetric bracing—both of which would become standard. He could name among his personal clients Andrés Segovia, the world's most noted concert guitarist.

In 1988, José III handed the business down to his son, José IV, who in addition to his hand-crafted heritage launched a range of student guitars built to exacting standards by outside contractors, but quality-assured and set up at the Ramírez workshop.

Laurindo Almeida played a guitar by José Ramírez III. Almeida enjoyed success as both a classical and jazz player.

▼
José Ramírez III marketed a "Segovia model" claimed to be identical to the guitar he made for the maestro's concert performances.

| | |
|---|---|
| **Body style:** | Spanish classical style |
| **Materials:** | Brazilian rosewood back; Brazilian rosewood sides reinforced with cypress; American red cedar soundboard; ebony neck reinforcement |
| **Dimensions:** | Lower bout width 14 ½", upper bout width 11 ⅛", depth 4 ¼" |
| **Fretboard:** | Ebony |
| **Frets:** | 19 (including partial fret) |
| **Scale:** | 26 ⅛" |
| **Width at nut:** | 2 ⅛" |
| **Width at 12th fret:** | 2 ¼" |
| **Bridge:** | Ebony; bone saddle |
| **Bracing:** | Asymmetrical (stiffer on treble side) |

# REPUBLIC HIGHWAY 61 2009

When we think of resonator guitars, it is the National and Dobro designs from the late 1920s that generally come to mind. Indeed, few other names have penetrated this niche market.

For Texan teenager Frank Helsley, hearing Johnny Winter playing acoustic blues on a resonator was the start of a lifelong obsession, both as player and designer. In 2007, frustrated at the poor quality of the affordable options available to the modern resonator enthusiast, Helsley founded Republic Guitars, teaming up with a small workshop in China to build his designs.

The Republic range covers both classic single-cone and tri-cone models, adding features that give a modern dimension to these very traditional instruments, such as body cutaways and options of classic nickel or "distressed" metal finishes.

In 2009 Helsley came up with the Highway 61, a travel-size guitar with a single cutaway, loud, highly playable, and with a surprisingly rich tone for such a small instrument. A year later Helsley won a U.S. patent on the design.

Although a young company, Republic has already attracted celebrity names such as the Doobie Brothers, The Eagles, and Johnny Winter himself.

Johnny Winter, one of the great modern-day slide blues players, works out on the Republic Highway 61 travel-size resonator.

▼

On the Doobie Brothers' acclaimed *World Gone Crazy* (2010), guitarist John McFee uses Republic resonators on a number of tracks.

| | |
|---|---|
| **Body style:** | Hollow-body, single-cutaway resonator |
| **Materials:** | Bell brass or steel body set around mahogany neck |
| **Finish:** | Polished nickel (on brass body); swamp green and powder coat (on steel bodies) |
| **Fretboard:** | Rosewood |
| **Inlays:** | Acrylic dot |
| **Frets:** | 19 |
| **Scale:** | 22 ½" |
| **Width at nut:** | 1 ¹¹⁄₁₆" |
| **Nut:** | Bone |
| **Bridge:** | Maple saddle |
| **Resonator cone:** | Handspun "continental" |

# RICKENBACKER : THE STORY

①
**Adolph Rickenbacker studies one of the first "Frying Pan" lap steel guitars.**

**1936 Electric Spanish Guitar (Model B).** ②

**1956 Combo 400.** ③

**1959 4000 bass with cresting wave body design.** ④

A dolph Rickenbacher was born in Switzerland in 1886. Brought to America, he changed the spelling of his name to cash in on the celebrity of his distant cousin, World War I flying ace Eddie Rickenbacker. Adolph formed the Rickenbacker Manufacturing Company in 1925, and by the end of the 1920s his workshop was largely employed making metal bodies for National resonator guitars, meeting guitarist and inventor George Beauchamp and luthier Paul Barth.

After disagreements at National, in 1931 the three of them formed the Ro-Pat-In (Electro-Patent-Intruments) company. Beauchamp had previously experimented with the idea of an amplified guitar, and in 1931 he produced the world's first commercial electronic stringed instrument. The "Frying Pan" ① was a lap steel Hawaiian guitar fitted with a pickup constructed from two horseshoe magnets. Shortly after, the company was renamed the Electro String Instrument Corporation and the Rickenbacker brand applied to its instruments. In 1935, the Frying Pan's horseshoe pickup was applied to a regular Spanish guitar, creating in effect the first true electric guitar. ② Rickenbacker himself, however, was not convinced of its business potential and concentrated on lap steels until 1953, when he sold his company to Francis C. Hall.

Hall believed that Rickenbacker could produce solid-body electric guitars capable of rivaling any Fender or Gibson. The first important new Rickenbacker was the 1956 Combo 400 solid-body electric guitar, ③ which was significant for its straight-through neck construction that would be a standard feature on many future Rickenbackers. The following year, Rickenbacker's star luthier, Roger Rossmeisl, designed the 4000 bass—the first realistic competitor for the pioneering Fender Precision. Its "cresting wave" body shape is still in production. ④

The brand thrived in the 1960s, fueled by the unprecedented success of The Beatles, whose two guitarists—John Lennon and George Harrison —both favored Rickenbackers. In 1964, Harrison was sent a prototype of the new Rickenbacker 360-12, which he first used for the dramatic opening chiming chords of "Hard Day's Night." This prestigious demonstration of the instrument made Rickenbacker the de facto leader of the pack when it came to twelve-string electric guitars.

**1925** Adolph Rickenbacker founds his manufacturing company

**1931** Rickenbacker forms Ro-Pat-In after disagreements at National

**1931** Ro-Pat-In produces the "Frying Pan" lap steel Hawaiian guitar

**1935** Ro-Pat-In creates the world's first electric (Spanish) guitar

**1953** Rickenbacker sells his company to Francis C. Hall

**1953** Hall switches focus from lap steels to solid-body guitars

**1964** The Beatles popularize Rickenbacker 12-string guitars

# RICKENBACKER

## FAMILY TREE

# RICKENBACKER FRYING PAN 1931

Although most of George Beauchamp's previous work had been with guitars—either as a player or as co-inventor of the principles of the cone resonator, by 1930 America was in the grip of the first major "world music" craze—Hawaiian music. So, as strange as it may seem to us, with six decades of guitar-dominated popular music behind us, when Beauchamp developed his magnetic pickup it seemed more logical from a commercial perspective to apply it to a Hawaiian lap steel.

A small six-stringed instrument, the lap steel was usually played horizontally with pitch changes made not by pressing the strings against frets with the fingers, but by moving a small metal bar along the strings with one hand and picking with the other.

Beachamp had conceived several different approaches to the amplification of vibrating strings, but the one that seemed to work most successfully was a single coil of wire wrapped around two large "horseshoe" magnets. Vibrations in the instrument's strings induced an electric signal in the coil which could then be amplified. According to the recollections of Beauchamp's son, Nolan, once the pickup had been successfully tested he asked a colleague at National to build a wooden body and neck. Within hours the instrument was constructed and the electronics fitted. Noting its shape, Beauchamp christened it the "Frying Pan."

Beauchamp and fellow supporters Paul Barth and Adolph Rickenbacker formed the Ro-Pat-In Corporation to exploit the invention commercially.

The earliest Frying Pans came in two models, the A-25 and the shorter scaled A-22. They were constructed from cast aluminum rather than the maple used on the prototype.

The Frying Pan was certainly the first electric lap steel guitar to be produced commercially, and as such its historical significance is beyond doubt.

▼
Alvino Rey was one of the first to popularize Rickenbacker's electric lap steel guitar. He was playing the instrument in the popular Horace Heidt band as early as 1932.

| | |
|---|---|
| **Body style:** Circle | |
| **Materials:** The protype featured an all-in-one maple body and neck; first production models were built from aluminum | |
| **Finish:** Natural | |
| **Fretboard:** Maple | |
| **Frets:** 25 | |
| **Inlays:** Dot | |
| **Scale:** A-25 models, 25"; A-22 models, 22 ½" | |
| **Bridge:** Combined bridge and tailpiece | |
| **Pickups:** Horseshoe-magnet pickup using 1 ½" magnets | |
| **Electrics:** None on original instrument—connection to amplifier made by connecting 2 terminals; volume control added in 1934; tone control added in 1935 | |

# RICKENBACKER MODEL B LAP STEEL 1935

The Rickenbacker A-22 and A-25 models had two significant drawbacks. The first problem players faced was the instrument's weight—they were built from cast aluminum, making them very heavy. What was less immediately obvious, however, was that since metal expands or contracts depending on the temperature, it was difficult to keep the instrument in tune. Beauchamp's solution was to build them from Bakelite, one of the earliest types of robust plastic, commonly used at this time on domestic electrical products such as radios.

The first Bakelite lap steel emerged in July 1935. The new body shape of the Model B made it more recognizable as a guitar, although the basic construction, with the neck bolted on to a solid body, was much the same as on the Frying Pan models. The metal look of its predecessor was continued, as five distinctive chrome plates were attached to cover almost the entire body.

Variants on the Model B design continued to be manufactured long after the Hawaiian craze had passed. Indeed, when Rickenbacker sold the company in 1953, Bakelite lap steels remained in production for the next two decades.

Jerry Byrd, while adept at playing the lap steel in Hawaiian settings, also played on the recordings of country stars, such as Hank Williams.

▼

*King Of The Hawaiian Steel Guitar* (2006) covers Hawaiian lap steel player Sol Hoopii's acoustic and electric recordings from 1927 to 1936.

| | |
|---|---|
| **Body style:** | Figure-eight molded body with hollow cavities |
| **Materials:** | Bakelite with bolt-on/detachable neck |
| **Finish:** | Black with 5 symmetrically positioned chrome plates covering the cavities |
| **Fretboard:** | Bakelite |
| **Frets:** | 23 double frets molded as part of the neck |
| **Inlays:** | Dot |
| **Scale:** | 22 ½" |
| **Width at nut:** | 2 ¼" |
| **Bridge:** | Combined bridge and tailpiece |
| **Pickups:** | Single horseshoe-magnet pickup positioned at bridge |
| **Electrics:** | Volume control |

# RICKENBACKER ELECTRO SPANISH 1933

Shortly after the launch of the A-22 lap steel, Rickenbacker began fitting the same single-coil horseshoe-magnet pickups to guitars. These inauspicious-looking models, branded "Electro Spanish" were the first electric guitars to be sold. They were not, however, specifically designed as electric instruments, but were stock acoustic guitars with an added pickup. The first Rickenbacker models bore a close resemblence to the National Trojan—unsurprising since the major players behind Rickenbacker had only a few years before been a part of National. The guitars were supplied unbranded to each company by Harmony in Chicago, which also supplied (and was subsequently bought by) mail order giant Sears-Roebuck.

The first Electro Spanish models appeared in Rickenbacker's advertising literature in 1933. They were basic models featuring a plywood body with a shaded mahogany finish, and two small f-holes on the upper bout. Like the first lap steels, the pickup was connected directly to an amplifier, with no onboard volume or tone controls—these were added, with plastic knobs that were sometimes octagonal, in subsequent years.

In 1935, the same year as the Model B lap steel appeared, Rickenbacker produced a Spanish counterpart, again molded from Bakelite and featuring the same pattern of chrome plates on its body. A case could be made for the Electro Spanish Model B as being the first purpose-built electric guitar, even though its size and shape did not appeal to professional players, who found it difficult to hold (guitarists in bands and orchestras at this time invariably played sitting down).

Adolph Rickenbacker had little faith in the idea of the electric guitar. He continued to concentrate on lap steel guitars until deciding to sell the company in 1953.

▼
The Electro Spanish was made using existing bodies of the National Trojan (below). The unusual position of its f-holes was dictated by the central resonator unit, which left no other place for them.

| | |
|---|---|
| **Body style:** | Figure-eight Spanish |
| **Materials:** | Maple veneer with maple neck |
| **Finish:** | Sunburst |
| **Fretboard:** | Rosewood |
| **Frets:** | 20 |
| **Inlays:** | Block |
| **Scale:** | 24 ¾" |
| **Width at nut:** | 1 $^{27}/_{32}$" |
| **Bridge:** | Fixed |
| **Tailpiece:** | Trapeze |
| **Pickups:** | Single horseshoe-magnet pickup |
| **Electrics:** | None on original models; volume and tone controls added separately in subsequent years |

# RICKENBACKER 360-12 1964

The folk music revival of the early 1960s saw a huge resurgent interest in acoustic twelve-string guitars. Danelectro and Gibson had already dabbled in twelve-string electrics, and in 1963 Rickenbacker began its own experiments. The Beatles may not have formally endorsed Rickenbacker products, but the very fact that the world's most popular band played "Rickys" provided priceless publicity. In 1964, Francis C. Hall ensured that The Beatles received a prototype of one of the first 360-12 models, and George Harrison was immediately taken with the guitar.

Based on the hollow-body Model 360, the 360-12 was noteworthy for a radical headstock design by Dick Burke that combined a classical guitar's slotted style with a standard electric's solid peghead. This innovation meant that all twelve tuners could be fitted into a regular sized headstock.

George Harrison's opening chords to the song "A Hard Day's Night" were largely responsible for the popularization of the 360-12. The distinctive intro inspired U.S. band The Byrds, whose jangly Rickenbackers went on to all but define how folk rock should sound.

▲
**The Byrds' Roger McGuinn**, seen here playing a related 370-12 twelve-string Rickenbacker. Their cover of Bob Dylan's "Hey Mr. Tambourine Man" was a benchmark in the folk rock genre.

▼
The single "Eight Miles High," released in 1966, was a huge influence on the psychedelic rock scene.

| | |
|---|---|
| **Body style:** | Hollow-body double cutaway |
| **Materials:** | Maple carved body with white plasticbinding; set 3-ply maple neck (walnut neck used on some models) |
| **Finish:** | Mapleglo (natural), jetglo (black), fireglo (sunburst), midnight blue |
| **Fretboard:** | Rosewood |
| **Inlays:** | Rickenbacker triangle |
| **Frets:** | 21 |
| **Scale:** | 24 3/4" |
| **Width at nut:** | 1 11/16" |
| **Bridge:** | Adjustable |
| **Pickups:** | 2 single-coil pickups; 3-way switching |
| **Electrics:** | Separate volume and tone controls for each pick-up; small mixer control |

# RICKENBACKER COMBO 400 1956

In view of Rickenbacker's undisputed place in the history of the electric guitar, the company seemed slow to grasp the commercial potential of solid-body instruments. An important change came about in 1953 when Francis C. Hall bought the Electro String Music Corporation from Adolph Rickenbacker. Hall had sold Fender electric guitars the previous two years and knew this was the direction his company needed to take.

The first Rickenbacker solids appeared in 1954: the Combo 600 and Combo 800 models were the first to feature the now-famous pointed "swoosh" logo on the truss-rod plate—a design created by Hall's wife.

Rickenbacker's first important contemporary solid-body instrument appeared two years later. A budget "student" guitar, the Combo 400 was notable for abandoning the large horseshoe pickup that had been used since the Frying Pan days. More significantly, it was the first Rickenbacker constructed using a straight-through neck—where the center of the body and neck were cut from a single piece of wood, with the wings glued separately. This would become a standard feature on most models thereafter.

▲
The 1956 Rickenbacker catalog heralds the new Combo 400 model, the first to feature what collectors call the "tulip" cutaways. The straight-through neck construction was also a first for a production solid-body guitar—although the one-off instruments built by Paul Bigsby for country musician Merle Travis in the late 1940s also used this technique.

| | |
|---|---|
| **Body style:** | Double "tulip" cutaway solid body |
| **Materials:** | Maple body with straight-through maple neck; wings bolted and glued |
| **Finish:** | Cloverfield green, Montezuma brown, jet black |
| **Fretboard:** | Rosewood |
| **Inlays:** | Rickenbacker dots |
| **Frets:** | 21 |
| **Scale:** | 24 ¾" |
| **Width at nut:** | 1 ⅝" |
| **Bridge:** | Fixed |
| **Pickups:** | 1 single-coil pickup |
| **Machine heads:** | Grover |
| **Electrics:** | Master volume and tone control; tone switch on upper treble bout |

# RICKENBACKER 325 1965

and their two guitarists—George Harrison and John Lennon—played Rickenbackers. When Beatlemania hit the U.S. after their 1964 appearances on the Ed Sullivan Show, demand for Rickenbackers would rocket, the company even receiving its own fan mail from teenagers the world over!

John Lennon was the first Beatle to encounter a Rickenbacker. At a store in Hamburg in 1960 he bought a 1958 natural-finish Model 325—a semi-hollow three-quarter-scale instrument with three pickups that had been introduced as part of the Capri series.

The guitar shown here is one of the four 325's owned by John Lennon. His original guitar was heavily modified, the middle pickup disconnected (presumably so the selector switch could be used to blend the other two pickups) and, in 1962, given a black paint job by British guitar manufacturing legend Jim Burns.

Hall had carefully managed the growth of Rickenbacker throughout the 1950s. Little did he know, however, that public recognition of the brand was about to explode. A new English band called The Beatles were creating hysteria,

▲
The Rickenbacker Model 325 was so strongly linked with John Lennon during Beatlemania that it became widely known as the Rickenbacker "John Lennon Model."

▼
All of The Beatles' early albums—such as *A Hard Day's Night* (1964)—featured John Lennon's Rickenbacker 325 and George Harrison's 425 or 360-12 models.

| | |
|---|---|
| **Body style:** | Semi-hollow double cutaway "Capri" style with f-shape sound holes (a few very early models from 1958—such as John Lennon's—have no sound hole) |
| **Materials:** | Maple body with three-quarter-scale set maple neck |
| **Finish:** | Mapleglo (natural), jetglo (black), fireglo (sunburst) |
| **Fretboard:** | Rosewood |
| **Inlays:** | Acrylic dot |
| **Frets:** | 21 |
| **Scale:** | 20 ¾" |
| **Width at nut:** | 1 ⅝" |
| **Bridge:** | Height adjustable (not individual saddles) |
| **Tailpiece:** | Trapezoid |
| **Pickups:** | 3 single-coil "toaster" pickups; 3-position switch (each selecting 1 pickup) |
| **Electrics:** | 2 volume and tone controls; small mixer control (on later models) |

# RICKENBACKER 450-12 1965

T he Combo 400 was launched at the same time as the twin-pickup Combo 450. These models, with their distinctive "tulip" body shapes, were discontinued in 1958 and replaced by a new series of instruments that featured a cresting wave body shape. The new 450, with

a thinner and lighter body introduced in 1961, was a commercially successful instrument that went through several notable upgrades. Most noticeably, the metal pickguard that covered much of the body was replaced with thick white plastic, which is now seen as a fundamental part of the Rickenbacker look. Other options offered were a Boyd vibrato arm and a third pickup.

Like most of the Rickenbacker series, a twelve-string version of the 450 was introduced. In 1966 the 450-12 could optionally be fitted with one of Rickenbacker's more curious pieces of technology—the "comb" converter system. A metal contraption fitted beneath the neck pickup, and engaged from above by a lever, would push one of each of the pairs of strings down against the fingerboard so that it could be used as a six-string guitar. Most who tried the system discovered that it impeded their playing style: it was abandoned in 1974.

▲
Fred "Sonic" Smith, guitarist with Detroit agitators the MC5, used a Rickenbacker 450-12 as his main instrument. Curiously, he strung it as a standard guitar, with six strings.

▼
Released in 1970, The MC5's second album *Back In The USA* was almost a blueprint for punk rock.

| | |
|---|---|
| **Body style:** | Cresting wave solid body |
| **Materials:** | Maple body with straight-through maple neck; wings bolted and glued |
| **Finish:** | Sunburst, "fireglo," black, or natural |
| **Fretboard:** | Rosewood |
| **Inlays:** | Acrylic dot |
| **Frets:** | 21 |
| **Scale:** | 24 ¾" |
| **Width at nut:** | 1 ⅝" |
| **Bridge:** | Fixed |
| **Pickups:** | 2 single-coil pickups; 3-way pickup selector switch |
| **Machine heads:** | Grover |
| **Electrics:** | Volume and tone control for each pickup |

# RICKENBACKER 4000 1957

▲

Hailing from Canada, Bachman-Turner Overdrive were famed during the 1970s for their high-energy rock. Bassist/vocalist Fred Turner played a Rickenbacker 4000.

Although Leo Fender is historically tied to the birth of the solid-body electric guitar, a convincing argument could be built around the idea that he *truly* altered the path of music with the invention of the electric bass guitar in 1951. Fender was all but unchallenged in this field until Rickenbacker debuted the 4000 bass in 1957.

The instrument was designed by Roger Rossmeisl and adopted Rickenbacker's unique new approach to building guitars, with a straight-through neck cut from a single piece of wood—most commonly maple, although some early 4000s also appeared in mahogany and walnut. This gave the bass greater sustain than the "bolt-on" Fender Precision.

The body also provided a dramatic visual contrast with the Fender, the now instantly recognizable cresting-wave shape seeming positively futuristic by comparison.

The success of the Rickenbacker 4000 caused Fender to take a closer look at the Precision. The outcome was the birth of the Fender Jazz in 1960. Five decades later, the two Fenders and the descendants of the Rickenbacker 4000 remain the most popular and celebrated of bass guitars.

▼

Released in 1974, *Not Fragile* featured Bachman-Turner Overdrive's worldwide hit "You Ain't Seen Nothing Yet."

| | |
|---|---|
| **Body style:** | Solid body cresting wave shape |
| **Materials:** | Maple body with straight-through neck (early models also produced in mahogany and walnut); neck featured a double truss rod |
| **Finish:** | Mapleglo, fireglo, and assorted colors |
| **Fretboard:** | Rosewood (ebony used on some reissues) |
| **Inlays:** | Acrylic dot |
| **Frets:** | 20 |
| **Scale:** | 33 ½" |
| **Width at nut:** | 1 11/16" |
| **Bridge:** | Combined bridge and tailpiece |
| **Pickups:** | Single horseshoe-magnet pickup |
| **Machine heads:** | Open |
| **Electrics:** | Master volume and tone control |

# RICKENBACKER 4001 1961

T he Fender Jazz emerged in 1960, its twin-pickup arrangement enabling the player to achieve a vastly increased tonal range. Rickenbacker began to add a second pickup to its 4000 model in 1961 before taking the decision to create a new model—the 4001.

A high-end model, the 4001 not only had two pickups but deluxe features, such as a binding on the body and neck as well as the characteristic Rickenbacker triangle inlays. An optional feature on the 4001 was having the instrument wired for twin-output Rick-O-Sound—essentially enabling separate audio signals to be taken from each pickup. Players who embraced the system would often take a stereo cable from the 4001 and connect the two pickups to different amplifier channels—or even separate amplifiers. Rick-O-Sound was fitted as a standard feature from 1971.

The 4001 appeared in many variants, undergoing a redesign in 1979 which resulted in the 4003. The original 4001 was slowly phased out and production ended in 1986.

The list of notable musicians using the 4000 series is endless, its popularity as strong as ever among the current generation of bass players.

▲
**Chris Squire of Yes made full use of the the Rick-O-Sound power, often using his 4001 as a lead instrument.**

▼
**Recorded in 1971, *The Yes Album* heralded the progressive rock era. Chris Squire's Rickenbacker 4001 takes an unusually prominent role for a bass guitar.**

| | |
|---|---|
| **Body style:** | Solid body cresting wave shape |
| **Materials:** | Maple body with straight-through neck |
| **Finish:** | Mapleglo, fireglo, and assorted colors |
| **Fretboard:** | Rosewood |
| **Inlays:** | Rickenbacker triangle |
| **Frets:** | 20 |
| **Scale:** | 34" |
| **Width at nut:** | 1¹¹⁄₁₆" |
| **Bridge:** | Combined bridge and tailpiece; individual saddles adjustable for intonation and height |
| **Pickups:** | 2 horseshoe-magnet/single-coil pickups, 3-way selector switch |
| **Machine heads:** | Open |
| **Electrics:** | Dedicated volume and tone control for each pickup |

# RICK TURNER MODEL 1 1979

Rick Turner was one of the innovative luthiers who formed part of Alembic Inc. in 1969, the company that produced the first high-impedance active guitars.

Turner left Alembic in 1978 to set up his own custom guitar workshop. His first new design was the Model 1, which was built for Lindsey Buckingham, then enjoying worldwide success with Fleetwood Mac.

The body of the Model 1 was inspired visually by the nineteenth-century Viennese luthier Johann Stauffer, under whom Christian Frederick Martin had learned his trade before emigrating to the United States.

A unique feature of the Model 1 is Turner's Rotatron pickup. Cradled in what from a distance appears to be a sound hole—indeed, many Fleetwood Mac watchers assumed Buckingham to be playing a semiacoustic instrument—the unit can be rotated by the musician to fine-tune the tonal balance across the strings.

The Model 1 has remained in small-scale production. As Turner himself estimates, "We've made somewhere around 500 to 600 of them over thirty years, so there are just not that many of them around. We currently make about five a month . . . pretty steady."

▲
**Lindsey Buckingham played guitar with the "American" AOR version of Fleetwood Mac that dominated the world at the end of the 1970s.**

▼
**Fleetwood Mac's *Tusk* (1979) was the first album on which Buckingham played the Rick Turner guitar.**

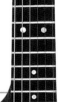

| | |
|---|---|
| **Body style:** | Single cutaway with solid body carved at top and back, inspired by Johann Stauffer |
| **Materials:** | Mahogany body with graphite-reinforced maple and purpleheart laminate set neck |
| **Finish:** | Natural |
| **Fretboard:** | Rosewood with black binding |
| **Inlays:** | Paua abalone dot |
| **Frets:** | 24 (medium jumbo) |
| **Scale:** | 24 ¾" |
| **Width at nut:** | 1 ¹¹⁄₁₆" |
| **Bridge:** | Turner design (previously used on his Alembic guitars) |
| **Pickups:** | Rotatable high-impedance humbucker |
| **Machine heads:** | Schaller M6-A |
| **Electrics:** | Master volume and tone controls; parametric EQ (with hardwire-bypass switch) with 150 Hz–3.5 kHz sweep and 12 dB boost/cut |

# ROCKINGER LADY 1983

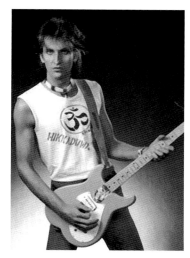

The Rockinger name, based in Hannover, Germany, is internationally established as a supplier of kits and parts for amateur luthiers or players wanting to hot-rod their guitars.

Founded in 1978, Rockinger achieved its greatest prominence two years later when it came to the attention of Dennis Berardi, the owner of the American Kramer brand—famed for its use of aluminum necks. He had been impressed with a demonstration of the Rockinger Tru-Tone tremolo—one of the first locking/fine-tuning systems to be produced—and licensed them for the new range of Kramer guitars. Also impressed was guitar superstar Eddie Van Halen, who consequently became a Kramer endorsee—indeed, the Rockinger system was introduced by Kramer as "The Edward Van Halen Tremolo." This success was quickly overshadowed, however, by the similar, less cumbersome Floyd Rose model, which was soon adopted universally.

Rockinger have also maintained a low-key guitar manufacturing operation, introducing models such as the Lady, featuring an offset waist, extended lower horn, and curious "dimple" on the lower bout.

▲
**German rock guitarist Carl Carlton (or Karl Walter Ahlerich Buskohl, to his family) seen playing a Rockinger Lady.**

▼
**Carlton is best known as German rock star Peter Maffay's sideman, and can be heard on *Tattoos* (2010), a greatest hits compilation.**

| | |
|---|---|
| **Body style:** | Offset-waist double cutaway solid body with extended lower horn |
| **Materials:** | Maple body with bolt-on maple neck |
| **Finish:** | Assorted colors |
| **Fretboard:** | Maple or rosewood |
| **Inlays:** | Acrylic dot |
| **Frets:** | 24 |
| **Scale:** | 25 ½" |
| **Width at nut:** | 1 ⅝" |
| **Bridge:** | Fixed |
| **Pickups:** | 1 or 2 single-coil pickups; 3-way pickup selector switch on 2-pickup models |
| **Electrics:** | Master volume and tone controls |

# ROLAND GS-500 1977

Roland's first guitar synth, launched in 1977, consisted of two parts. The GS-500 was an unremarkable guitar built by Ibanez; the onboard technology, however, was anything but. A twenty-four-way cable connected the guitar to an external synthesizer unit (the GR-500), enabling the knobs on the body of the guitar to control aspects of the synthesizer.

Critical to the technology was creating a pickup that could accurately convert the vibration of the strings into the control voltage data needed to drive the synthesizer. This entailed creating a "divided" pickup that sent a signal from each individual string to the unit—the sound of multiple strings is too complex to produce accurate pitch.

Requiring considerable adjustment in playing technique, the GS/GR-500 was not hugely popular. It remains, however, a bold and interesting attempt to fuse the disparate worlds of the guitar and the synthesizer.

The Japanese electronics giant Roland was, surprisingly, only founded in 1972. As befitting a company built around bringing innovative electronics to the masses, it's no surprise that Roland was the first (and only) company to mass-market a guitar-controlled synthesizer.

▲
**This promotional photograph from 1977 shows Roland's suggested stage setup, with the GR-500 unit on its own stand so it can be manipulated while playing the GS-500.**

▼
**U.S. session guitarist Chuck Hammer used the GS/GR-500 system throughout David Bowie's 1980 *Scary Monsters* album.**

| | |
|---|---|
| **Body style:** Single cutaway solid body | |
| **Materials:** Mahogany body with 2-piece maple top; set mahogany neck | |
| **Finish:** Natural | |
| **Fretboard:** Rosewood | |
| **Frets:** 22 | |
| **Scale:** 25½" | |
| **Width at nut:** 1 ¹¹⁄₁₆" | |
| **Pickups:** 1 humbucker (for guitar output); divided pickup for control of external GR-500 unit; 3-position switch (guitar/both/synthesizer) | |
| **Electrics:** Master volume and tone controls with 3-way EQ switch | |
| **Synthesizer controls:** Polyensemble, bass, solo melody, external; synth remote switch; portamento switch | |

# ROLAND G-707 1984

in 1984 Roland's GR-700 was a stomp-box unit housing banks of preset sounds that could be recalled from a footswitch. These sounds could also be programmed and stored by the user.

The issue of performance was also addressed on the G-707 guitar. Converting a vibrating string into consistent control data had been a problem: Roland's solution was a graphite support bar that connected the upper horn to headstock, making the neck more stable and thus avoiding data being corrupted by unintended movement. This also gave the instrument a futuristic appearance that fitted the mood and music of the time (but would appear absurdly dated only a few years later).

This was the last mass-market guitar synth. Roland later focused on pickups that can be fitted to any guitar and send generic MIDI data.

Roland showed admirable persistence with the idea of the guitar synthesizer. One of the reasons the 500 series had failed (and why it is still so prized by guitar-synth enthusiasts) was that it was too complex to use. Following the evolution of keyboard synthesizers,

▲
Steve Stevens is a long-standing member of Billy Idol's band. He was seen using the G-707 on stage in music videos during the 1980s.

▼
Billy Idol was a surprising success in the U.S. during the 1980s. Steve Stevens used the G-707 extensively on the 1983 album *Rebel Yell*.

| | |
|---|---|
| **Body style:** | Single cutaway solid body with stabilizing bar |
| **Materials:** | Alder body; maple set neck; graphite stabilizer bar |
| **Finish:** | Silver, red, black |
| **Fretboard:** | Rosewood |
| **Frets:** | 22 |
| **Scale:** | 25 ½" |
| **Width at nut:** | 1 ¹¹⁄₁₆" |
| **Pickups:** | 2 humbuckers; 3-way switching; divided pickup fitted alongside bridge |
| **Electrics:** | Master volume and tone controls; balance control mixing guitar and synthesizer |
| **Synthesizer controls:** | Cut-off frequency control; Resonance control; low-frequency oscillator (vibrato depth) control |

# SANTA CRUZ TONY RICE 1982

The Californian Santa Cruz Guitar Company is a uniquely American business. Seemingly founded on the West Coast hippie ideals of the 1960s, Santa Cruz has fused a traditional approach to craftsmanship with a strong desire to innovate. And, true to the company's origins, a willingness to share information with other luthiers.

In the early 1970s, young guitarist Richard Hoover moved to Santa Cruz, California. When his Martin D-28 was stolen he was unable to buy another, so Hoover decided to learn the basics of guitar-making from a local luthier.

In 1976, teaming up with William Davis and Bruce Ross, Hoover formed Santa Cruz Guitar Company to compete with the Martins and Gibsons that dominated the steel-string market. Santa Cruz quickly became brand of choice for an emerging new generation of progressive steel-string players, such as Tony Rice, Dale Miller, and Will Ackerman. The company's roster of artists now reads like a "who's who" of American country and folk.

Tony Rice has used Santa Cruz guitars since the 1980s. Dating from 1982, the signature model produced for him is a dreadnought shape designed with an enhanced treble and midrange for Rice's rapid single-note playing style.

▲
Tony Rice is one of the most influential modern American acoustic guitarists; his progressive Bluegrass style is sometimes referred to as "Newgrass."

▼
Rice's *Cold On The Shoulder* (1984) added vocals to his guitar skills, but dysphonia, a voice disorder, ended his singing in the early 1990s.

| | |
|---|---|
| **Body style:** | Dreadnought |
| **Materials:** | Indian rosewood body with zipper stripe and ivaroid binding; Sitka spruce top |
| **Bracing:** | Scalloped |
| **Finish:** | Clear top, clear gloss back and sides, clear matte neck |
| **Fretboard:** | Ebony |
| **Inlays:** | Black side dots; Santa Cruz Guitar Company logo on 12th fret; herringbone rosette and purfling |
| **Frets:** | 21 |
| **Scale:** | 25 3/8" |
| **Width at nut:** | 1 11/16" |
| **Pickguard:** | Tortoiseshell |
| **Machine heads:** | Nickel, open-back |

# SELMER MACCAFERRI 1932

The Selmer guitar—more widely known as the Selmer Maccaferri—is uniquely associated with the incomparable Belgian-born, Romani gypsy jazz guitarist, Django Reinhardt.

The "Maccaferri" was first produced in 1932 by the French Selmer company. The body of the guitar was shaped to accommodate an internal resonator unit created by Italian luthier Mario Maccaferri—remembered mainly because Selmer's London showroom advertised the guitar as The Maccaferri. (In fact, the resonator was only fitted to early models, as players complaining of rattling requested them to be removed.)

The body of the Selmer is visually distinctive for two reasons: the unusual perpendicular cutaway that allowed easier access to the upper frets, and the Art Nouveau styling of the D-shaped sound hole—often called *la grande bouche* (the big mouth).

In 1936, the Selmer Maccaferri underwent a redesign. The scale length was increased from 25 ½ inches to 26 ⅖ inches, the internal ladder bracing was revised, and the sound hole reduced to a small oval shape. Known as the Modéle Jazz, this is widely regarded as the Selmer in its definitive form, and remained in production until 1952.

**Django Reinhardt was Europe's first celebrated jazz guitarist. He used the Selmer Maccaferri through most of his career.**

**Reinhardt's driving, rhythmic guitar style, both solo and with jazz ensembles, is showcased on many good compilations.**

| | |
|---|---|
| **Body style:** | Hollow body with single perpendicular cutaway and gently arched top with D-shaped sound hole (small oval sound hole from 1936) |
| **Materials:** | Laminated Indian rosewood back and sides; French spruce top; ladder-bracing; walnut neck |
| **Finish:** | Natural |
| **Fretboard:** | Ebony |
| **Frets:** | 23 (not including zero fret; frets 21–23 on top 2 strings only) |
| **Scale:** | 25 ½" (26 ⅖" after 1936) |
| **Width at nut:** | 1 11/16" |
| **Bridge:** | Floating |
| **Tailpiece:** | Brass |

# SHERGOLD MARATHON 1976

concentrated on producing woodwork for other guitar companies. From 1969, they were designing and providing woodwork for the new Hayman guitar company; when this collapsed in 1974 they decided to continue themselves.

Much of the Shergold range is derived directly from the four Hayman designs, and is unusual in that the bodies were crafted from obeche, a West African tree that produces a lightweight wood.

The Shergold Marathon bass evolved from the Hayman 4040 bass, and was available in four-string (fretted and fretless), six-string, and eight-string versions. The pickup is a split humbucker wired to a stereo jack output socket: using a splitter cable, the two signals could be sent to separate amplifiers, or plugged into a stereo channel for wider separation.

Struggling in a troubled British economic climate, Shergold finally ended production in 1982.

Producing guitars between 1975 and 1982, Shergold was Britain's last significant mass-producer of electric guitars.

Shergold Woodcrafts was founded in 1967 in East London by two former Burns employees, Jack Golder and Norman Houlder. At first the company

▲
**Mike Rutherford often used Shergold double-necked guitars when he was bassist for Genesis. One of his Shergolds combined bass and twelve-string necks.**

▼
**Released in 1980, *Smallcreep's Day* was Mike Rutherford's first solo album. He played all of the bass and guitar parts.**

| | |
|---|---|
| **Body style:** | Double cutaway solid body with extended curved horns |
| **Materials:** | Obeche body with maple bolt-on neck |
| **Finish:** | Maple |
| **Fretboard:** | Rosewood (ebony used on some reissues) |
| **Inlays:** | Acrylic dot |
| **Frets:** | 20 on 4-string; 24 on 6-string and 8-string; or fretless as shown |
| **Scale:** | 34" |
| **Width at nut:** | 1 9/16" |
| **Bridge:** | Combined bridge and tailpiece |
| **Pickups:** | 1 split humbucker wired to stereo output socket |
| **Electrics:** | Master volume and tone controls |

# SILVERTONE 1457 AMP-IN-CASE 1965

The brand has a special place in the affections of many American guitarists, who learned their chops on cheap but playable Silvertone models sourced from guitar manufacturers such as Danelectro, National, Harmony, Kay, and Teisco.

The most significant Silvertones were the "Amp-In-Case" models, which emerged in 1962 with the three-quarter scale 1448. The guitar itself was a standard-issue single-pickup Danelectro, built using a cheap poplar wooden frame covered in masonite hardboard. With the complete beginner in mind, however, the 1448 also came with a sturdy carrying case that housed a neat five-watt amplifier and an 8-inch loudspeaker. The range was offered in five varieties, uppermost being the twin-pickup, standard-scale 1457.

The Silvertones represented amazing value: the 1448 package came in at $69.99—a Gibson SG Custom at the same time retailed for $450.

The Silvertone brand name was owned by Sears Roebuck, the well-known American mail order and department store chain. First appearing on a phonograph in 1915, the name adorned the company's own line of musical instruments and sound equipment until 1972.

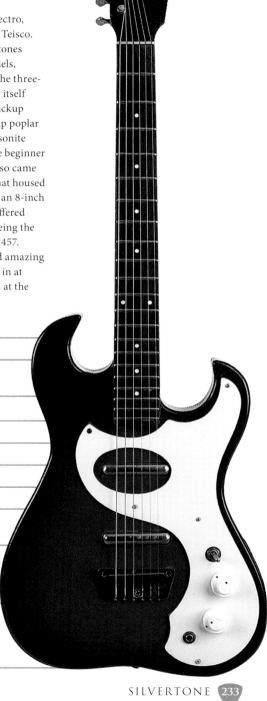

**Perhaps in an act of retro perversity, Beck Hansen uses a Silvertone as his main guitar. Hansen plays a single-pickup 1448, the original "Amp-In-Case" model.**

▼

**The Silvertone can be heard on Beck's 2008 album *Modern Guilt*.**

| | |
|---|---|
| **Body style:** | Double cutaway semi-solid |
| **Materials:** | Stapled poplar center-block and frame; masonite top and back; poplar bolt-on neck |
| **Finish:** | Red "sparkle" |
| **Fretboard:** | Rosewood |
| **Frets:** | 21 |
| **Scale:** | 24 ¾" |
| **Width at nut:** | 1 ¾" |
| **Bridge:** | Danelectro notched bridge with rosewood saddle |
| **Pickups:** | 2 Danelectro "lipstick tube" single-coil pickups; 3-way selector switch |
| **Electrics:** | Master volume and tone control |
| **Amplifier:** | Built into guitar case—5 watts, 3 valves, 8" speaker, gain and tone controls, tremolo (speed and strength), 2 inputs, and 1 foot-switch |

# STEINBERGER GM4T 1985

Launched in 1979, and variously described as a broomstick or cricket bat, these were extremely fashionable during the first half of the 1980s. More conventional-looking guitars such as the GM4T would emerge later.

Steinberger guitars were unique. For starters, the neck was made entirely of the "Steinberger Blend," a proprietary mix of graphite and carbon fiber. This made for a material that was harder than wood but extremely lightweight. Of course, the most visually arresting feature of any Steinberger is the headstock—or lack of one. The specially-made double-ball-ended strings are threaded from behind the nut, and tuned from behind the bridge.

Steinberger's third significant innovation appeared in 1984. The Trans-Trem is a vibrato unit that detunes strings in parallel tension—entire chords can be "bent" but remain perfectly in tune.

American luthier Ned Steinberger is one of an elite set who have produced an instrument that was both revolutionary in design *and* commercially successful.

The first Steinbergers to appear were the period-piece L-series instruments.

▲
**Unusual in the area of metal, there is a distinct jazz influence to the high-speed playing of Cynic's Paul Masvidal.**

▼
**Cynic's 1993 album *Focus* was a huge influence on the progressive metal scene. The band's two guitarists were Steinberger users.**

| | |
|---|---|
| **Body style:** Double cutaway solid body | |
| **Materials:** Maple body with bolt-on Steinberger Blend graphite/carbon fiber composite neck | |
| **Finish:** Black, pearl white, candy apple red, electric blue | |
| **Fretboard:** Phenolic | |
| **Inlays:** Acrylic dot | |
| **Frets:** 24 (not including zero fret) | |
| **Scale:** 25 ½" | |
| **Width at nut:** 1 ⁵/₉" | |
| **Bridge:** Steinberger R-Trem | |
| **Pickups:** Seymour Duncan Hotrail/ Custom combination or EMGs; 5-way selector switch | |
| **Tuning:** Headless double-ball micrometer system | |
| **Electrics:** Master volume and tone controls | |

# SYNTHAXE 1986

Although it barely qualifies as a guitar in its own right, the Synthaxe is a historically significant piece of technology in that it approached the idea of a guitar synthesizer in a unique way.

First appearing in 1986, the Synthaxe was brainchild of Bill Aitken, a former BBC Radiophonic Workshop composer/experimenter. In the early 1980s, the synthesizer hybrid was still thought by some to be the guitar's next evolutionary phase. The problem with earlier attempts was inaccurate note tracking: the standard approach had been to take the signal from the string and convert it to control data, but this could easily be corrupted. The Synthaxe featured two independent sets of strings: the short group on the body was used to trigger notes; the set on the neck determined the pitch of the note. However, the pitch data was generated electronically, the frets themselves forming part of the circuit when the string was pressed down.

Produced in small numbers, the Synthaxe carried a price tag of around $13,000. It was also an unintuitive instrument for many guitarists to play, not least because of the differing angles of the string sets and the fact that the frets were spaced equally.

Since the Synthaxe is primarily a controller, it can't be said to have a sound of its own. Most of its noted users have operated in the jazz/fusion arena—names such as Al Di Meola, Pat Metheny, or Allan Holdsworth.

▲
**Electro-percussionist Roy "Future Man" Wooten converted a Synthaxe into a hand-operated drum kit, the "Drumitar."**

▼
**The Synthaxe was showcased on Allan Holdsworth's album *Atavachron* (1986).**

| | |
|---|---|
| **Body style:** Ax shape | |
| **Materials:** Fiberglass covering a metal chassis; metal neck | |
| **Finish:** Metallic blue, green, red, gold | |
| **Frets:** 24 (not including zero fret) | |
| **Scale:** 24 ¾" | |
| **Upper-bout controls:** Master trigger key; left-hand trigger enable switch; 2 treble-group trigger keys; 6 bass-group trigger keys | |
| **Lower-bout controls:** Assignable tremolo arm (can be used for altering assorted MIDI parameters); left-hand trigger enable switch | |

# TAKAMINE GB7C 1996

surprise that 150 years later one of the world's most respected acoustic guitar manufacturers is based in Japan.

The workshop from which Takamine emerged began life in 1959, in Gifu, central Japan. Success came with the Western folk music boom that hit Japan toward the end of the 1960s.

The key figure in Takamine's history is Mass Hirade, a well-respected Japanese luthier, who joined the company in 1968, boosting the quality to the brand. Seven years later he became company president and quickly set about turning Takamine—then unknown outside of Japan—into an international force. His success can perhaps be gauged by the very *existence* of the GB7C Dreadnought model shown here—a signature guitar created with Garth Brooks, American country music's biggest star, and one of the world's biggest selling recording artists: since 1996 Brooks has rarely been seen onstage without a Takamine.

The guitar may have been born in southern Europe, but developments from the 1850s onwards have made the steel-string acoustic a quintessentially American musical instrument. However, given the way the electric guitar market evolved, it should come as little

▲
**Country singer and songwriter Garth Brooks has played his Takamine signature model exclusively since it was introduced in 1996.**

▼
**By the time of the 1998 concert album** *Double Live*, **Garth Brooks was one of the biggest-selling artists in the world.**

| | |
|---|---|
| **Body style:** | Dreadnought with single cutaway and guitar-shaped sound hole |
| **Materials:** | Rosewood back and sides, solid cedar top; mahogany neck |
| **Finish:** | Natural |
| **Fretboard:** | Rosewood |
| **Inlays:** | None |
| **Sound hole:** | Rosette |
| **Frets:** | 21 (including partial fret) |
| **Scale:** | 25 ⅜" |
| **Width at nut:** | 1 ¹¹⁄₁₆" |
| **Tuners:** | Gold with amber pearloid buttons |
| **Bridge:** | Rosewood |
| **Electrics:** | CT4B 3-band graphic equalizer/ chromatic tuner |

# Taylor RNSM 2003

A t the age of eighteen, with no woodcraft qualifications to speak of, Bob Taylor was taken on at the tiny American Dream guitar workshop in San Diego, California. Two years later, in 1974, he and two other employees had bought out the business and began making acoustic guitars bearing his name. By the turn of the century, Taylor would be one of the most important names in the world of steel-string acoustic guitars, with two production plants employing over 500 staff.

The Taylor brand initially pitched itself as an affordable alternative to a Martin—the benchmark for a flat-top acoustic guitar. Taylors had a fine, balanced sound and featured low-profile necks, offered in a choice of widths. Furthermore, they were constructed with necks bolted on, making them easier to reset or repair.

Taylor has successfully used celebrity endorsements to market its guitars. An early signatory was steel-string maestro Leo Kottke; in the rock field, Taylor produced a beautiful koa double-neck acoustic for Bon Jovi's Ritchie Sambora. The RNSM shown here, in an attractive green finish, was developed in 2003 with Rick Nielsen of U.S. rock band Cheap Trick.

▲
Better known for his five-necked electric guitars, Cheap Trick's Rick Nielsen was awarded a Taylor signature acoustic model in 2003.

▼
More than two decades after their commercial peak, Cheap Trick's 2006 album, *Rockford*, was rated by *Rolling Stone* as one of the albums of the year.

| | |
|---|---|
| **Body style:** | Jumbo with Venetian cutaway |
| **Materials:** | Big-leaf maple back and sides, Sitka spruce top; hard rock maple neck |
| **Bracing:** | Scalloped X-brace |
| **Finish:** | Green or black |
| **Fretboard:** | Ebony |
| **Inlays:** | Breakaway checkerboard |
| **Sound hole:** | Abalone |
| **Frets:** | 20 |
| **Scale:** | 25 ½" |
| **Width at nut:** | 1 ¾" |
| **Nut:** | Tusq |
| **Bridge:** | Ebony bridge with Tusq saddle |
| **Tuners:** | Gold-plated Grovers |

# TEISCO DEL REY MAY QUEEN 1968

NEW MODEL

VAMPER セミ・ホロー・ギター

DELUXE GUITAR
VAMPER
¥40,000

AMPLIFIER
CHECK-MATE - 60
¥ 90,000

CM-60

MAY QUEEN

DELUXE GUITAR
MAY-QUEEN
¥ 32,500

Teisco was a major Japanese guitar manufacturer, whose exports to Europe and the United States helped fuel the electric guitar boom of the 1960s. Founded in 1946, the company was known under a variety of names until 1964, when it became the Tokyo Electric Instrument and Sound Company—which was abbreviated to Teisco.

Teisco guitars were ubiquitous starter instruments in the 1960s, being exported bearing brand names such as Silvertone, Jedson, Kent, Lyle, Tulio, Arbiter, Audition, Kay, and Top Twenty. In most cases these guitars were low-end imitations of Strats, Teles, and Les Pauls.

Branded in the U.S. as Teisco Del Rey, the 1968 hollow-body May Queen is one of the more unusual Japanese copies, not least because the instrument on which it was loosely based—the Vox Mandoguitar—was itself rather obscure. The most striking visual features of the May Queen are its so-called artist's palette body shape and the cat's-eye sound hole.

Teisco was taken over by the Kawai Corporation in 1967, and two years later ceased guitar production. These "cheap" Japanese guitars are now surprisingly collectible.

▲
The Teisco May Queen in a 1969 catalog—with details in both Japanese and English.

▼
The Vox Mandoguitar—a twelve-string electric mandolin—inspired the shape of the May Queen.

| | |
|---|---|
| **Body style:** | Hollow-body, single-cutaway artist's pallette shape |
| **Materials:** | Laminate body with 4-hole bolt-on maple neck |
| **Finish:** | Red, white, and black |
| **Fretboard:** | Rosewood |
| **Inlays:** | Acrylic dot |
| **Frets:** | 22 (not including zero fret) |
| **Scale:** | 25 ½" |
| **Width at nut:** | 1 ¹¹⁄₁₆" |
| **Bridge:** | Adjustable bridge; tailpiece with Bigsby-inspired vibrato |
| **Pickups:** | 2 single-coil pickups; 3-way selector switch |
| **Electrics:** | Master volume and tone controls |

# TEUFFEL BIRDFISH 1995

In 1995, Ulrich Teuffel, a Bavarian luthier who had previously been a student of industrial design, launched his first instrument, the Birdfish. It remains one of the most radical reinventions the electric guitar has ever seen. Teuffel's starting point was brutally fundamental: "I reduced the guitar to its basic functional elements." The resulting instrument was constructed rather like a frame of interconnecting modules.

The core of the body consists of two distinct aluminum sculptures that Tueffel calls "the bird" and "the fish." These are joined by a pair of strong wooden tonebars. The neck is bolted on to the upper element—the bird—while the lower fish carries the electronics. The wooden bars provide the guitar's tonal characteristics, and can be interchanged—the Birdfish ships with one pair made from alder and another from maple. Although the structure would appear to be dangerously fragile

and liable to fall apart, it is in fact extremely strong.

The same modular approach is applied to the pickups. The Birdfish comes with two single-coils and three humbuckers, any of which can be fitted into the three available slots.

Not only is the Birdfish a versatile guitar, it is also a deeply satisfying piece of design. It is arguably the perfect contemporary electric guitar for any modern musician—although with a retail price of up to $15,000, one with suitably deep pockets.

Teuffel has produced two other instruments. The Tesla and Coco guitars are more conventional in appearance but still have the look of design artifacts. Only twenty-three Cocos were made, as Teuffel discovered that he had an allergic reaction to the epoxy used in its composite body. The ill-fated guitar was succeeded by a version made of wood, called the Niwa.

▼
**Billy Gibbons of U.S. rock band ZZ Top owns a Teuffel Birdfish. Talking about his band's new album in 2003, Gibbons enthused over the role of the guitar: "The Birdfish really shines on *Mescalero* ... because of that dirty, raunchy tone."**

| | |
|---|---|
| **Materials:** | Aluminum "bird" and "fish" joined by a pair of interchangable tonebars made from alder or maple; bolt-on asymmetrically V-shaped bird's eye maple neck |
| **Finish:** | Apricot, fire, sapphire, olive, charcoal |
| **Fretboard:** | Maple |
| **Inlays:** | 2-tone glow-in-the-dark side dots |
| **Frets:** | 22 |
| **Scale:** | 25 3/5" |
| **Width at nut:** | 1 22/31" |
| **Bridge:** | Gotoh or Schaller Tune-o-matic |
| **Pickups:** | 2 single-coil pickups, plus 3 different humbuckers to fit into any of 3 body slots; 5-way Schaller "Megaswitch" |
| **Electrics:** | Master volume/tone controls |

# TOKAI TST 50 1982

Much of the early Japanese "copy" industry was of dire quality, but by the late 1970s the quality gap between America and Japan had narrowed to a disturbing degree. The moment of truth arguably arrived in 1982 with the launch of the Tokai TST range. These guitars were *blatant* Stratocaster imitations—right down to the angled bridge pickup and the mimicking of the stylized Fender logo on the headstock. But they sounded and played every bit as sweetly as an early 1980s Fender. And they sold at around half the price.

After much bluster and threats of legal action, Fender came up with a solution—if they were to produce a range of cheaper Japanese Fenders, then surely nobody would *want* to buy the copies. Thus Fender launched the Japanese Squier range built at the same factories that had previously been building copies, quite literally putting an end to the competition.

M usical instrument manufacturer Tokai Gakki was founded in 1947 in the city of Hamamatsu, Japan. Like every other Japanese manufacturer of the period, Tokai produced copies of the most popular American designs in addition to its own original models.

▲
**Relative labor costs meant that Fender's U.S. models had not been able to compete with Japanese copies.**

▼
**The unusual Hummingbird, Tokai's first electric guitar, produced in 1968.**

| | |
|---|---|
| **Body style:** | Solid body with double cutaway |
| **Materials:** | Alder body; bolt-on maple neck |
| **Finish:** | Standard Fender finishes |
| **Fretboard:** | Rosewood or maple |
| **Inlays:** | Acrylic dot (black on maple neck; white on rosewood) |
| **Frets:** | 21 |
| **Scale:** | 25½" |
| **Width at nut:** | 1 11⁄16" |
| **Bridge:** | Fender-style vibrato |
| **Pickups:** | 3 single-coil MK-2 pickups laid out in Stratocaster style; 3-way selector switch |
| **Electrics:** | Single volume control and 2 tone controls |

# TOM ANDERSON DROP T 1991

Until the 1980s, most professional guitarists played mass-produced instruments from one of the big American names. A decade earlier, small workshops began a trend toward customization: hot-rodding production guitars or building instruments tailored to needs that weren't being met by the big guns.

Having struggled to make a living as a guitarist, in 1977 Tom Anderson went to work for Schecter Guitar Research, a repair shop in Van Nuys, California. Schecter manufactured replacement necks, bodies, and hardware, eventually, in 1979, offering its own fully-assembled electric guitars based on Fender designs. They were both high quality and very expensive.

When the Schecter operation was scaled up and materials increasingly sourced from Japan, Anderson chose to set up his own business. In 1984, Tom Anderson Guitarworks was born, initially based in Anderson's garage,

where he made pickups and necks. His first break came when Dave Schecter commissioned 300 American-made Strat pickups. As Anderson recalled: "I set up a little pickup-making shop in the kitchen . . . After I got through making necks and bodies in our garage during the day, we sat up making pickups every night."

By 1990, Tom Anderson Guitarworks had moved into a small factory space and switched completely to making completed instruments. Its impressive artist roster includes the Rolling Stones, Vernon Reid, The Eagles, Steve Miller, Richie Sambora, and Carlos Santana.

The Drop T is a startlingly attractive high-performance Telecaster-style guitar featuring a versatile Anderson H-Series pickup array wired with every switching option imaginable. Since all Tom Anderson guitars are custom-built instruments, the tonewood options are also endless.

▼
Bob Seger is a long-standing aficonado of Tom Anderson guitars—notably on his sixteenth studio album, *Face The Promise* (2006).

| | |
|---|---|
| **Body style:** | Single cutaway solid body (hollow body on Hollow T models) |
| **Materials:** | Alder, swamp ash, basswood, or mahogany body; quilt or flame maple, koa, or walnut top; maple neck |
| **Finish:** | Natural |
| **Fretboard:** | Maple, rosewood, or pau ferro |
| **Inlays:** | Dot |
| **Frets:** | 22 |
| **Scale:** | 25 ½" |
| **Width at nut:** | 1 ⅝" or 1 ¹¹/₁₆" |
| **Bridge:** | Fixed; vintage tremolo or Floyd Rose locking tremolo |
| **Pickup:** | Tom Anderson H-Series humbucker/single/humbucker array (S-Series, M-Series or T-Series optional); Switcheroo switching options (5-way selector optional) |
| **Electrics:** | Volume and tone with push-pull options |

# TORRES (FIRST EPOCH) 1858

Antonio de Torres Jurado—usually referred to simply as "Torres"—is the single most important figure in the evolution of the Spanish guitar. Instruments created by Torres, between 1852 and 1892, are revered historically and artistically in much the same way as violins fashioned by Antonio Stradivari. Torres was born in 1817 in La Cañada de San Urbano, Almería, and at the age of twelve years he began an apprenticeship as a carpenter. Married with a family by the time he was twenty, Torres struggled to make ends meet during the civil unrest of the Carlist Wars and often had to take on different means of employment.

In 1842, Torres is thought to have learned about building guitars while employed by José Pernas in Granada, and shortly afterward opened his first shop in Seville. It was not until the early 1850s, on the advice of the noted guitarist and composer Julián Arcas, that Torres concentrated wholly on building musical instruments.

Torres would remain in his Seville workshop until 1870, creating what amounts to a template for the modern classical guitar. The instruments he built during this time are said to date from Torres' "First Epoch."

▲
**Miguel Llobet, one of Spain's leading guitarist/composers in the early twentieth century, owned the guitar known as "FE09" built by Torres in 1859. It is now held at the Museu de la Música in Barcelona.**

▼
**Llobet's playing style was thought to be rather old-fashioned by the time he recorded in the 1920s.**

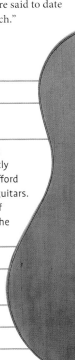

**Body style:** Classical Spanish "figure-8"

**Materials:** Maple back and sides; spruce top; mahogany neck

**Notes on materials:** In spite of his reputation as the Stradivari of the guitar, Torres frequently lived in poverty and was not always able to afford the best quality woods for the bodies of his guitars. Consequently he worked with a wide range of woods, often using cypress or rosewood for the back and sides

**Finish:** French polish

**Fretboard:** Rosewood (ebony used on other models)

**Frets:** 19

**Scale:** 25 $\frac{13}{22}$"

**Bridge:** Two-part; rosewood bridge and bone saddle

# TORRES (SECOND EPOCH) 1882

Italian concert guitarist Stefano Grondona has often used the 1887 Torres guitar known as "SE107."

T orres invented few of the great innovations associated with his guitars. His achievement was in refining others' ideas to create the radical new instrument from which the modern classical guitar has evolved.

The most striking feature of a Torres guitar when compared to earlier instruments is the size of its body: the soundboard of a Torres concert guitar was some 20 percent larger. This is reflected in the fullsome curves of both upper and lower bouts that give us the now familiar figure-of-eight form. Torres also reduced the thickness of the soundboard, giving added strength by arching in both directions, supported by a series of internal fan struts. Torres had thus improved the tone and volume of the concert guitar.

Other innovations included the use of machine heads rather than tuning pegs, and the separation of the saddle from the bridge, enabling very fine adjustment of string height.

Despite having built guitars for some of Spain's greatest players, Torres remained poor, and in 1870 he returned to Almería to open a china shop. Within five years, however, he had returned to guitar making. The period until his death in 1892 is known as the "Second Epoch."

Stefano Grondona uses the Second Epoch Torres guitar on his 1996 album *La Guitarra De Torres.*

| | |
|---|---|
| **Body style:** | Classical Spanish "figure-8" |
| **Materials:** | Maple back and sides; spruce top; mahogany neck |
| **Finish:** | French polish |
| **Fretboard:** | Ebony |
| **Frets:** | 19 (including partial fret) |
| **Scale:** | 25 $^{13}/_{22}$" |
| **Bridge:** | Two-part; ebony bridge with bone saddle |

**Notes on labels:** Torres is thought to have built no more than around 320 guitars in his lifetime, of which some 100 are known still to exist. These guitars are not always easy to authenticate since Torres did not sign or label them until his Second Epoch. Since instruments from the First Epoch are most attractive to players and collectors, a number of convincing fakes exist on the market

# VOX PHANTOM 1962

The British Vox company, first a specialist in amplification and electronics, began to make guitars in 1959—cheap Fender imitations. When company boss Tom Jennings decided to produce an original model in 1962, he came up with an unusual pentagonal body and ideas for more onboard circuitry than usually found on a guitar. The first models were built in the U.K. before relocating to the EKO factory in Italy.

The Vox Phantom appeared in a number of different combinations (a mid-1960s twelve-string Phantom XII is shown at right), with two or three single-coil pickups, open-back tuners, and a bridge modeled on the Gibson Tune-o-matic. Optional extras included a Bigsby-style vibrato unit designed by Jennings.

Although the Phantom included a round leather-coated pad on the back for comfort while playing, the guitar was not the most practical of instruments, poorly balanced, and—like many unorthodox body shapes—difficult to play while sitting down.

Jennings' new circuitry included a stereo option that enabled the guitar to be connected to two amplifiers simultaneously, so complex panning and switching effects could be heard.

▲
Ian Curtis of Joy Division performs with a Vox Phantom. Curtis and the band's main guitarist, Bernard Sumner, often swapped their instruments in the studio. Sumner played a British Shergold Masquerader.

▼
After Curtis' death, Sumner played his Vox on the New Order single "Everything's Gone Green" (1981).

| | |
|---|---|
| **Body style:** | Solid body, pentagonal design |
| **Materials:** | Maple or ash body with set maple neck |
| **Finish:** | Black, white, green, pale blue, red (custom colors were also produced in small numbers) |
| **Fretboard:** | Rosewood |
| **Inlays:** | Acrylic dot |
| **Frets:** | 22 (not including the zero fret) |
| **Scale:** | 25" |
| **Width at zero fret:** | 1 3/4" |
| **Bridge:** | Tune-o-matic style; optional Vox-designed vibrato arm available on later models |
| **Pickups:** | 2 or 3 single-coil pickups; switching dependent on model |
| **Electrics:** | At most basic, master volume and tone controls; other options include stereo sound, panning, and in-built effects, such as fuzz |

# VOX PHANTOM MARK III 1964

Just as The Beatles had all but established the Rickenbacker name with the music-buying public, one musician had much the same impact on Vox guitars—Brian Jones of the Rolling Stones. The founder and leader of the band (until Mick Jagger and Keith Richards began writing hit records), Jones used a prototype of the Teardrop—hand-built for him in late 1963 by Vox designer Michael Bennett—until 1966, when he largely switched to playing Gibsons. The Teardrop we see in many iconic images of the Stones differs from the models that went on sale (as the Mark VI) in its slightly elongated body.

At the time, advertisements could justifiably brag, "Vox: it's what's happening." But since the mid-1960s the brand has changed hands many times and, although the name lives on with its seminal range of amplification, with the exception of occasional limited-edition reissues, large-scale guitar manufacture ended in the 1970s.

The first Vox Phantoms became popular with British beat groups such as The Kinks and The Hollies. At the start of 1964, Vox came up with a second unusual body shape. Broadly based on the appearance of a Renaissance lute, the Phantom Mark III (and its related instruments) became known as the "Teardrop"—the most famous Vox guitar.

▲
**Brian Jones of the Rolling Stones switched to the Vox Teardrop in 1964; prior to that he used a Gretsch Double Anniversary.**

▼
**Jones played all of the lead guitar parts on *The Rolling Stones No. 2* using his prototype Vox Teardrop.**

| | |
|---|---|
| **Body style:** | Solid lute-style body |
| **Materials:** | Mahogany body with bolt-on maple neck |
| **Finish:** | Sunburst, 3 white options, black, salmon, light blue, red |
| **Fretboard:** | Rosewood |
| **Frets:** | 21 |
| **Scale:** | 25" |
| **Width at nut:** | 1¾" |
| **Bridge:** | Tune-o-matic style |
| **Tailpiece:** | Stop bar or combined vibrato |
| **Pickups:** | 2 or 3 single-coil pickups; 3-way switching |
| **Electrics:** | Master volume and separate tone controls for bass and treble |

# WASHBURN PS 1800 1999

 The Washburn brand likes to trade on its early links to development of Chicago blues. The company was founded in 1883 by George Washburn Lyon, its factory indeed located a few blocks from Chicago's Maxwell Street—the epicenter of the Delta Blues movement of the early 1920s. The first Washburn instruments were ornate rosewood and spruce flat-tops, modeled closely on the fine Martin guitars of the period. The company went bankrupt with the 1929 Wall Street Crash and for the next decade the brand name was used on cheap mass-produced instruments before being abandoned altogether.

The Washburn brand as we know it today has only been in existence since 1974. Although still a Chicago-based company, Washburn electric guitars were originally built in Japan, but later echoed the tiered approach of other major manufacturers, with high-end models built in the U.S. and budget Washburns coming in from Korea.

The company has specialized in producing celebrity-tied instruments for such names as Bootsy Collins, Dimebag Darrell, and Sonny Smith. Perhaps the most successful has been the Paul Stanley PS range, created in conjunction with the Kiss guitarist.

▲
**Paul Stanley of premiere glam metal stars Kiss plays a signature Washburn PS 1800 guitar.**

▼
**In 2009 Washburn celebrated a decade of working with Stanley with an anniversary edition of the PS 1800. That year Kiss also recorded *Sonic Boom*, their first twenty-first-century album.**

| | |
|---|---|
| **Body style:** | Single cutaway solid body with extended treble horn |
| **Materials:** | Mahogany body with set mahogany neck |
| **Finish:** | Black gloss, white gloss |
| **Fretboard:** | Rosewood |
| **Inlays:** | Mother-of-pearl dot |
| **Frets:** | 22 |
| **Scale:** | 24 ¾" |
| **Width at nut:** | 1 ¹¹⁄₁₆" |
| **Bridge:** | Tune-o-matic |
| **Pickups:** | 2 humbuckers; 3-way selector switch |
| **Electrics:** | Volume control for each pickup; master tone control |

# WASHBURN STEALTH ST-3 2000

A hugely influential player, Dimebag had established his reputation in Pantera, one of America's top-selling metal bands.

The Washburn Stealth series was based on the Dean ML that Dimebag had made famous in the 1990s. The body shape of the ML resembled a Gibson Flying V combined with the upper half of a Gibson Explorer. Mirroring the body was a V-shaped headstock. The Stealth took all of these features but exaggerated each of the points. Launched in 2000, it was available as the ST-2, a budget Korean model with a bolt-on neck, or the U.S.-built set-neck ST-3.

The Dimebag Darrell story ended in tragedy in 2004 in Columbus, Ohio. While onstage with his new band Damageplan, a paranoid schizophrenic ran riot, killing Dimebag and four others. Diaries later showed that the gunman had become convinced that the band were "stealing" his thoughts.

Although Washburn continues to produce acoustic and electric hollow-body guitars, the brand has been most successfully established in the world of metal.

In 2000, Washburn teamed up with "Dimebag Darrell" Abbott, then one of the metal scene's leading shredders.

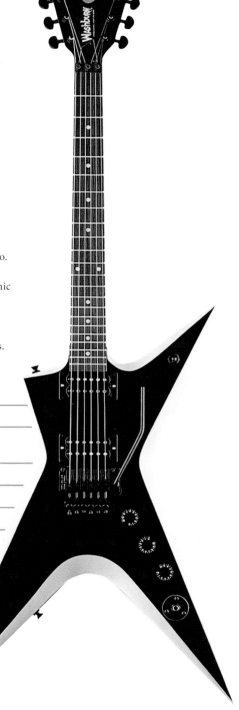

▲
**Dimebag Darrell (1966–2004), one of the all-time great shredders.**

▼
**Pantera's break-up in 2003 was widely attributed to vocalist Phil Anselmo's escalating heroin addiction. Dimebag then formed Damageplan, who recorded one album before the guitarist's murder in 2004.**

| | |
|---|---|
| **Body style:** | Solid body with single cutaway |
| **Materials:** | Mahogany body; set mahogany neck (bolt-on neck on ST-2) |
| **Finish:** | Black |
| **Fretboard:** | Ebony |
| **Inlays:** | Dot or none |
| **Frets:** | 22 |
| **Scale:** | 25 ½" |
| **Width at nut:** | 1 ⅝" |
| **Bridge:** | Schaller Floyd Rose locking tremolo |
| **Pickups:** | Bill Lawrence L500XL/Seymour Duncan '59 pickups; 3-way selector switch |
| **Electrics:** | Volume controls for each pickup; master tone control |
| **Tuners:** | Grover 18:1 |

# YAMAHA SG5A "FLYING SAMURAI" 1966

F ounded in Japan in 1887 as the Nippon Gakki Company, Yamaha began as a maker of pianos and reed organs. The company first began building classical guitars in 1941 and during Japan's "eleki" pop boom of the mid-1960s, introducing its first electric guitars in 1966.

As with many Japanese guitar manufacturers of the time, the early models were strongly influenced by the instruments that had crossed the Pacific with bands such as The Ventures. Unsurprisingly, then, the first Yamaha electrics bore more than a passing resemblance to the Ventures' own Mosrite signature models, with the reverse body shape and extended lower horn. However, these visual curiosities were more than mere copies, the asymmetric curves and hooked end on the lower horn giving a distinctly oriental flavor. The most original feature was the narrow headstock, which resembled the handle of a katana sword—little wonder these guitars became known as "Flying Samurai."

Although these instruments were exported to the West, it was in Japan itself where they prospered, aided in no small measure when the country's top guitarist, "Terry" Terauchi, packed away his Mosrite in favor of an SG5A.

▲
**Like many Japanese teenagers, Takeshi "Terry" Terauchi took up the guitar after hearing U.S. surf group The Ventures. Terauchi's fast and frantic style has earned him a reputation as Japan's first guitar hero.**

▼
**Terauchi was a founder of Terry and His Blue Jeans— Japan's top "eleki" group of the 1960s.**

| | |
|---|---|
| **Body style:** | Solid double cutaway with extending lower horn |
| **Materials:** | Alder body with bolt-on maple neck |
| **Finish:** | Sunburst (other finishes available later) |
| **Fretboard:** | Rosewood |
| **Inlays:** | Acrylic dot |
| **Frets:** | 22 (not including zero fret) |
| **Scale:** | 24 ¾" |
| **Width at nut:** | 1 ⁷⁄₁₆" |
| **Bridge:** | Adjustable |
| **Tailpiece:** | Separate from bridge with integral Yamaha vibrato unit |
| **Pickups:** | 3 single-coil pickups (2 on bridge wired as one); 3-way selector switch |
| **Electrics:** | Master volume and tone control, mix control governing the balance between the 2 single coils of the bridge pickup) |

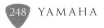

# YAMAHA SG2000 1976

One of the factors behind the success of Yamaha's electric guitars was that they represented quality at a fair price. Yet the volume of cheap, barely playable plywood knock-offs that began to flood the West from Japan seriously tarnished the reputations of Japanese instruments as a whole. By the mid-1970s, however, the big names of the American guitar world—Fender and Gibson—were having problems of their own, with a widespread perception that quality had dropped following corporate takeovers. Yamaha saw an opportunity to make a bold statement, and hired Carlos Santana to endorse a Japanese-built instrument intended to match the best of the West.

The instrument that emerged was the SG2000. It had a double cutaway body that strongly resembled a certain classic Gibson guitar but with such deluxe features as a straight-through neck, gold-plated hardware, opulent binding, and a radical "T Cross" neck construction.

The SG2000 proved beyond all doubt that construction of high-end electric guitars was not the sole province of America. Noting the threat, Gibson later took legal action to prevent Yamaha using the letters "SG."

▲
**It is testament to Carlos Santana's global reputation that so many guitar makers have sought his approval. Santana used the SG2000 extensively until he met Paul Reed Smith in the 1980s.**

▼
***Moonflower* captures Santana's fine live playing with the SG2000 in 1977.**

| | |
|---|---|
| **Body style:** | Double cutaway solid |
| **Materials:** | Carved maple top with maple and mahogany back; straight-through 3-piece mahogany and maple neck |
| **Finish:** | Sunburst, black, burgundy (other colors introduced later) |
| **Fretboard:** | Rosewood |
| **Frets:** | 22 |
| **Scale:** | 24 3/4" |
| **Width at nut:** | 1 11/16" |
| **Inlays:** | Split wing |
| **Bridge:** | Yamaha T-O-M |
| **Pickups:** | 2 Alnico V-covered humbuckers; 3-way selector switch |
| **Electrics:** | Dedicated volume and tone controls for each pickup |

# ZEMAITIS 1971

Zemaitis set up his first workshop in 1955, and by the end of the 1960s he had built up an impressive client roster that included Jimi Hendrix, George Harrison, and Eric Clapton.

A landmark year for Zemaitis was 1970. In an attempt to combat the problem of microphonic feedback, he began experimenting with placing a metal shield on the top of the body. A year later, when Ronnie Wood of The Faces used one of these eye-catching instruments on the TV show *Top Of The Pops*, the Zemaitis order-book quickly began to bulge. Shortly afterward, Zemaitis commissioned gun engraver Danny O'Brien to produce intricate etchings on the metal panels, making his guitars, quite literally, works of art.

Since his death in 2002, some of Zemaitis's guitars have become highly collectible, with engraved models—even non-celebrity instruments—fetching over $30,000 at auction.

Born in London to Lithuanian parents, Antanas Kazimieras "Tony" Zemaitis learned his craft taking a five-year cabinet-making apprenticeship. His successful future career emerged when he applied this training to a damaged guitar found in the attic of his family home.

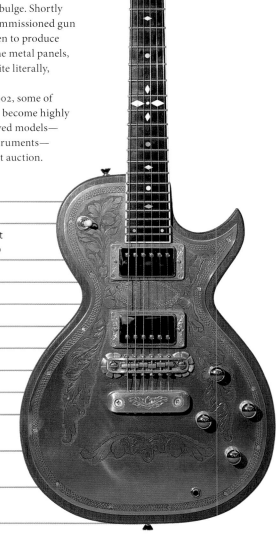

The Faces enjoyed a reputation as one of the world's greatest rock bands in concert. Guitarist Ronnie Wood and bassist Tetsu Yamauchi are seen here with instruments built by Tony Zemaitis.

▼

The Faces' love affair with guitars made for them by Tony Zemaitis lasted long after *A Nod Is As Good As A Wink . . .* (1971), their third album.

| | |
|---|---|
| **Body style:** | Single cutaway solid body |
| **Materials:** | Honduran mahogany body and set mahogany neck; hand-etched Duralumin top |
| **Finish:** | Natural |
| **Fretboard:** | Ebony |
| **Inlays:** | Abalone diamond and dot |
| **Frets:** | 24 |
| **Scale:** | 25" |
| **Width at nut:** | 1 11/16" |
| **Bridge:** | Hand-crafted Duralumin |
| **Tailpiece:** | Hand-crafted etched Duralumin stop |
| **Pickups:** | 2 humbuckers; 3-way selector switch |
| **Electrics:** | Dedicated volume and tone controls for each pickup |

# ZON LEGACY ELITE 4 1982

Zon bass guitars are especially noted for their neck design, in particular the use of "composite" materials, which, beside enhancing clarity in the lower bass register, also provide greater consistency from one bass to another. The base material used on the necks is a carbon fiber, developed for the aerospace industry, which is then, according to Zon, "rayon-extruded under extreme heat and pressure, a process that changes its molecular structure on a subatomic level." This process maximizes the ratio of strength to weight, making Zon necks extremely strong and stable but also very light. The fingerboard is also unorthodox, using what Zon calls "phenowood"— namely birch or maple that has been injected with a carbon resin, heated to an extremely high temperature, and then compressed.

Unsurprisingly, these custom-built instruments are aimed squarely at the well-heeled professional player.

Zon was established in 1981 in Buffalo, New York, growing out of a music retail store that had developed a reputation for high-quality repair work. Luthier and bass player Joe Zon set out with the aim of producing upscale bass instruments using unorthodox materials.

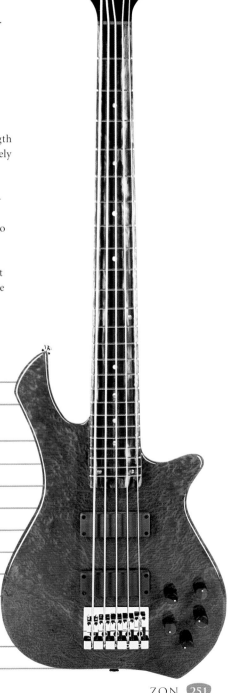

▲
**Leader Tetsuya of L'Arc-en-Ciel, one of Japan's biggest rock bands, plays a variety of Zon Elite basses.**

▼
**Ark was one of a pair of albums released by L'Arc-en-Ciel on the same day in 1999. It went straight to the top of the Japanese charts—one up from its sister album, Ray.**

| | |
|---|---|
| **Body style:** Double cutaway body | |
| **Materials:** 2-piece mahogany body with "master grade" figured top; composite carbon fiber set neck | |
| **Finish:** Natural, with satin covering | |
| **Fretboard:** Phenowood | |
| **Frets:** 24 (medium) | |
| **Scale:** 34" | |
| **Width at nut:** 1.532" | |
| **Bridge:** Zon machined brass | |
| **Pickups:** Bartolini soapbar style (exclusive to Zon) | |
| **Electrics:** Polyfusion ZP-2DM active preamp powered by 9-volt battery; master volume, pickup blend, bass, treble, and mid-range controls with +/- 15dB boost/cut | |
| **Tuners:** Gotoh GB-7 | |

# INDEX

# Picture Credits

Every effort has been made to credit the copyright holders of the images used in this book. We apologize for any unintentional omissions or errors and will insert the appropriate acknowledgment to any companies or individuals in any subsequent editions of the work.

Key r = right / tl = top left / bl = bottom left / t = top / c = center / b = bottom

2 MARKA/Alamy 7 Zakk Wylde 10 r Outline Press Ltd. 11 tl Getty Images 11 r Outline Press Ltd. 12 tl Redferns/Getty Images 12 r Outline Press Ltd. 13 tl Redferns/Getty Images 13 r Outline Press Ltd. 14 bl Outline Press Ltd. 14 r Outline Press Ltd. 15 tl Redferns/Getty Images 15 r Outline Press Ltd. 16 tl AF Archive/Alamy 16 r Outline Press Ltd. 17 tl VintAxe 17 r Outline Press Ltd. 18 r Outline Press Ltd. 20 bl Quintessence Editions Ltd. 20 r Quintessence Editions Ltd. 21 r Outline Press Ltd. 22 tl FilmMagic/Getty Images 24 tl Michael Ochs Archives/Getty Images 24 r Outline Press Ltd. 25 r Outline Press Ltd. 26 r Outline Press Ltd. 27 tl Getty Images 27 r Redferns/Getty Images 28 b Outline Press Ltd. 29 t VintAxe 29 c Outline Press Ltd. 29 b Getty Images 32 bl Burns Guitar Museum 32 r Outline Press Ltd. 33 tl Getty Images 33 r Outline Press Ltd. 34 tl Getty Images 34 r Outline Press Ltd. 35 tl VintAxe 35 r Outline Press Ltd. 36 tl Bob Shimizu/John Buscarino 36 r Outline Press Ltd. 38 r Outline Press Ltd. 39 r Outline Press Ltd. 40 tl erikamatthias 40 r Outline Press Ltd. 41 tl Redferns/Getty Images 41 r Quintessence Editions Ltd. 42 tl Getty Images 42 r Outline Press Ltd. 43 tl Redferns/Getty Images 43 r Outline Press Ltd. 44 tl WireImage/Gett Images 44 r Outline Press Ltd. 45 r Outline Press Ltd. 46 c VintAxe 50 tl VintAxe 50 r Outline Press Ltd. 51 tl 2010 George W. Burrows 51 r Outline Press Ltd. 52 tl Michael Ochs Archives/Getty Images 52 r Outline Press Ltd. 53 tl Redferns/Getty Images 53 r Outline Press Ltd. 54 tl Redferns/Getty Images 54 r Outline Press Ltd. 55 tl Mosaic Records 55 r Outline Press Ltd. 56 tl Redferns/Getty Images 56 r Outline Press Ltd. 57 bl Chip Stern 57 r Outline Press Ltd. 58 tl VintAxe 58 r Outline Press Ltd. 59 tl VintAxe 59 r Outline Press Ltd. 60 3_right Outline Press Ltd. 61 r Outline Press Ltd. 62 t VintAxe 62 b Redferns/Getty Images 64 tl Getty Images 64 r Outline Press Ltd. 65 tl VintAxe 65 r Quintessence Editions Ltd. 66 tl VintAxe 66 r Outline Press Ltd. 67 tl Redferns/Getty Images 67 r Outline Press Ltd. 68 tl Redferns/Getty Images 68 r Outline Press Ltd. 69 tl Epiphone 69 r Outline Press Ltd. 70 tl Amblin/Universal/The Kobal Collection 71 r Outline Press Ltd. 72 t Jacques Torregano/Dalle/Retna Pictures 73 t VintAxe 73 c Futura 74 t Fender 74 b vintageguitars.org.uk 75 t Outline Press Ltd. 75 b Michael Ochs Archives/Getty Images 76 t Paul Slattery/Retna Pictures 76 b Getty Images 77 tl Redferns/Getty Images 77 r Outline Press Ltd. 78 tl Ian Dickson/Rex Features 78 r Outline Press Ltd. 79 tl vintageguitars.org.uk 79 r Outline Press Ltd. 80 tl Redferns/Getty Images 80 r Outline Press Ltd. 81 tl Ian Dickson/Rex Features 81 r Outline Press Ltd. 82 tl Rex Features 82 r Outline Press Ltd. 83 tl Getty Images/Time & Life Pictures 83 r Outline Press Ltd. 84 tl Getty Images 84 r Outline Press Ltd. 85 tl Ilpo Musto/Rex Features 85 r Outline Press Ltd. 86 tl Ian Dickson/Rex Features 86 r Outline Press Ltd. 87 tl Redferns/Getty Images 87 r Outline Press Ltd. 88 tl Redferns/Getty Images 88 r Outline Press Ltd. 89 tl Redferns/Getty Images 89 r Outline Press Ltd. 90 tl vintageguitars.org.uk 90 r Outline Press Ltd. 91 tl Getty Images 91 r Outline Press Ltd. 92 bl Outline Press Ltd. 92 r Outline Press Ltd. 93 tl Redferns/Getty Images 93 r Outline Press Ltd. 94 c Outline Press Ltd. 94 b VintAxe 96 tl Ray Stevenson/Rex Features 96 r Outline Press Ltd. 97 tl Getty Images 97 r Outline Press Ltd. 98 tl Clayton Call/Retna Ltd./Corbis 98 r Outline Press Ltd. 99 tl Redferns/Getty Images 99 r Outline Press Ltd. 100 tl Michael Ochs Archives/Getty Images 100 r Outline Press Ltd. 101 tl Redferns/Getty Images 101 r Outline Press Ltd. 102 tl VintAxe 102 r Outline Press Ltd. 103 tl Outline Press Ltd. 103 r Outline Press Ltd. 104 r Outline Press Ltd. 105 tl Redferns/Getty Images 105 r Outline Press Ltd. 106 t Gibson 109 t VintAxe 109 c Redferns/Getty Images 109 b vintageguitars.org.uk 110 t Outline Press Ltd. 110 c Jim Snyder/Getty Images 111 tl Pictorial Press Ltd/Alamy 111 r Outline Press Ltd. 112 tl VintAxe 112 r Outline Press Ltd. 113 tl Michael Ochs Archives/Getty Images 113 r Outline Press Ltd. 114 tl Redferns/Getty Images 114 r Outline Press Ltd. 115 tl Redferns/Getty Images 115 r Outline Press Ltd. 116 tl Getty Images 116 r Outline Press Ltd. 117 tl Redferns/Getty Images 117 r Outline Press Ltd. 118 tl Redferns/Getty Images 118 r Outline Press Ltd. 119 tl Redferns/Getty Images 119 r Outline Press Ltd. 120 tl Redferns/Getty Images 120 r Outline Press Ltd. 121 tl Redferns/Getty Images 121 r Outline Press Ltd. 122 tl Redferns/Getty Images 122 r Outline Press Ltd. 123 tl Michael Ochs Archives/Getty Images 123 r Outline Press Ltd. 124 tl Redferns/Getty Images 124 r Outline Press Ltd. 125 tl WireImage/Gett Images 125 r Outline Press Ltd. 126 tl Michael Ochs Archives/Getty Images 126 r Outline Press Ltd. 127 tl Redferns/Getty Images 127 r Outline Press Ltd. 128 tl Michael Ochs Archives/Getty Images 128 r Outline Press Ltd. 129 tl Redferns/Getty Images 129 r Outline Press Ltd. 130 tl Michael Ochs Archives/Getty Images 130 r Outline Press Ltd. 131 right Outline Press Ltd. 132 tl Redferns/Getty Images 132 r Outline Press Ltd. 133 tl Redferns/Getty Images 133 r Outline Press Ltd. 134 tl Michael Ochs Archives/Getty Images 134 r Outline Press Ltd. 135 tl Redferns/Getty Images 135 r Outline Press Ltd. 136 tl WireImage/Getty Images 136 r Outline Press Ltd. 137 tl Getty Images 137 r Outline Press Ltd. 138 tl Redferns/Getty Images 138 r Outline Press Ltd. 139 tl Getty Images 139 r Outline Press Ltd. 140 right Outline Press Ltd. 141 2_bottom left Outline Press Ltd. 141 3_right Outline Press Ltd. 143 tl Michael Ochs Archives/Getty Images 143 r Outline Press Ltd. 144 r Outline Press Ltd. 145 tl Redferns/Getty Images 145 r Outline Press Ltd. 147 tl Redferns/Getty Images 147 r Outline Press Ltd. 148 tl Getty Images 148 r Outline Press Ltd. 149 tl Redferns/Getty Images 149 r Outline Press Ltd. 150 tl Redferns/Getty Images 150 r Outline Press Ltd. 151 tl Redferns/Getty Images 151 r Outline Press Ltd. 152 tl Getty Images 152 r Outline Press Ltd. 153 left Phil Mucci/Retna Ltd./Corbis 153 right Outline Press Ltd. 154 tl Getty Images 154 r Outline Press Ltd. 155 tl Redferns/Getty Images 155 r Outline Press Ltd. 156 right Outline Press Ltd. 157 tl WireImage/Gett Images 157 r Outline Press Ltd. 158 tl Popperfoto/Getty Images 158 r Outline Press Ltd. 159 tl Michael Ochs Archives/Getty Images 159 r Outline Press Ltd. 160 tl VintAxe 160 r Outline Press Ltd. 161 tl Redferns/Getty Images 162 t VintAxe 162 b FilmMagic/Getty Images 164 bl Outline Press Ltd. 164 r Outline Press Ltd. 165 tl WireImage/Gett Images 165 r Outline Press Ltd. 166 tl Getty Images 166 r Quintessence Editions Ltd. 167 r Outline Press Ltd. 168 c Michael Ochs Archives/Getty Images 170 tl Getty Images 170 c Outline Press Ltd. 171 tl Redferns/Getty Images 171 r Outline Press Ltd. 172 r Outline Press Ltd. 173 tl Getty Images/Time & Life Pictures 173 r Quintessence Editions Ltd. 174 r Outline Press Ltd. 176 3_centre below Redferns/Getty Images 177 right Outline Press Ltd. 178 right Outline Press Ltd. 179 right Outline Press Ltd. 180 tl Redferns/Getty Images 180 r Outline Press Ltd. 181 tl Getty Images 181 r Outline Press Ltd. 182 tl Getty Images 182 r Outline Press Ltd. 183 tl Getty Images 183 r Outline Press Ltd. 184 right Outline Press Ltd. 185 tl FilmMagic/Getty Images 185 r Outline Press Ltd. 186 tl Redferns/Getty Images 186 r Outline Press Ltd. 187 tl Michael Ochs Archives/Getty Images 187 r Outline Press Ltd. 188 bl VintAxe 188 r Outline Press Ltd. 189 tl Photofest/Lebrecht Music & Arts 189 r Outline Press Ltd. 190 r Outline Press Ltd. 191 tl Redferns/Getty Images 191 r Outline Press Ltd. 192 r Outline Press Ltd. 193 tl Redferns/Getty Images 193 r Outline Press Ltd. 194 bl VintAxe 194 right Outline Press Ltd. 195 r Outline Press Ltd. 198 tl Redferns/Getty Images 198 r Redferns/Getty Images 199 tl Redferns/Getty Images 199 r Outline Press Ltd. 200 tl Redferns/Getty Images 200 r Outline Press Ltd. 201 tl Redferns/Getty Images 201 r Outline Press Ltd. 202 r Outline Press Ltd. 203 tl Redferns/Getty Images 203 r Outline Press Ltd. 205 t Outline Press Ltd. 205 c Outline Press Ltd. 205 b Outline Press Ltd. 208 tl Getty Images 208 r Outline Press Ltd. 209 tl Redferns/Getty Images 209 r Outline Press Ltd. 210 bl VintAxe 210 r Outline Press Ltd. 211 tl Redferns/Getty Images 211 r Outline Press Ltd. 212 bl VintAxe 212 r Outline Press Ltd. 213 tl Getty Images 213 r Outline Press Ltd. 214 tl Redferns/Getty Images 214 r Outline Press Ltd. 215 r Quintessence Editions Ltd. 217 right Private Collection/Lebrecht Music & Arts 218 r Outline Press Ltd. 219 r Outline Press Ltd. 220 tl Redferns/Getty Images 220 r Outline Press Ltd. 221 tl VintAxe 221 r Outline Press Ltd. 222 tl Redferns/Getty Images 222 r Outline Press Ltd. 223 tl Michael Ochs Archives/Getty Images 223 r Quintessence Editions Ltd. 224 tl Redferns/Getty Images 224 r Redferns/Getty Images 225 tl Getty Images 225 r Outline Press Ltd. 226 tl Redferns/Getty Images 227 r Outline Press Ltd. 228 r Outline Press Ltd. 229 tl Redferns/Getty Images 229 r Outline Press Ltd. 230 tl Getty Images 230 r Outline Press Ltd. 231 tl Michael Ochs Archives/Getty Images 231 r Outline Press Ltd. 232 tl Redferns/Getty Images 232 r Quintessence Editions Ltd. 233 tl Getty Images 233 r Outline Press Ltd. 234 tl Redferns/Getty Images 234 r Outline Press Ltd. 235 r Outline Press Ltd. 236 tl WireImage/Gett Images 236 r Outline Press Ltd. 237 tl Getty Images 237 r Outline Press Ltd. 238 3_right Outline Press Ltd. 239 right Outline Press Ltd. 240 tl VintAxe 240 2_bottom left Outline Press Ltd. 240 3_right Outline Press Ltd. 241 right Quintessence Editions Ltd. 242 r Outline Press Ltd. 243 r Outline Press Ltd. 244 tl Redferns/Getty Images 244 r Outline Press Ltd. 245 tl Redferns/Getty Images 245 r Outline Press Ltd. 246 tl Redferns/Getty Images 246 r Outline Press Ltd. 247 tl WireImage/Getty Images 248 r Outline Press Ltd. 249 tl Getty Images/Sony Music Archive 249 r Outline Press Ltd. 250 tl Redferns/Getty Images 250 r Outline Press Ltd. 251 tl Joe Zon 251 r Joe Zon

# Acknowledgments

THE AUTHOR would like to thank everyone at Quintessence: Jane Laing; Tristan de Lancey; Philip Contos; Frank Ritter; Simon Hartley; Simon Ward; Tom Howey; and Alison Hau. Enormous gratitude also goes to Nigel Osborne for the use of his extensive picture library. Martin Howells provided additional picture research, loaned guitars, and frequently prevented work with the lure of food and alcohol. Thanks also to Ben Way for his magnificently thorough fact-checking; Simon Pask and Neil Davis for their photography; Frank Helsley, the resonating man from Republic Guitars; Joe Zon, bass luthier supreme; Dean Campbell of Campbell American guitars; Mark and Tom Erlewine; and Chalize Zolezzi of Taylor Guitars.